GATEKEEPING
Your Marriage
COVENANT

TAQUETTA BAKER

PRAISE ASEMOTA

Kingdom Wellness Counseling and Mentoring Center

Christian Counseling

Ebook Products

GATEKEEPING YOUR MARRIAGE COVENANT

Dr. TAQUETTA BAKER

COACH PRAISE ASEMOTA

Amazon Publications
Muncie, IN

Kingdom Wellness Counseling and Mentoring Center
Learning Applicable Relationship Tools

This manual is based on over 24 years experience in professional counseling.

kingdomwellnesscenter@gmail.com

Kingdomshifters.com

KSWU.NET

Connect with Taquetta via Facebook or YouTube

Copyright 2025 – Kingdom Wellness Counseling & Mentor Center. All rights reserved.

Images are either copyright free, public domain images or used with permission of the graphic artist.

This book is protected by the copyright laws of the United States of America. This book may not be reprinted for commercial gain or profit. The use of occasional page copying for personal or group study is permitted and encouraged. Permission will be granted with written request.

TABLE OF CONTENTS

VISION STATEMENT vi
MANUAL SYNOPSIS vii
KINGDOM AUTHOR BIOS viii
FOREWORD BY BISHOP MICHAEL HUTTON-WOOD
.... xiv
FOREWORD BY GLORIA BROADOUS xvii
TAQUETTA'S BENEFITS OF MARITAL MENTORSHIP 1
PRAISE'S BENEFITS OF MARITAL MENTORSHIP 5
SURE FOUNDATION 7
I AM ENGAGED NOW WHAT? 45
DATING & ENGAGEMENT STRATEGIES 52
CHOOSING A GODLY MATE 55
GODLY SUBMISSION 77
MY HELP MEET 93
GODLY VISION FOR MARRIAGE 111
LEAVING & CLEAVING 129
BALANCING RELATIONSHIPS WITH IN-LAWS 139
GODLY VISION MARRIAGE ACTIVATION 145
WISDOM KEYS FOR MARRIED COUPLES 149
BALANCING MARRIAGE & DESTINY 151
BUILDING FINANCIAL MATURITY 155
FREEDOM FROM IMPURE ENTANGLEMENTS .. 160
RELATIONSHIP DESTROYING DEMONS 214

SEXUAL PERVERSION IN MARRIAGE *235*
HEALTHY COMMUNICATION SKILLS *260*
PURSUING GOD'S UNCONTAINABLE LOVE *282*
MARITAL INTIMACY BY AKEYSHA *294*
MARITAL INTIMACY BY PRAISE *296*
MARITAL INTIMACY BY TAQUETTA *299*
WAYS TO INCREASE AROUSAL *316*
I AM DIVORCED NOW WHAT? *326*
MANUAL REFERENCES *349*
MARRIAGE GATEKEEPING INDEX *350*

VISION STATEMENT

Kingdom Wellness offers a revolutionary theory of bridging mental and physical health with biblical truths, faith-based counseling, deliverance and healing principles. This is a holistic ideology of the total person – body, soul (mind, will, emotions), and spirit becoming one.

"Psychological theories are valuable for guiding practice in education, mental health, business, and other domains. They provide answers to intrinsically interesting questions concerning many kinds of thinking including perception, emotion, learning, and problem-solving."

MANUAL SYNOPSIS

God created marriage and family. God designed marriage to reflect his love, unity, blessing, delight, and faithfulness. In Ephesians 5, marriage symbolizes Christ's relationship with the church, built on love, sacrifice, and mutual respect. Marriage is a partnership where the husband and wife grow together in purpose divine vision and destiny, while honoring and serving one another as unto the Lord. When we follow God's design, marriage becomes more than a commitment. It becomes a testimony of His unmerited favor and eternal salvation covenant.

This manual is for anyone who is preparing for marriage, dating, engaged, or married. It is designed to teach you and your partner how to build a solid foundation of godly covenant marriage. You will be able to uproot and rebuild if necessary or build a sure foundation if you are waiting or dating. You will be able to avoid pitfalls and overthrow demonic enemies and systems that seek to break your marriage covenant. This manual will journey with you and your spouse throughout your marital union, as the activations within each chapter are utilized to sustain in a healthy, fulfilling, evolving, purpose driven, covenant relationship with God and one another.

KINGDOM AUTHOR BIOS

DR. TAQUETTA BAKER

As an adopted child, Taquetta knows the lifelong journey of appreciating both spiritual and natural relationships and encounters. She understands being strengthened by the pain that life can bring while embracing the joy of unexpected connections. Taquetta has transformed her experiences to establish a legacy of pioneering and fearlessly leading others.

Taquetta Baker is the founder of Kingdom Shifters Ministries (KSM), Kingdom Shifters Empowerment Church, and Kingdom Wellness Counseling and Mentoring Center. She has authored over 50 books and two prayer CDs. Taquetta has a Doctorate in Ministry, a Master's Degree in Community Counseling with an emphasis on Marriage, Children and Family Counseling, a Bachelor's Degree in Psychology and Associates Degree in Business Administration. Taquetta has a Therapon Belief Therapist Certification from the Therapon Institute, which provides faith-based counseling and ministry training. She is a certified Leadership & Executive Life Coach and has written her own Kingdom Wellness Counseling & Life Coaching theory and curriculum.

Taquetta serves in the mental health field as a Behavioral Consultant. She enjoys working with individuals and families who experience a broad range of psychological, emotional, social, relational, and spiritual challenges. Her outreach demonstrates cultural agility across a spectrum of ages, ethnicities, and socio-economic backgrounds. She is committed to empowering others with launching ministries, businesses, and books. She provides mentoring, counseling and vision launching through her Kingdom Wellness Counseling and Mentoring Center. With over 22 years of faith-based and professional counseling experience, her reputation is one who transforms lives and families through balancing biblical principles with applicable tools and strategies.

Taquetta serves on the Board of Directors for New Day Community Ministries, Inc. and is a graduate of the Eagles Dance Institute under Dr. Pamela Hardy with a license in liturgical dance. Before pioneering her own ministry, Taquetta was a dedicated member of Christ Temple Global Ministries for 14 years. She served pioneered Shekinah Expressions dance ministry and served in the role of prophet, teacher, presbytery board member, and overseer of the Altar Workers Ministry. Taquetta receives mentoring and ministry covering from Bishop Jackie Green, Founder of JGM-National Prayer Life Institute (Phoenix, AZ), and was ordained as an Apostle on June 7, 2014.

The Bible is full of stories that are centered around digging or receiving from wells which represent stability and deep places of renewal. Taquetta flows through the spiritual wells of warfare, worship, counseling and deliverance. Taquetta's mantle is an apostolic directive of judging and establishing God's kingdom in people, ministries, communities, and regions. Taquetta travels in foreign missions and throughout the United States. She has mentored and established dance teams, altar workers, counseling programs, and deliverance and prophetic ministries. Taquetta ministers in the areas of fine arts, systems of prayer, fivefold ministry, deliverance, healing, miracles, atmospheric worship, and counseling. Her mission is to empower and train others to identify and embrace their destiny.

COACH PRAISE ASEMOTA

Praise Asemota was ordained by World Evangelism Bible Church and licensed by Trans-Atlantic Pacific Alliance of Churches (TAPAC) as a Reverend Minister. Her sixteen years of working with Christian communities and leaders has ignited a passion for leadership development, health, wellness, and coaching of men and women to reach their full potential. Her focus at present is relationships, families, and women's empowerment. Praise has expertise in herbalism which has brought healing and stability to the lives of those she coaches. Praise can intertwine counseling, inner healing, intercession, and life application practices into her life coaching process to break people free from hard cases.

Praise Asemota has led daily prayers with the Ephratah Church community for ten years. Within the last four years, this mandate has expanded into a global reach on the Clubhouse social media platform. Praise's crafted gift of exhortation keeps people actively tuning in to her prayer movement daily! Praise has authored three books and blogs scriptural revelations for the daily prayers and teachings that are conducted on her Clubhouse platform.

This global prayer movement has greatly impacted people from all walks of life as consistent testimonies are shared unto the glory of God.

Praise oversaw Pastoral Care for Kingdom Connections Community formed by House of Light for two years. She facilitated a marriage preparation course for two years called, "*The Eligibles.*" This course prepared people for different stages of romantic relationships - dating, courtship, engagement, and marriage. For the last three years and counting, Praise has been a key expert for the *Singles and Married Nations Ministry*. She is a constant panelist and relationship coach who provides deliverance, healing, wisdom, and strategies to people inquiring advice on relationships. Her unique and practical approach has changed lives by freeing people from relationship bondages and restoring them on pathways to healthy relationship wellness.

Praise has nine years of professional experience in hosting her own show in media production. Praise is innovative, self-motivated, and proactive. She is an entrepreneur, pioneer, while being able to give others vision for their life and ministry mandates. Praise is dedicated to positively impacting the lives of the people she encounters daily and within her sphere of influence. She is without a doubt a leader of leaders and a builder and confident for leaders. God has called her to wardrobe leaders and to journey with them as a prayer and accountability partner as they release their ministry and business mandates in the earth.

With over the past years in the marketplace ministry and business endeavors, Praise has worked with individuals of all ages. Her experience spans to customer service, business administration, training, management, change management, and time management. She is deeply committed to delivering excellence and thrives on embracing new challenges. Praise is passionate about problem-solving and possesses a proactive *'let's just do it'* mentality.

Shift!

FOREWORD BY BISHOP MICHAEL HUTTON-WOOD

Many people jump into marriage relationships moved by the initial looks, feelings, physique, romance, promises, butterfly feelings without checking backgrounds, history, characters, asking the right and relevant questions or engaging in wise investigations as listed comprehensively in this book.

This book written by these two authors is quite detailed in presentation, wisdom, knowledge, experience, counsel, giving warnings, revealing red flags to avoid, and what the readers should be aware of so as not **TO MARRY THIS PERSON OR THAT PERSON**, while also gives keys to satisfaction and fulfilment in marriage.

This quote in the book is also key:

*The Bible says that both the **HUSBAND** and the **WIFE** should care to please one another as they work together in these areas revealing **AGAPE I.E. GOD'S UNCONDITIONAL LOVE** which is crucial to add to*

friendship love, romantic love and family love that we must demonstrate toward each other.

Another vital key in this book caught my eye is as follows:

Your mate should find you doing the work of the Lord.

- *Doing what pleases God!*
- *Doing ministry!*
- *Doing destiny!*
- *Demonstrating an intimate personal relationship with God!*
- *Demonstrating the God identity*

When the person comes into your life, they should not be drawing you from that work but learning about who you are in God as they watch you continue to build and evolve in your relationship and destiny with God.

Many will save themselves from a lot of heartache and regrets by thoroughly going through the content in this manual addresses God's true heart for marriage.

One of the things most people focus on before and in marriage is love but what builds and keeps marriages in addition to love is **WISDOM** as King Solomon said in ***Proverbs 24:3-4***, *"By wisdom a house (or marriage) is built, and by understanding it (marriage) is established; through knowledge its rooms (marriage rooms) are filled with rare and beautiful treasures."*

There are a lot of wisdom nuggets throughou this manual, including teamwork which is essential for a succcess marriage.

You will be doing yourself a great deal of justice to settle down and read, study, understand, practice, and live the contents of this manual and apply it so that you become **GATEKEEPERS OF YOUR MARRIAGE COVENANT!**

Covenant Blessings,

A KINGDOM
MARRIAGE
GATEKEEPER & MENTOR!

Bishop Michael Hutton-Wood

- Senior Pastor of House of Judah City Church in Croydon – UK
- President of Michael Hutton-Wood Ministries
- Author of 44 books to be purchased on Amazon or www.michaelhutton-wood.org
- Books to consider:

  - *What Husbands Want & What Wives Really Want*
  - *200 Questions To Ask Before You Say I Do*
  - *No Ringy, No Dingy*
  - *50 Common Mistakes Singles Make*
  - *101 Tips For A Great Marriage*

FOREWORD BY GLORIA BROADOUS

It is an honor to write a foreword for Apostle Taquetta Baker, whom I love dearly as a daughter and covenant ministry partner. Apostle Taquetta Baker flows through the spiritual wells of warfare, worship, counseling & deliverance with fluidity. Journeying with her in life and watching God "**SHIFT**" through her is truly a delight and a wonder. God has given Apostle Taquetta a clear apostolic directive of judging and establishing his kingdom in people, ministries, communities, and regions. This magnificent manual is a continuous of her mandate in building and establishing HIS Kingdom remnant "**BEFORE**" they say "**I DO**" in marriage covenant.

This manual will disciple you as a believer even as it prepares and establishes you in a solid foundation of covenant marriage. You cannot have a successful home built unless the foundation has been properly laid. That is what is being taught in this manual – **SOLID KINGDOM FOUNDATION**. Taking you back to what God says about you, for you, and for marriage, and teaching you how to live, build, and evolve in what he has said it divine plan for you and your union.

You will be challenged, provoked, and disrupted in your thinking to gain a better **OUTCOME** for a proper personal and marital foundation and how to build with God and your partner as you establish and mature in your life and marriage covenant. I am reminded of this scripture passage the helped me before I got married and sustained me throughout my marriage:

Psalm 127:1 *says "Except The Lord build the house, they labor in vain that build it: except The Lord keep the city, the watchman wakes but in vain (**KJV**)."*

*"If God does not build the house, the builders only build <u>shacks</u>. If God does not guard the city, the night watchman might as well nap (**MSG**)."*

Without question, the absolute most important aspect of a building is to BUILD with the Lord. My late husband, Apostle William T. Broadous and I did not want to build a "SHACK" for a marriage. This is what you have when you build without God. You will not be able to withstand the storms, tests, trials, and/or tribulations that will come. I believe this is why most marriages fail as they are a SHACK. They have not laid a proper godly foundation. Allow me to share what I have learned in my marriage journey regarding the importance of gatekeeping covenant marriage that is a home and not a SHACK.

When the trials and storms of an emergency appendectomy, degenerative rheumatoid arthritis, both hips & knees being replaced with bone growing over the joints, pulmonary embolisms in both lungs resulting in a vena cava filter being placed; bowel obstruction with colostomy bag for 6 months, diagnosis of Acute Myelogenous Leukemia (AML; 2 months to live), aggressive chemo, Hickman Catheter, biopsies, bone marrow transplant, autoimmune cytopenia, IVIG-Gamma guard monthly (build up & boost platelets), 2ND type of cancer came and was cut out, pneumonia which eventually led to respiratory failure, comatose, carbon monoxide poisoning, and ventilator with intubation, (spanning from 1986-2015), entered our marriage covenant;

I AM JUST LETTING YOU BREATHE IN MY REALITY FOR A MOMENT!

WOW! BUT GOD!

My husband and I were able to stand and keep standing because of the foundation of Jesus Christ we had established in our marriage covenant. THANK YOU, LORD!

I know in the natural, it would be difficult for most **WIVES** to stand or remain with their spouse. In some cases, **HUSBANDS** would have left. Many say, "*I didn't sign up for this*!" Please know that I did not expect this or know it was what I was signing up for either. I did not know this was part of how we would further build our personal destiny foundations and how the vision of our covenant marriage would manifest.

Even though the doctors were not hopeful, I had to **"LIFE"** with my husband through the Bible, prayer, worship, faith, and trusting God to be the healer of him, me, and our home.

I AM ALLOWING YOU TO BREATHE IN MY REALITY OF COVENANT MARRIAGE FOR A MOMENT!

FOR YOU SHALL LIFE IN COVENANT MARRIAGE WITH YOUR PARTNER!

This is what covenanting, submitting, surrendering, sacrificing, nourishing, and evolving with your mate entails. This is what **"GATEKEEPING"** your marriage covenant looks like in real time.

Throughout these trials, tribulations, and storms, God delivered him out of them all and raised him up each time. Talk about resurrection power! WE GOT TO WITNESS, ENDURE, LIVE OUT, AND BE GOD'S RESURRECTION POWER!

What is the vision God is giving you and your mate? Are you able to live it out no matter how it unfolds? This manual will help you do just that.

Our walls to our foundation were the Bible, vision of God, prayer, constant communication, trust, faith, worship, daily devotions with one another, fasting, intimacy, with the roof of **"UNCONDITIONAL ENDURING SELFLESS LOVE"** holding us together. These were the nutrients and vitamins to continuously nourish and strengthen our marriage.

- ✓ We cleaved to God and each other.
- ✓ We swept nothing under the rug.

Not saying we did not have differences, but we took them to God in prayer and examined the Bible for resolution, then we came together to resolve them.

Our marriage was a **"COVENANT"** marriage & not a **"CONTRACT"** marriage.

Our marriage was being built daily and God blessed it for thirty-seven ½ years as death we did part in 2016.

Many do not think or talk about sickness and/or disease entering in and how to manage it when it comes. Every part of our vows was honored including "*In sickness and in health*." Even through my own eleven surgeries, having children, and blending a family, we still were able to stand up under it because of our foundation being on **JESUS CHRIST, THE SOLID ROCK!**

Apostle Paul instructs us about the foundation:

1Corinthians 3:11 "Another foundation can no man lay than that which is laid which is Christ Jesus."

As you read this book, remember that a life built on the foundation of **JESUS CHRIST, THE BIBLE, AND HIS MARRIAGE VISION** is one that can withstand **ALL** the trials, tests, storms, and challenges, while leading to spiritual maturity and eternal security. All other ground is sinking sand.

Though my prayer is that your marriage covenant does not entail what my testimony is sharing, I am praying that through this manual, you embody the solid foundation to build a true fiery relationship that allows you to stay the course with **GOD** and your mate in **EVERYTHING GOD AND LIFE PRESENTS TO YOU!** This manual will equip you and your mate as you **GATEKEEP MARRIAGE WITH GOD!**

Still Standing,
A LIVE OUTLOUD MARRIAGE GATEKEEPER!
Apostle Dr. Gloria Broadous

TAQUETTA'S BENEFITS OF MARITAL MENTORSHIP

For over twenty-two years, I have had the privilege of mentoring couples as they date, move to engagement, and then to marriage. God has gifted me to help couples access his will and purpose for their lives personally and as a union such that they are successful in their marital journey. Thankfully, every couple I have mentored thus far is still married and reaping the fruit of the foundation they have cultivated through their personal and marital mentorship with me.

Whether seeking to be married or already married, I want to encourage couples to take their personal and marital foundation seriously and to prioritize having a mentor. It will significantly aide in the wellness fortification of your marriage journey.

***Titus 2:3-8** Older women similarly are to be reverent in their behavior, not malicious gossips nor addicted to much wine, teaching what is right and good, so that they may encourage the young women to tenderly love their husbands and their children, to be sensible, pure, makers of a home [where God is honored], good-natured, being subject to their own husbands, so that the word of God will* *not be dishonored. In a similar way urge the young men to be sensible and self-controlled and to behave wisely [taking life seriously]. And in all things show yourself to be an example of good works, with purity in doctrine [having the strictest regard for integrity and truth], dignified, sound and beyond reproach in instruction, so that the opponent [of the faith] will be shamed, having nothing bad to say about us.*

The Benefits of A Marriage Mentor Are As Followed:
1. Get to learn biblical realities, truths, and standards for marriage! Yay!
2. Get to live out the true interpretation of the scriptures as you become disciplined in loving, submitting to, and honoring your partner and marriage covenant! Yay!
3. Get to do life and marriage God's way! Yay!
4. Able to identify, discern, and live through the standards God has for your life, your purpose, the mate he has for you, and your marriage.
5. Able to maintain your purity and godly standards, while being prepared for marriage and the mate God has for you.
6. Learn God's will and purpose for your life, for marriage, and the reason he has personally called you to be married.

7. Able to identify and overthrow generational bondages, curses, covenants, and dedications that would litigate your ability to be married and your marriage covenant.
8. Learn healthy communication skills, conflict resolution skills, anger management skills, coping skills, interpersonal skills, social skills, emotional wellness, financial wellness, parenting skills, marital boundaries and safeguards that fortify your interactions, connection, and communication with one another and within the marriage.
9. Reduces constant division, discord and the risk of divorce, because you all have accountability and divine guidance to help you navigate challenging seasons of your lives and marriage covenant.
10. Can receive biblical truth that marriage continuously evolves, and there will be seasons of restructuring, realignment, maturing, and growing personally and together to sustain where the marriage has SHIFTED into.
11. Able to address and resolve common marital challenges quickly.
12. Allows for proactive guidance, goal setting, strategies, measurable daily habits, and operations in dealing with matters that would come to challenge the marriage covenant.
13. Can make more cohesive and assertive decisions regarding marital and life situations.
14. Increases the shared meaning, responsibility, accountability, empowerment, hope, optimism, and fulfillment of the marriage as both parties commit to doing whatever is necessary, including mentoring, counseling, etc., to safeguard their marriage covenant, their future, and the achievement of a healthy marriage.

15. Increase in intimacy, sexual relationships, and marital satisfaction.
16. Able to become more effective parents and godly trainers for your children.
17. Able to help set a standard for healthy marital covenant in your family life and gatekeep this area with sustaining success.
18. Have a voice that keeps you rooted in the sacrifice of marriage and the truth that it is not just about you, but about your partner and God's will and purpose for your marriage! Yay!
19. Remind and help you to celebrate personal and marital milestones and destiny moments.
20. Help you and your partner keep God first so he can be the head of your lives and marriage! Yay!

PRAISE'S BENEFITS OF MARITAL MENTORSHIP

1. **Embrace Your Singleness:** But if anyone thinks he acts unbecomingly toward the virgin, if she passes the bloom of youth, and things must be so, let him do what he wishes; he does not sin. Let them marry. But he who stands firm in his heart, having no necessity, but has power over his own will, and has so determined in his heart that he will keep his virgin, does well. (1 Corinthians 7:36-37)

2. **Find Joy in God:** The joy of the Lord is your strength. (Nehemiah 8:10)

3. **Cultivate Healthy Relationships:** Do not forsake the assembly of yourselves, as is the manner of some, but exhort one another, and so much the more as you see the Day approaching. (Hebrews 10:25)

4. **Pursue Spiritual Growth:** But grow in the grace and knowledge of our Lord and Savior Jesus Christ. (2 Peter 3:18)

5. **Practice Self-Discipline:** But the fruit of the Spirit is love, joy, peace, longsuffering, kindness, goodness, faithfulness, gentleness, self-control. (Galatians 5:22-23)

6. **Set Boundaries:** Flee youthful lusts and pursue righteousness, faith, love, peace, with those who call on the Lord out of a pure heart. (2 Timothy 2:22)

7. **Trust in God's Timing:** Be still and know that I am God. (Psalm 46:10)

8. **Focus on Your Purpose:** For we are God's workmanship, created in Christ Jesus for good works, which God prepared beforehand that we should walk in them. (Ephesians 2:10)

9. **Cultivate Patience:** Be patient, therefore, brethren, until the coming of the Lord. See how the farmer waits for the precious fruit of the earth, being patient in it, until he receives the early and latter rain." (James 5:7)

10. **Seek God's Wisdom:** If any of you lacks wisdom, let him ask of God, who gives to all liberally and without reproach, and it will be given to him." (James 1:5)

SURE FOUNDATION

From: Why Is It Important to Have a Strong House Foundation? - Roar Engineering

> **When Building A Home:**
> A foundation refers to the lower part of a structure, which is designed to distribute the weight of the new building evenly and provide a firm footing. If it weren't there, your house would sink into the ground, leading to cracks and damage. A proper foundation does more than support a house. Building foundations prevent moisture from entering, provide insulation, and keep the earth from moving around the home.
>
> **Holding The Building:**
> The primary purpose of a foundation is to support the entire structure. As a result, it needs to be properly shaped and reliable so that the rest of the house can remain upright.
>
> By not investing adequately at this stage, you may have to deal with costly repairs and modifications

later in the process, a situation which you could have avoided earlier

WHEWWW!

Matthew 7:24-29 The Amplified Bible *"So everyone who hears these words of Mine and acts on them, will be like a wise man [a far-sighted, practical, and sensible man] who built his house on the rock. And the rain fell, and the floods and torrents came, and the winds blew and slammed against that house; yet it did not fall, because it had been founded on the rock. And everyone who hears these words of Mine and does not do them, will be like a foolish (stupid) man who built his house on the sand. And the rain fell, and the floods and torrents came, and the winds blew and slammed against that house; and it fell—and great and complete was its fall."*

When Jesus had finished [speaking] these words [on the mountain], the crowds were astonished and overwhelmed at His teaching; for He was teaching them as one who had authority [to teach entirely of His own volition], and not as their scribes [who relied on others to confirm their authority].

Sure Foundation Activation:
1. Journal what you learned from reading the truth of having a strong house foundation.
2. Spend time with your partner discussing and journaling what you learned about a sure foundation.
3. Consider the firm foundation picture. What is right with how the couple is building? What is wrong with how the couple is building?
4. Study *Matthew 7:24-29*. Journal what God speaks to you about a strong foundation.
5. Spend time asking God what is solid and what is missing or unstable in the foundation of you personally and in your relationship with your partner.

Proper Foundational Planting

Isaiah 33:6 *And wisdom and knowledge shall bethe stability of thy times, and strength of salvation: the fear of the LORD is his treasure.*

<u>Stability</u> in Greek is *emûnâ;* or (shortened) אֱמֻנָה *'emunah, em-oo-naw«* and means:

1. literally firmness; figuratively security; morally fidelity
2. faith (-ful, -ly, -ness, (man)), set office, stability, steady, truly, truth, verily
3. firmness, fidelity, steadfastness, steadiness

New International Bible *He will be the sure foundation for your times, a rich store of salvation and wisdom and knowledge; the fear of the LORD is the key to this treasure.*

The Amplified Bible *And He will be the security and stability of your times, A treasure of salvation, wisdom and knowledge; The fear of the LORD is your treasure.*

The Message Bible *GOD is supremely esteemed. His center holds. Zion brims over with all that is just and right. GOD keeps your days stable and secure—salvation, wisdom, and knowledge in surplus, and best of all, Zion's treasure, Fear-of-GOD.*

Foundation is the natural or prepared ground, groundwork, initial stages, or base on which some structure rests.

Whatever you plant and build into the foundation of your relationship determines the stability, capability, sufficiency, and impact of that relationship.

This is the reason you must have a strong foundational relationship with God. Every other relationship is birthed from the foundation of this relationship.

Psalm 1:1-3 *Blessed is the man that walketh not in the counsel of the ungodly, nor standeth in the way of sinners, nor sitteth in the seat of the scornful. But his delight is in the law of the LORD; and in his law doth he meditate day and night. And he shall be like a tree planted by the rivers of water, that bringeth forth his fruit in his season; his leaf also shall not wither; and whatsoever he doeth shall prosper.*

Relationship Activation:

1. Did you have a relationship with God before you entered your relationship with your mate and what does that relationship look like? Does it or did it have a sure foundation?

2. Search out your relationship with God. Do you really have a healthy relationship with him that demonstrates a sure foundation such that all your other relationships, especially with your mate flow through that relationship with him?

3. Take a moment to journal three good things that are in your foundation and three things you need to gut out of your foundation to restabilize it? Work on those areas that need to be uprooted in your foundation.

4. Set time to build your foundation. Make time and schedule in time to check and continue to build effectively in your foundation. Quality time to build a continuous solid foundation.

5. Your foundation activates your standard. What is God's standard for your life and the relationship you are in?

6. Your foundation activates your standard. What is God's standard for your life and the relationship you are in?

   A. Friendship Intimacy
   B. Engagement Intimacy
   C. Marriage Intimacy

Singles Care for What Pleases God!

It is ideal for a person to have a relationship with God before you enter a relationship with them. If they do not have one and if you do not have one, it is essential to work on building a solid relationship with God and then filter your relationship with one another through a relationship with him.

If you are already dating or married, you can still implement this principle. Doing so will expose, snuff out, and reorder your perception of yourself, your life, your destiny, your focus, your relationship with God, people and that person. This is the reason people experience shook as they tend not to have the ideal experience. Many things are revealed that should have been dealt with in the secret chambers with God. The person needs to have grace with themselves, the person they are in a relationship with and with the relationship itself. Patience is vital to allowing God to still work and produce his exceeding weight of glory as he completes his perfect work in a not so ideal situation.

1Corinthians 7:32-35 But I would have you without carefulness. **He that is unmarried careth for the things that belong to the Lord, how he may please the Lord:** *But he that is married careth for the things that are of the world, how he may please his wife. There is difference also between a wife and a virgin.* **The unmarried woman careth for the things of the Lord, that she may be holy both in body and in spirit:** *but she that is married careth for the things of the world, how she may please her husband. And this I speak for your own profit; not that I may cast a snare upon you, but for that which is comely, and that ye may attend upon the Lord without distraction.*

The Message Bible *I want you to live as free of complications as possible.* **When you're unmarried, you're free to concentrate on simply pleasing the Master.** *Marriage involves you in all the nuts and bolts of domestic life and in wanting to please your spouse, leading to so many more demands on your attention. The time and energy that married people spend on caring for and* *nurturing each other, the unmarried can spend in becoming whole and holy instruments of God. I'm trying to be helpful and make it as easy as possible for you, not make things harder. All I want is for you to be able to develop a way of life in which you can spend plenty of time together with the Master without a lot of distractions.*

<u>Careth</u> in Greek is <u>merimnaō</u> and means:
1. to be anxious about: — (be, have) care(-ful), take thought
2. to be anxious, to be troubled with cares
3. to care for, look out for (a thing)
4. to seek to promote one's interests
5. caring or providing for

<u>Please</u> is <u>areskō</u> in Greek and means:
1. (through the idea of exciting emotion)
2. to be agreeable (or by implication, to seek to be so): — please
3. to please to strive to please to accommodate oneself to the opinions, desires and interests of others

Your mate should find you doing the work of the Lord.

- ✓ Doing what pleases God!
- ✓ Doing ministry!
- ✓ Doing destiny!
- ✓ Demonstrating an intimate personal relationship with God!

✓ Demonstrating your God identity and your God inheritance!

When the person comes into your life, they should not be drawing you from that work but learning about who you are in God as they watch you continue to build and evolve in relationship and destiny with God.

If someone is:

- Detering
- Deflecting
- Disregarding - making light of
- Dishonoring - to deprive of honor; disgrace; bring reproach or shame on, to fail or refuse to honor or pay honor
- Disrespecting - speaking against, insulting, belittling
- Distracting
- Drawing you away from
- Rejecting
- Competing
- Comparing
- Defiling
- Mishandling

Your walk with God - **RUN!** - This is a huge red flag. **RUN FOR YOUR LIFE!**

If the person is really sent by God, they should want to experience you in your lifestyle walk with him. Your walk will speak volumes to who you are as a person, in God, in obedience to him, and your ability to evolve in destiny and in covenant relationship with God and that person.

As the relationship grows, accommodations can be made to make room for what God is doing between the two people. But to initially demand and require a SHIFT can bring a hinderance to learning things about one another and to allow God to naturally grow and mature each of you personally and in relationship together.

The word says when an unmarried person cares for the things of God, this keeps them holy in body and in spirit.

Holy in this scripture is *hagios* in Greek and means:
1. sacred (physically, pure, morally blameless or religious, ceremonially, consecrated)
2. (most) holy (one, thing), saint

When a single person cares for the things of God, it keeps them consecrated and focused on him and the things that concern him. This focus helps them to maintain a sacred walk of purity and holiness where their bodies - flesh stay under subjection and their spirit remains rooted in God. They are being cleansed and ceremonially cleaned through their posture of keeping God first and abiding in him.

As God is the catalyst and governor of that person's life, they can be delivered and healed and SHIFTED into wholeness.

Wholeness means complete and healthy in God identity and in a continual evolving of allowing God to perfect those things which concerns you.

This is such a beautiful principle because we tend to think that being in a relationship makes us whole. However, we should be pursuing wholeness with God. This allows us to enter a relationship as a whole person joining in oneness with another whole person.

If I am not in pursuit of wholeness but you are then I am a half person bringing half of who God wants me to be and trying to join it with a whole person. It can cause us to be unequally yoked or have a lot of trials because what I am lacking or needing to make me whole must come from God. I am trying to get you to give me something only God can give. It places weights and burdens on the person and the relationship that God is not requiring.

LET'S JUST PONDER THIS FOR A MOMENT!

It is important to be mindful to heal and not use relationships to fulfill voids, as doing so can cause the relationship to become unhealthy. Especially if those relationship expectations and desires cannot be met by your partner. Your pursuit of fulfilling voids will become the vision and false god of the relationship instead of what God is requiring. Expecting someone to fulfill voids that should be filled by God, your own personal self-care, healing of trauma wounds and unresolved issues, or that may be unrealistic ideas regarding a relationship, can lead to idolatry. These voids are often fantasies or expectations that do not belong in a relationship or should be balanced as they are met. When you are operating through voids, you will want and need them fulfilled continuously to keep you in a place of satisfaction. Since they are being met in an unhealthy way, drainage, frustration, and conflict tends to enter the relationship as the desire for voids to be constantly fulfilled by one's partner becomes an idol in the relationship. An idol is that which is being created to bring fulfillment rather than relying on God the creator. You are idolizing the idea of what a partner and that relationship should be and do for you, rather than the reality of what that relationship and potential marriage is, what you are to give and receive in a relationship, and the truth of what a marriage covenant is.

LET'S JUST PONDER THIS FOR A MOMENT!

When we are not whole, we look for people to fulfill parts of our personality to make up for where identity is void and incomplete. We were never meant to live through personalities as this causes us to operate through parts of ourselves, not the totality of who we are.

LET'S JUST PONDER THIS FOR A MOMENT!

Relationship Activation:
1. If you are already dating or married, were you whole when you came into the relationship? Explain in detail? How has this impacted your identity and destiny? Your relationship with God? Your relationship with your partner?

2. What are the voids in your life right now?

3. What areas does God need to make whole in you that you have been trying to achieve in your relationship with your mate?

You do not want to take a person out of their abiding place in God. You want to learn about this place and then seek him in where you fit into his plans for your mate and who you all are together.

This posture helps the relationship to evolve in holiness and in gaining and maintaining vision for what and where God wants to take the relationship.

It allows you all to maintain your relationships with God while he uses the two of you to sharpen and further perfect one another into his likeness.

***Proverbs 27:17** tells us that "Iron sharpens iron, so a man sharpeneth the countenance of his friend."*

Sharp is *hadad* in the Hebrew and means "*to be fierce, to be alert, keen, piercing.*"

Iron is "*strong, tough, resilient, fortified, firm, robust, sound, solid - of a steel material, composite, or nature.*"

This describes two steel - iron like people strengthening one another.

When sharpened, you are empowered to be the best you that you can be. If there is a cutting away of who you are, it is only too perfect the essence of who you are in a greater measure. You should always become better through those you are in a relationship with. If you become less and even stagnant where you are no longer growing and being empowered to grow, then the relationship should be reevaluated. Either you all are not being who you are to be to one another, or you are holding on to the relationship for other reasons that have no true defined divine purpose. Be okay with letting go and allowing God to connect you with relationships that can sharpen you.

The Message Bible *You use steel to sharpen steel, and one friend sharpens another.*

Proverbs 27:17 tells us that, "*Iron sharpens iron, so a man sharpeneth the countenance of his friend.*" Iron is sharpened by rubbing it against another piece of sharp iron. When two pieces of iron, especially iron blades, rub together, both become sharper. Also, equipping is occurring as both are empowering the other through the connection they have with one another. Both begin to change and transform while becoming more refined. Each of them is more efficient for use.

Sharp means, "to become *keen, acute, alert, watchful, defined, cutting edge, swift, tapered, fierce.*"

When people do not sharpen one another, the relationship becomes dull, slow, lazy, un-useful and blurred in vision. Feelings are easily hurt due to unspoken and unmet expectations flaring. These expectations tend to outweigh the level of iron production manifesting in the relationship. If the relationship is unfruitful or not beneficial, check the iron production. For whatever reason, either you or the other person is not investing in the relationship. Someone has to start sharpening the other for production to manifest, so if you are waiting for the other person, then you are already demonstrating that you have some issues with investing in relationships or in that person.

Examine yourself and that relationship and be okay with releasing it if necessary or doing what is necessary to sharpen it so it can produce what God has required of it.

Deliverance From Soulties
From my manual, *"Deliverance From Soulties."* Soul ties can be godly or ungodly in nature. In the same way that  generational curses are passed down, soul ties are interchangeable and transferable between you and another person. Soul ties can be formed through close friendships and interactions, covenants, vows, commitments, promises, and physical intimacy. You can also have a soul tie by having an unhealthy attachment to something or someone that has taken the place of God in your life or that has become an addiction in your life. Your soul, heart, mind, and body can be intertwined, bound, knitted, or in covenant with that person, place, or thing. In addition, you exchange parts of yourself with the person that is part of your soul tie. Parts of their personality, soul, heart, thoughts, mindsets, character, nature, and other deposits infuse you and begin to influence and live in you and vice versa. Also, whomever they have had a relationship with and have not cleansed themselves of is passed between the two of you.

It is also important to be delivered from soul ties and errored mindsets about relationships and marriages. This will also help with breaking free of sin issues that would hinder a pure foundation from being built in the relationship and the marriage.

When soul ties are present:

- ✓ You will want to refer to their past experiences to assess what they want and do not want in a relationship.

- ✓ You will have a hard time letting go of pleasures that do not align with God.

- ✓ You will want your partner to do and perform in ways that feed your flesh, appetites, addictions, and habits.

- ✓ If you have traumas or unresolved issues, you will be operating through those experiences and the fears tied to them. You will demand your partner prove that they will not hurt you or repeat the experiences of your previous partners. This is because your soul is still tied to those people and those experiences.

Until they are broken, you will have faulty perceptions about how the relationship should and should not be, and regarding what is needed so you will not get hurt. These pain triggers will cause conflicts and outbursts, while also hindering you from being able to trust God with the relationship and to trust him for the vision for the relationship. They will cause you to want to hold on to the past, rather than SHIFTING to being completely purified of your past sins and transgressions and learning what God requires so you and your partner can build a healthy, holy, God designed marriage covenant.

Want what God wants for you and your relationship more than you want to hold on to things you learned in the world, in trauma, or outside the will of God. God gives the best gifts. He created you, relationships, and marriage. He knows how to fulfill you. He can give you a healthy foundation and healthy relationship that will not cross boundaries with him yet make you the happiest man or woman alive.

Relationship Activation:
1. What is the iron production you have with God?
2. What is the iron production you have with your mate?
3. What have you learned from observing your mate's relationship with God?
4. How does the relationship your mate have with God impact you? Challenge you? Reveal about them, You? God?

5. What has God revealed that needs to be changed as you have grown in relationship with your mate as it relates to who they are in God?
6. What unresolved issues and soul ties do you need to be delivered from to become healthy in trusting God and your partner as you build a solid foundation. Spend time seeking God, breaking soul ties, and healing in these areas. Seek counseling, deliverance, and inner healing from a minister or a professional if necessary.

Married Couples Care for What Pleases Their Mate!

1Corinthians 7:32-35
But I would have you without carefulness. He that is unmarried careth for the things that belong to the Lord, how he may please the Lord: ***But he that is married careth for the things that are of the world, how he may please his wife.*** *There is difference also between a wife and a virgin. The unmarried woman careth for the things of the Lord, that she may be holy both in body and in spirit:* ***but she that is married careth for the things of the world, how she may please her husband.*** *And this I speak for your own profit; not that I*

may cast a snare upon you, but for that which is comely, and that ye may attend upon the Lord without distraction.

The Message Bible *I want you to live as free of complications as possible. When you're unmarried, you're free to concentrate on simply pleasing the Master.* ***Marriage involves you in all the nuts and bolts of domestic life and in wanting to please your spouse, leading to so many more demands on your attention. The time and energy that married people spend on caring for and nurturing each other,*** *the unmarried can spend in becoming whole and holy instruments of God. I'm trying to be helpful and make it as easy as possible for you, not make things harder. All I want is for you to be able to develop a way of life in which you can spend plenty of time together with the Master without a lot of distractions.*

<u>*Careth*</u> in Greek is *merimnaō* and means:
1. to be anxious about
2. (be, have) care(-ful), take thought
3. to be anxious, to be troubled with cares
4. to care for, look out for (a thing)
5. to seek to promote one's interests
6. caring or providing for

<u>*Please*</u> is *areskō* in Greek and means:
1. (through the idea of exciting emotion)
2. to be agreeable (or by implication, to seek to be so): — please
3. to please, to strive to please, to accommodate oneself to the opinions, desires and interests of others

When you are married you are attentive to building a life together where both parties are pleased.

- ✓ Please means that I am in agreement with what pleases my mate and in helping my mate to seek or pursue a life of that pleasure.

- ✓ Please means I will sacrifice myself to make sure what pleases my mate is fulfilled in their life even if it is not something that pleases me.

- ✓ Please means that I take an active interest in investing time and attention to what pleases my mate. I am in agreement that pleasing them is essential to their wellbeing and the healthiness of our marriage covenant.

LET'S JUST PONDER THIS FOR A MOMENT!

If you do not have a heart and desire to please a person, **DO NOT MARRY THEM!**

If you are more challenged by what interests them, what fulfills them, what brings them pleasure, than wanting to accommodate them, **DO NOT MARRY THEM!**

If you are just tolerating their interests and pleasures, more than regarding them, honoring, and understanding that this is apart of who they are, **DO NOT MARRY THEM!**

If you are just tolerating their interest and pleasures and have believed a lie that:

- Their interest and pleasures will change when you all are married.

- You can change their interest and pleasures once you are married.

- You do not have to demonstrate an invested – accommodating interest - in what pleases them (e.g. I can just be doing other things while they are doing that, oh that is their thing, etc.).

You are in error. **DO NOT MARRY THIS PERSON!** Of course, you won't love all the same things or want to do all of the same things all the time. However, the word says you are to have an invested accommodating interest in what pleases your spouse.

I believe the Bible emphasizes this revelation because so many people marry and do not take into account how this can be an open door to someone else or something entering and validating, empowering, covenanting with your spouse in this area.

Also, people tend to tolerate things during dating and engagement and even demonstrate interest only to become inconsistent or nonexistent once married. You have instilled a false narrative in your foundation that is an open door for your spouse to get this need and desire met outside the marriage covenant when this passage of scriptures reveals that this is the essence of the marriage covenant. It is what sustains marriage.

> **PLEASING YOUR SPOUSE IS WHAT SUSTAINS THE MARRIAGE!**

JUST PONDER THIS FOR A MOMENT!

Now domestic life entails the home, household affairs, and family. The domestic life are the daily living customs, situations, and experiences. They entail shared responsibilities of household chores, managing finances, parenting children, pets, hobbies, habits, interests, job/entrepreneurial endeavors, decision-making on daily matters, creating a home environment together, extended family and friend relationships, and supporting each other through life's trials and tribulations.

The Bible says that both the HUSBAND and the WIFE care to please one another as they work together in these areas. Many homes strive to have traditional roles of what a wife should do and what a husband should do domestically. Often, these traditional roles cause lots of contention in the home because they are the doctrines of religion or the customs of the world rather than the pleasures and interests of the married couple. To ensure a solid foundation, it will be important for you and your spouse to search out a domestic plan that both of you all can accommodate.

JUST PONDER THIS FOR A MOMENT!

There also needs to be a heart posture to please your spouse and to love him or her as God loves them. This should be developed and cultivated in dating and engagement then evolve as your marriage covenant progresses. This is where submission and loving one another as God loves takes precedence. It is also necessary to ask God how to please your partner, so you can give them what God wants and desires rather than what you think they desire. This also SHIFTS you beyond just fulfilling what they say they need and desire as truly God created us, God created relationships, God created marriage. He is truly the only one who really knows what he needs to be fulfilled and to be successful in our relationship and marriage covenants.

(Study the Godly Submission chapter in this manual to further understand what it means to please your spouse the ways God requires. Once you have studied submission, return to reading and studying this chapter).

Intentionality is vital in pleasing your spouse. Intentionality entails the quality and ability of being able to do something on purpose or with intent. Such a posture requires an attitude and heart posture of purposefulness, consciousness, and commitment to deliberate action. When you are intentional, you do not become too familiar where you take your partner and your relationship for granted or become relaxed where you do not regard the work, energy, and ingenuity it takes to constantly evolve in a healthy thriving relationship. **With that being said, it is essential to understand that relationships, especially marriage, takes work. If you do not want to work, do not enter a relationship and by all means, do not get married.**

in·ten·tion·al
adjective: done on purpose; deliberate

JUST PONDER THIS FOR A MOMENT!

God never promised that relationships, especially marriage would be easy. He did say that if a man finds his wife, he finds a good thing and obtains favor from him.

> **What Efforts look like in a MARRIAGE**
> - Following through with what you say
> - Showing affection, non-sexual included
> - Listening and actually hearing your spouse
> - Asking how you can help your spouse
> - Staying interested and excited about your spouse
> - Apologizing and changing when wrong
> - Initiating love making and showing desire
> - Prioritizing emotional connection
> - Encouraging and uplifting your spouse
> - Learning and speaking their love language
> - Caring
> - If your marriage is in trouble and your man is becoming cold, losing interest or pulling away then you can check out my free ebook to make your man obsessed with you. Link in bio.

Proverbs 18:22 *He who finds a wife finds a good thing and obtains favor from the LORD.*

Obtains in the Hebrew means: "secure, furnish, affords, promote, draw out, bring out, cause to draw out."

> **MEN YOU ARE PROMOTED TO CONTINUOUSLY OBTAIN FAVOR WHEN YOU FIND YOUR GOOD THING!**

The man is already favored by way of sonship but draws out even greater secure favor with the Lord when he finds his good thing. WHEWWW!

MEN - When you find your good thing, you should want to work to receive the good from her and the extra SECURE FURNISHED favor God has for you.

WOMEN - When you are found to be a good capture, you should want to work to receive the good from it and the favor God has for you.

So many couples remain bound in their personal ideologies, traumas, pet peeves, flawed personalities, prideful and puffed-up ways, that they spend more time working to destroy their good thing and the favor God has for them, than they do embracing their good thing and receiving the favor of God. They wear themselves out fighting against what it means to be good and favorable – what it means to be delightful and pleasing to them and to God. When you find yourself engaging in this behavior, it is an indicator that you:

- You need deliverance from unresolved issues.
- You need deliverance and healing in the areas of trust, giving, and receiving love.
- You need deliverance from the spirit of inadequacy and healing in your identity.
- You are not convinced that you have found your good thing.
- You do not know how to identify a good thing.
- You do not understand God and who he is as a blessing God.
- You do not know how to be blessed and to rest in blessings. You need to address your issues of self-sabotage and victimization.
- You are not ready to share your life with someone in a marriage covenant.

KINGDOM WOMEN – When you know you have worked with God to be a good thing, do not allow ANYONE to come and destroy the truth of his goodness in you. Trust who you are and require honor. If a man is not willing to do the work to SHIFT into the reality of who you are, RUN!

You may not be his good thing and that is okay. The man who is capable of discerning and honoring your truth is on the way. But by all means, do not compromise and do not allow ANYONE to manipulate you, sweet talk you, break your will where you cannot discern your own truth, or destroy God's goodness in you. God will send THE ONE who knows and is willing to work to honor you as a good thing and to obtain favor from God so you all can live in his fulfilled goodness.

When God sends a mate, he is sending you his good thing – his best gift to you. You do not have to fear being pleased or fulfilled because God has chosen that person to be able to fulfill you, bless you, and be an extension of you. You do not have to hold on to old sin desires, especially sexual ones as God created sex. He knows what will please and fulfill you. You do not have to yield to sin to make sure your partner can please you. He or she is **NOT** a car, so you do not need to test drive them to make sure they are what you want and need, or to make sure they work properly. God will make sure you are blessed in this marriage as you and your partner work together to build a solid foundation. You just need to posture in the truth and fruit that this is your good thing, and you are ready to build life, destiny, and purpose with them. Everything else will unfold beautifully as you submit to God, submit and surrender to one another, and do the work to take care of the good and favored blessing God has given you all in one another.

JUST PONDER THIS FOR A MOMENT!

Pleasing Your Mate Activation:
1. What did you learn about the importance of posturing to please your mate?
2. Ask God what pleasing him in a relationship looks like. Journal what he reveals.
3. Ask God for insight on what pleases your partner. Journal what he reveals.
4. Ask God what your place is in caring for your mate and how that will help you to evolve in Christlikeness? Journal what he reveals.
5. Ask God to reveal whether your motives and intentions are to please him and or to please yourself as it relates to your partner? As it relates to the relationship itself? Ask him to deliver you from motives and intents that do not align with him. Journal three goals you can consistently work on to resist these motives and intents as they would try to arise later in your relationship.
6. Ask God to reveal to you any areas where your heart is broken from past relationships with ex-girlfriends and

boyfriends or life in general. Spend time journaling on these experiences and allow God to heal them.

7. Ask God to reveal to you any way your love is broken, or your perception of love is broken. Spend time journaling on these experiences and allow God to heal them.

8. Spend time falling out of agreement with making your present partner fulfill mindsets you have that are based on past relationships and past partners. Ask God to give you a clean slate to start in a new place with your present partner where you can build and love from his design and not past traumas issues, wants and needs, pleasures and desires. Desire to build from the new place and trust that it will fulfill you. Journal what God reveals and your process of healing and starting new in this area with God.

Team Building In Relationship

It is essential to build a team and partner concept while dating and during engagement so that this will be the essence of the flow of your relationship as you SHIFT to marriage. Honoring one another through a team and honoring what each brings to the team is vital in knowing that you all are an extension of God, and an extension of one another. ***(Study the Help Meet chapter in this manual for more insight into being a team).***

***Ephesians 4:9-12** Two are better than one; because they have a good reward for their labour. For if they fall, the one will lift up his fellow: but woe to him that is alone when he falleth; for he hath not another to help him up. Again, if* *two lie together, then they have heat: but how can one be warm alone? And if one prevail against him, two shall withstand him; and a threefold cord is not quickly broken.*

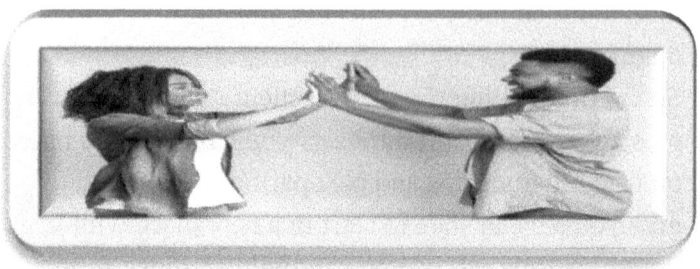

In this scripture we learn that when two work together, they:

- Ensure that they each receive the rewards of their labor, the works of their hands, destiny, sonship, and living in alignment with God (Rewards for their labor).
- Catch one another before you fall.
- Pick one another up when you fall.
- Encourage and lift one another.
- Be a support and carry one another.
- Can cover one another.
- Comfort one another.
- Give and receive from one another in times of adversity (Lend heat to one another; keep one another warm).
- Protect one another from dangers, trials, tribulations, calamities seen and unseen.
- Deliver and heal one another.
- Bring breakthrough to one another.

- Aide one another in enduring and withstanding trials and tribulations.
- Complete one another.
- Keep one another whole and safe in God, in destiny, and in the relationship (Not easily broken).

Truth is, how you engage in your general relationships is an indication of whether you have the capacity to work this scripture in a marriage. So many people claim they desire marriage, however, they are not good friends. God says this about friendships.

> ***Proverbs 27:9-10 The Amplified Bible*** *Oil and perfume make the heart glad; So does the sweetness of a friend's counsel that comes from the heart. Do not abandon your own friend and your father's friend, And do not go to your brother's house in the day of your disaster. Better is a neighbor who is near than a brother who is far away.*
>
> ***The Message Bible*** *Just as lotions and fragrance give sensual delight, a sweet friendship refreshes the soul. Don't leave your friends or your parents' friends and run home to your family when things get rough; Better a nearby friend than a distant family.*
>
> ***Colossians 3:12-14*** *Put on then, as God's chosen ones, holy and beloved, compassionate hearts, kindness, humility, meekness, and patience, bearing with one another and, if one has a complaint against another, forgiving each other;*

as the Lord has forgiven you, so you also must forgive. And above all these put on love, which binds everything together in perfect harmony.

Proverbs 27:17 *Iron sharpeneth iron; So a man sharpeneth the countenance of his friend.*

Proverbs 17:9 *Whoever would foster love covers over an offense, but whoever repeats the matter separates close friends.*

Proverbs 17:17 *A friend loveth at all times, and a brother is born for adversity.*

2Kings 2:2 *And Elijah said unto Elisha, Tarry here, I pray thee; for the LORD hath sent me to Bethel. And Elisha said unto him, As the LORD liveth, and as thy soul liveth, I will not leave thee. So they went down to Bethel.*

Proverbs 18:24 *A man that hath friends must shew himself friendly: and there is a friend that sticketh closer than a brother.*

New Living Bible *One who has unreliable friends soon comes to ruin, but there is a friend who sticks closer than a brother.*

Proverbs 27:5-6 *Better is open rebuke than hidden love. Faithful are the wounds of a friend; profuse are the kisses of an enemy.*

Philippians 2:3 *Do nothing from selfish ambition or conceit, but in humility count others more significant than yourselves.*

Proverbs 13:20 *He that walketh with wise men shall be wise: but a companion of fools shall be destroyed.*

Job 6:14 *To him that is afflicted pity should be shewed from his friend; but he forsaketh the fear of the Almighty.*

The Amplified Bible *For the despairing man there should be kindness from his friend; So that he does not abandon (turn away from) the fear of the Almighty.*

Job 42:10 *After Job had prayed for his friends, the LORD restored his fortunes and gave him twice as much as he had before.*

Proverbs 22:24-25 *Make no friendship with an angry man; and with a furious man thou shalt not go: Lest thou learn his ways, and get a snare to thy soul.*

Romans 12:9-10 English Standard Bible *Let love be genuine. Abhor what is evil; hold fast to what is good. Love one another with brotherly affection. Outdo one another in showing honor.*

***1Peter 4:8-10** And above all things have fervent charity among yourselves: for charity shall cover the multitude of sins. Use hospitality one to another without grudging. As every man hath received the gift, even so minister the same one to another, as good stewards of the manifold grace of God.*

***John 15:12-15 English Standard Bible** This is my commandment, that you love one another as I have loved you. Greater love has no one than this, that someone lay down his life for his friends. You are my friends if you do what I command you. No longer do I call you servants, for the servant does not know what his master is doing; but I have called you friends, for all that I have heard from my Father I have made known to you.*

I chuckle when people claim they want to be married but suck at being a good friend. They are incapable of giving and receiving love, often seek to control the relationship, and their interactions are more transactional than relational.

They cannot give themselves fully to a friendship yet have convinced themselves they are ready for the work it takes to BUILD a marriage. Love, patience, kindness, grace, sacrifice, forgiveness, support, empowerment, and aide are foundational keys of any relationship, especially friendships.

We have been told to look at whether a person has a good relationship with their momma or their daddy, but I say look at whether a person can be a friend – how do they treat their friends. Though parenting relationships are important, a person chooses to have friends or not. They also choose to be friendly or not. Their friendships speak volumes to how they were raised and what their pain points are as it relates to their parents and upbringing.

Cultivating friendship is vital to your marriage. When you build friendship, it enables you to become a TEAM. Team means we are in this together. Team means, **"I AM A BETTER ME WHEN I HAVE YOU!"**

Friendship Activation:
1. Study the scriptures on friendship separately and then with your partner. Journal what you learn about yourself, your partner, and God as you meditate and examine the scriptures.

2. Journal the truth about your engagement in your friendships and whether you possess the qualities in the scriptures. Journal where you need to improve. Set and work three goals to improve your relationships with your closet friends. Share these goals with your partner when you all work on this activation.

3. Journal the truth of what you have witnessed regarding your partner's friendships. Journal where you feel they need improvement. Discuss with them the reason these areas are lacking in their relationships. Ask them to set three goals to improve their relationships with their closest friends. Make a commitment to hold one another accountable to the goals you all set to improve their relationships. Grant them grace as they work on improving in this area.

4. If you and your partner do not have friends, examine the root of this. Pray for one another in this area and encourage one another to pursue relationship counseling or guidance in this area. Commit to working on pursuing and building friendships outside of one another and with other couples. It would be good to ask God to lead each of you to the right people that are best for you personally and together. Please know this is healthy and needful. Though you all will put one another before others, **YOU ALL CANNOT BE EVERYTHING TO EACH OTHER.** Not having balanced healthy relationships opens the door to possession, abuse, jealousy, covetousness, suspicion, and constant discord. Close the doors by building a community around you that breeds joy and destiny fulfillment.

Relationship Pleasing One Another Activation:
1. Spend time journaling what pleases and interests your partner.
2. Spend time asking your partner what pleases them.

3. Spend time journaling what pleases and interests you.
4. Spend time allowing your partner to ask what pleases you.
5. Spend time examining and repenting for anyway you all have not been accommodating to one another's interests and pleasures. Deal with toleration, inconsistency, lack of time, attention, and failure to create opportunities for that person to be pleased and built up in what pleases them.
6. Spend time examining what you need from one another to accommodate one another's pleasures and interests.
7. Spend time as a couple discussing your personal strengths and weaknesses as it relates to domestic matters. Journal a foundational plan that would work for you all as it relates to pleasing, accommodating, supporting, and building one another even as you would build your domestic home life together.

I AM ENGAGED NOW WHAT?

From Dr. Taquetta Baker's *"The Power Of Purity"* Manual.

Engagement Means Just That - ENGAGE!

"Engaged In War!"

Dictionary.com defines *engage* as:
1. to bring (troops) into conflict; enter into conflict with
2. to cause (gears or the like) to become interlocked
3. interlock with, to attach or secure
4. to entangle or involve
5. to cross weapons
6. enter into conflict
7. choosing to involve oneself in or commit oneself to something
8. a hostile encounter between military forces

When becoming engaged, you enter a battle for divine covenant and for the blessings of God to be upon it. You enter a battle because of who you are, what you do for God, what you will do for God, and how your union will produce covenant marriage and family that will glorify God.

The devil hates covenant marriages, so he seeks to destroy them before they get started. This battle starts while we are still single and waiting, ramps up when we begin to date and consider godly marriage, and increases into a full assault as we enter the engagement stage before marriage.

Because most couples are not aware of the assault on their engagement, much of their joy about being married is stolen by the petty, continuous attacks the enemy sends to weary and drain the love and life out of the foundation of the marriage. Many of them have a false image and fantasy mindset about marriage. Much of this is clouded by their desires for a fairytale wedding. Many couples are also more focused on planning for their wedding day and making it perfect than on building a solid foundation for their future marriage. The lack of God- ordained focus opens the doors to attacks. Even conflicts surrounding wedding planning can complicate the engagement process. A lack of premarital counseling or being counseled by someone who can truly posture the couple in foundational truths that ground the marriage in God, can be a factor to how the couple is able to weather the engagement process.

People, especially those who are oppressed or influenced by familiar spirits that operate in the family line, can have those spirits rear their ugly heads during the engagement process. These voices are good for making comments and engaging in behaviors that suck the celebration right out the engagement process. One essential key I constantly remind the couple of, especially the bride, is to remain in a place of celebration and not to let anyone steal their time of joy and being honored by God to be chosen as a bride or a groom. I express to them constantly that they cannot get this time back. Once this season is over, they do not want to look back in dread at what they experienced. I express that it is important to focus and draw close to those who are celebrating them, while guarding from familiar spirits and those who are more critical than encouraging at this time in their lives. I encourage them to tell people they are in premarital counseling and that they respect their opinions and wisdom, but they are not needed at this time. This helps them to bond closer to God, their mate, and to the vision that God is desiring to reveal to them concerning their marriage covenant.

Couples, war for this right to have a space to focus on celebration, processing, and building a godly foundation. Familiar spirits, and those who are used to speaking whatever they desire into the couple's lives, do not value the boundaries that are being set to help the couple leave and cleave, while having joy in the SHIFT that God has done in their lives. When they are not considerate, the enemy will further use them as an open door to engage the couple in battle regarding their marriage covenant. I actually believe this is a plus for the couple. They are having the generational strongholds around marriage revealed that are among them and that will come for them as they marry and do life with their mate. They can spend this time closing doors to how these familiar spirits and voices would try to operate in their marriage covenant and cleanse them out of their bloodline. Sadly, many do not recognize that this is an asset. They result in engaging in fights in the natural rather than spiritual battles against the true enemies raging against their marriage covenant. These battles in the natural complicate their lives and the engagement. Many of them also seek to people please, thus allowing the familiar spirits and voices to make decisions about their engagements, wedding planning, and marriage that God may not be wanting and that the couple does not really desire to do. They lend themselves to false loyalties and false obligations that cause them to dread their time of engagement and even dread decisions that they make about their wedding day. Many couples enter marriage having to cut out familiar spirits and voices that entered in during dating and engagement. These people are used to speaking and tend to wreak havoc in the marriage until the couple takes a stand and implements boundaries that weed them out the marriage covenant.

My prayer is that as those preparing to date for marriage, as well as the couples that are already engaged, would take the insights from this chapter and guard themselves and their relationships once they enter the engagement process.

Deliverance Activation:

- Journal your thoughts as you consider the insights in this chapter.

- Study the definitions of engage and engagement. Journal your insights regarding the definitions.

- Journal what God reveals to you and the conflict that you may experience or are enduring in this time of engagement from your family line, your personal life, the things you are still growing in and working on with your partner.

- Journal your current image and marriage in general. Journal your image of marriage regarding your partner. Spend time asking God if your images are fantasy or reality. Study the false images of marriage in the *"Kingdom Marriage"* manual by Apostle Jackie Green, and journal what you learned. Search out areas where you need to mature using the revelation regarding the marriage maturity list she shares in the manual. Journal where you need to grow personally, where your partner needs to grow, and where you think your engagement relationship needs to grow in these areas.

- Sit with God and write the vision of the reason he gave you your chosen mate and how you are to evolve with him or her in purpose and covenant marriage.

- Spend time in prayer birthing a love and heart for your chosen mate in your spirit. It is not enough to have feelings for them, to know they are a good person, or even that they are ordained by God. You want to also carry them in your spirit, and, through the spirit of God. You want to love, engage and be able to govern, submit to, and cover them. Birth for this dimension of covenant marriage with them via prayer, personally and together.

- Spend time with God journaling about the familiar spirits, familiar voices, personal and generational destiny killing spirits and patterns that have and will come for you. Seek God for strategy on shutting the doors to these areas and strongholds that are operating in your engagement and marriage.

- Ask God to give you a love and unmerited honor for the voice and God-identity of your future spouse. Practice loving, honoring, and adhering to their voice and God-identity as you work on leaving and cleaving in your engagement process.

- Journal on the importance of enjoying the journey of a bride or a groom and what it is like to be chosen by God to represent his marriage covenant.

- Journal on the challenges that come with being a bride or a groom. Seek God for revelation on how to thwart or process through these challenges.

- Identify and journal personal and generational patterns in your life and how destiny killing spirits will come for your engagement and marriage covenant. Seek God for strategies to contend and overthrow these destiny killing spirits and operations.

- Journal five attributes you need to work on to solidify the foundation during this time of your engagement to further cultivate a solid relationship with the Lord.

- Study the scriptures on submission, unconditional love, leaving and cleaving. Journal what you learn. Journal the challenges you have in these areas. Explore and journal five goals to help you posture according to God's will and purpose in these areas.

DATING & ENGAGEMENT STRATEGIES

From Dr. Taquetta Baker's *"Sustaining The Vision Workbook."*

***Relationship Activation:** As you and your partner consider these nuggets, set goals to apply them to your relationship.*

If you are dating or engaged, be honest about your ministry schedule and your times of prayer and study with the Lord. Role model your schedule, rather than giving the impression that you have free time that you do not really have. Let the person know the reason God has required the specific disciplines for you so they can pray concerning what you are sharing and have a clear vision of who you are in God.

Seek the Lord together for any changes you each need to make in each of your spiritual walks to make time for one another.

Create a vision plan for cultivating your relationship and commit to working it.

Schedule prayer and study time together. This will help with your transition if you have been single for a while and are used to spending a lot of time praying, studying and doing ministry. This will also help you build one another up in the Lord.

Have a balance between attending ministry activities and leisure time. Be cognizant of not just spending time together at ministry events. Schedule leisure events that you both may enjoy, but do not hinder or jeopardize your walk with the Lord.

Communicate when you feel neglected or torn between the relationship and ministry. Encourage the other person to do the same. Commit to not holding back your thoughts and feelings in this area as it will cause an open door to division and strife. Communication is key to giving your thoughts and feelings a voice in the relationship, and to getting your needs and desires met. You must be able to communicate, because the Lord will not tell you everything no matter how anointed you are. This will cause you to grow in honesty and vulnerability with one another in your desires, needs, and standards.

If you are dating or engaged, the Lord will give you grace to sustain the relationship. In busy seasons, time will be stretched. You must set aside special time for one another knowing God has given you the grace to walk in the relationship. He released the relationship in due time knowing you could balance ministry, work life, and personal relationship. Therefore, be okay with working through these seasons.

Be intentional to celebrate one another. You are not in competition with one another but there to support, strengthen, and esteem each other greater than yourselves as you move forward in unity. No one wants to date or become engaged with someone who cannot genuinely celebrate their successes. You must be willing to gut out any subtle jealousy, inadequacy, or revenge of wanting to perform better than your potential spouse.

Please know that whatever you root in your foundation will be difficult to pluck out in the future. It is important to have a balanced healthy foundation that your relationship can stand on.

CHOOSING A GODLY MATE

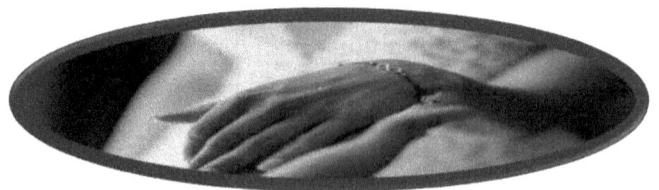

From Dr. Taquetta Baker's *"The Power Of Purity"* Manual.

Often society, and even the church, alludes to the idea that because men are pursuers and women are to be pursued, that women should play a passive role in the choosing of their mate. We often hear things like:

- Just wait for your godly mate, he will find you.
- You're a man, you can keep dating until you decide which woman you want.
- You do not have to do anything; God will reveal your mate to you.
- If you learn the expected female gender roles such as cooking, cleaning, beautifying yourself etc., the right man will choose you.
- If you learn the expected male gender roles of having a good job and provider, the right woman will want you.
- If you have a great relationship with God, you will easily find a man who is equally yoked.

- If you are committed to the work of God, you will quickly be rewarded with a mate.

All these notions sound great in theory but are more optimistic in nature than spiritually factual.

- You can wait years for a godly mate but if you have not spent that time in the secret place with God asking him what he desires for you to have as a mate, you can still miss him.

- You can dedicate years to being sold out for God, obedient to his will, and dedicated to purpose, but if the timing is not right, God will not send you a mate as some form of reward for your obedience to him. God honors your obedience, but the obedient are not the only ones who get a mate.

- You can have an excellent relationship with God, but this does not mean that only excellent believers of God will pursue you. You must be vigilant and watchful for the signs and standards of a godly mate.

I have watched many women who were on fire for God and completely sold out for him sell out for less than God's best. Most often it is not because they do not love God; they simply do not know what they deserve, need, or desire. They also did not intimately know and/or love themselves, so they were seeking a man to fulfill areas they were void, or uncertain in. They did not account for areas such as fear, ungodly timelines, negative mindsets, unworthiness, emotionalism, and other barriers that make women think that they are either not good enough or that there are not enough good, godly men around, so they must settle.

I have also seen godly men not really know what they desire in a mate so they just date and fumble in relationships until they either get tired, settle, or choose a trophy wife. A trophy wife is someone that validates their manhood and makes them look good in appearance and stature, but the relationship is not the will and plan of God for him or that woman. The woman is wooed and accoladed for her anointing, intellect and success so she is unaware that she is being postured as a trophy wife versus being honored for the good thing she is as a potential wife. Often, such men have compromised God's standards for holiness for themselves and for that woman, broken the hearts of good women, experienced heartbreak themselves, or they are just hoping for the best with the woman they chose as a mate.

It is important to understand that God has a very active role for you to play in this process or preparation for a godly mate. God wants you to identify and learn the standards you need for your life and a godly mate. He also wants you to live in these standards as a lifestyle, while you cultivate destiny with him in singleness, and as you SHIFT to dating, engagement, and marriage.

> **You need godly standards to help guide and keep you focused on your journey as you prepare, consider, pursue, and evolve with a potential mate.**

Your standards must be birthed out of covenant relationship, prayer, and journeying in destiny as a lifestyle with God. God knows what, and who you need in your life so that you flourish, evolve, and sustain in life, giftings, callings, purpose, anointing, and design. General standards do not work for unique and extraordinary people. You must first align with God's standard, then actively build a standard around your relationships that builds and evolves you in God-identity with them.

Psalm 138:8 *The Lord will perfect that which concerneth me: thy mercy, O Lord, endureth for ever: forsake not the works of thine own hands.*

When we SHIFT into salvation with God, we are not living our best life according to our standards, will, and desires. We are not perfecting ourselves by becoming challenged and overwhelmed when we do not, or cannot, live up to the religious or personal burdens we have put on ourselves. We are to be resting in the process of evolving in salvation and destiny with God and allowing him to guide us in what is to be perfected in us and concerning us. We now agree with God that he is our Lord and Savior, our Creator, our Father, our deliverer, our healer. He knows what is best for us because he made us in his likeness and his image, and we now want to live for him and in relationship with him so we can become what he created us to be.

Genesis 1:26-27 *And God said, Let us make man in our image, after our likeness: and let them have dominion over the fish of the sea, and over the fowl of the air, and over the cattle, and over all the earth, and over every creeping thing* *that creepeth upon the earth. So God created man in his own image, in the image of God created he him; male and female created he them.*

As we agree with God and learn his ways through personal relationship with him, studying his word, and living as he desires, we posture ourselves for him to perfect us in God-identity. We allow him to teach us what our God-identity is, and we SHIFT with him into embracing and living his will, standard, and purpose as a destiny lifestyle.

This information on standards is from my "*Kingdom Keys To Governing Relationships*" manual:

Isaiah 59:19 *So shall they fear the name of the Lord from the west, and his glory from the rising of the sun. When the enemy shall come in like a flood, the Spirit of the Lord shall lift up a standard against him.*

<u>*Standard*</u> is *nus* in Hebrew and means:
1. to flit (to move lightly and swiftly, fly, change one's address)
2. vanish away (subside, escape; causatively, chase, impel, deliver) (disappear quickly, make invisible, disappear by ceasing to exist; come to an end)
3. abate (annul, extinguish, suppress), away, be displayed, (make to) flee (away,- ing)
4. put to flight, hide, lift up a standard
5. to drive hastily, to cause to disappear, hide

When we know God's standard, and we STAND in it, our standard becomes the weapon to abate, send fleeing, drive away, vanish, and put an end to the challenging or potentially fiery trials in our life.

A standard is an approved model. In this case, it is a model approved by God which guarantees that it aligns with his word and will.

<u>Dictionary.com defines *standard* as:</u>
1. something considered by an authority or by general consent as a basis of comparison
2. a rule or principle that is used as a basis for judgment
3. an average or normal requirement, quality, quantity, level, grade, etc.
4. standards, those morals, ethics, habits, etc., established by authority, custom, or an individual as acceptable

A flood is a great overflowing or outpouring of water that abundantly covers, fills, submerges, overwhelms, overtakes, damages, destroys, or drowns land, people, structures, and material things.

When the enemy comes in like a flood, his objective is to:

- Make himself comparable to or above God.
- Become governor and ruler of a thing by covering and overtaking it.
- Flood a person's life with people, things, conditions, and situations that are not of God.

- Overwhelm people so they become weary, pressured, and weighty while giving into drowning by what has consumed them.
- Damage the identity and purpose of a person or thing.
- Destroy the identity and purpose of a person or thing.
- Cause settling and compromise that leads to death.

Most structures cannot withstand a flood because the influx of water has great destructive powers. When flood waters settle on land, they cause erosion to occur in the soil. This destroys the foundation of buildings, causing cracks to develop that can lead to buildings tumbling to the ground. As continual flooding occurs, erosion wears on the land while causing the land to become compromised. This eventually kills the natural state and inhabitants of the land, kills the nutrients in the soil, and can even change the natural composition and proposition of whatever it flooded (changes the identity and purpose of a thing).

Education.nationalgeographic.org states the following: *Floods can cause even more damage when their waters recede. The water and landscape can be contaminated with hazardous materials, such as sharp debris, pesticides, fuel, and untreated sewage. Potentially dangerous mold can quickly overwhelm water-soaked structures.*

As flood water spreads, it carries disease. Flood victims can be left for weeks without clean water for drinking or hygiene. Another effect of flooding includes outbreaks of deadly diseases.

In essence, the flood is a thief, while the standard gives life and that more abundantly. ***John 10:10*** says, *"The thief cometh not, but for to steal, and to kill, and to destroy: I am come that they might have life, and that they might have it more abundantly."*

Standards Prevent:
- The enemy from stealing, killing, and destroying the identity and purpose of a person or thing.
- The person from settling and compromising for less than God's identity and purpose for their life.
- The person from cycling into old behavioral patterns.
- The person from failing and aborting their success and progress.
- The person from developing new sin issues, unhealthy behaviors, and experiencing trials and challenges that God did not intend.
- Health hazards and disease from emotionally, spiritually, and naturally infecting a person.
- The person from becoming consumed and transformed by the identity of the enemy while being transformed into something God did not intend.

A levee is used to keep water within its respective habitats and borders. Standards provide clear boundaries that serve as a levee to the floods of the enemy. When we set and live by the standards the Lord has established for our lives, the spirit of the Lord can raise these standards up against the enemy when he sends floods into our lives. If we have no standards, minimal standards, compromised standards, contaminated standards, or confused standards, then our levee can easily be overtaken by the flood of the enemy. It is important to know who we are and what God's standards are for our lives, so we live a fortified lifestyle that sustains our success and progress.

The Amplified Bible *So [as the result of the Messiah's intervention] they shall [reverently] fear the name of the Lord from the west, and His glory from the rising of the sun. When the enemy shall come in like a flood, the Spirit of the Lord will lift up a standard against him and put him to flight [for He will come like a rushing stream which the breath of the Lord drives].*

The Message Bible In the west they'll fear the name of GOD, in the east they'll fear the glory of GOD, For he'll arrive like a river in flood stage, whipped to a torrent by the wind of GOD.

If the enemy came in with a person who was not up to your standards, can you stand?

GODLY MATE DESTINY ACTIVATION

1. Journal your understanding of having a standard.

2. Journal your understanding of standards being a levee.

3. If the enemy came into your life right now, what ways would his flood overtake your:

   a. Destiny
   b. Purity
   c. Standards or lack of thereof

4. Spend time using the revelation below to seek God and journal what your gifts, talents, callings, and purposes in life are.

   Calling – Calling is what you are anointed or appointed to do on the earth.

   Purpose – Our calling entails our purpose. We were all born with a specific purpose. Our calling allows us to have Kingdom impact so we can impart our God-identity onto the earth. What impact does your calling have on your family, people, lands, communities, regions, and spheres of influence? That is your purpose.

Destiny – Destiny is where we are going in life. Destiny is a progressive journey with God. We all have destiny moments of success, but destiny is a lifestyle journey with the Lord.

Genesis 1:26-28 *And God said, Let us make man in our image, after our likeness: and let them have dominion over the fish of the sea, and over the fowl of the air, and over the cattle, and over all the earth, and over every creeping thing that creepeth upon the earth. So God created man in his own image, in the image of God created he him; male and female created he them. And God blessed them, and God said unto them, Be fruitful, and multiply, and replenish the earth, and subdue it: and have dominion over the fish of the sea, and over the fowl of the air, and over every living thing that moveth upon the earth.*

Proverbs 19:21 *Many plans are in a man's mind, but it is the Lord's purpose for him that will stand.*

Psalm 119:105 *Your word is a lamp to my feet, and a light to my path.*

Natural & Learned Talents - Talents are skills and abilities that you do well. All talents are not listed in the Bible, but they are a grace, uniqueness, and ability to do something with supernatural uniqueness and ability that others may or may not have, and, even if they do have it, it is not a prototype of you or your talent. An example of talent would be playing the piano, a musical instrument, singing, being a great athlete, being a genius, skilled at math, etc. If you do it well and it comes naturally to you, it is probably a talent that God supernaturally gifted you with.

Skill & Expertise - Expertise falls under natural talents. Expertise entails an expert skill or knowledge, expertness, field of study, passion, or compassion, or know-how regarding a topic, population of people, region, arena, or sphere of influence. This expertise can be learned through personal experience, watching, and assisting others who have experienced it, educational learning, training, equipping, and self-teaching. The person can also have a natural knack for learning on different subjects, thus becoming an expert. Because of a person's spiritual gifts, they can see a need and become an expert by fulfilling that need. Please understand that God blesses talents and expertise even as he blesses spiritual gifts. He will also fill us with skill and abilities.

Exodus 31:6 *And behold, I Myself have appointed with him Oholiab, the son of Ahisamach, of the tribe of Dan; and in the hearts of all who are skillful I have put skill, that they may make all that I have commanded you:*

***Exodus 35:35** He has filled them with skill to perform every work of an engraver and of a designer and of an embroiderer, in blue and in purple and in scarlet material, and in fine linen, and of a weaver, as performers of every work and makers of designs.*

Spiritual Gifts - Spiritual gifts are in the Bible. They are gifts empowered in us through God's Holy Spirit. They are gifts that God has given us for the purpose of saving the lost, bringing deliverance and healing to people, lands, and regions, and establishing God's Kingdom on the earth. Though you are born with some gifts, you can ask the Holy Spirit for other gifts, and he can awaken them in you as he desires. Studying the word and pursuing the gifts can always activate and mature them in you.

***Romans 12:6-8** Having then gifts differing according to the grace that is given to us, whether prophecy, let us prophesy according to the proportion of faith; Or ministry, let us wait on our ministering: or he that teacheth, on teaching; Or he that exhorteth, on exhortation: he that giveth, let him do it with simplicity; he that ruleth, with diligence; he that sheweth mercy, with cheerfulness.*

***1Corinthians 12:8-10** For to one is given by the Spirit the word of wisdom; to another the word of knowledge by the same Spirit; To another faith by the same Spirit; to another the gifts of healing by the same Spirit; To another the working of miracles; to another prophecy;*

to another discerning of spirits; to another divers kinds of tongues; to another the interpretation of tongues:

1Corinthians 12:28-31 *And God hath set some in the church, first apostles, secondarily prophets, thirdly teachers, after that miracles, then gifts of healings, helps, governments, diversities of tongues. Are all apostles? are all prophets? are all teachers? are all workers of miracles? Have all the gifts of healing? do all speak with tongues? do all interpret? But covet earnestly the best gifts: and yet shew I unto you a more excellent way.*

Gifts and talents operate through the wells of our calling. Many people operate in their gifts and talents but lack understanding in their calling, so they err, or fail to walk in their divine purpose. It is important for you to know your calling and the spiritual gifts and natural talents you have. It is equally important to know the reason a person is called to release the vision or endeavor you are assisting with, how it impacts the earth, and how to awaken their gifts and talents so they will flourish in their calling through that vision.

5. Spend time seeking God and journaling what your calling and purpose is.

6. Practical ways to create standards for a Godly mate. Spend time praying and asking God to reveal the areas in which he wants to evolve and heal you as a mate.
Proverbs 8:17 *I love those who love me, and those who seek me diligently find me.*

Deuteronomy 4:29 *But from there you will seek the Lord your God and you will find him, if you search after him with all your heart and with all your soul.*

- There is a guarantee that if you have a desire to create godly standards, God desires even more to give them to you.
- Seeking God for personal growth and areas of healing is essential because it allows you to see the areas where he wants to raise the standard within you first. Once you know that you are living at the standard of excellence that God desires from you, it is easier to believe that you deserve this in a mate.
- Journal areas for personal growth, healing, and development in the following areas: spiritually, mentally, emotionally, and financially.

7. Spend time asking God what you specifically need in a kingdom partner and a mate.

   - What type of prayer partner do you need?
   - Where does the person you build your life with need to be financially to build and advance the kingdom?
   - What mindsets, habits, and character strengths should they have?
   - What type of father or mother qualities should they display?
   - What should their devotion to God look like?
   - What should their interactions with family, friends, and loved ones be like?

- How should they navigate times of distress or hardship?
- What type of qualities do they need to possess when it comes to workmanship?

8. Spend time seeking God and journaling what your standards need to be in relationship to your destiny and calling.

9. Spend time journaling about what type of mate you need to walk alongside of you in your destiny and calling.

10. Spend time journaling what that mate would look like five years from now, ten years from now.

11. Spend time journaling what you would look like five years from now, as well as ten years from now as you journey in life with God and that mate?

12. **Mark 12:30-31** *And thou shalt love the Lord thy God with all thy heart, and with all thy soul, and with all thy mind, and with all thy strength: this is the first commandment. And the second is like, namely this, Thou shalt love thy neighbour as thyself. There is none other commandment greater than these.*

When a person aligns with this scripture, they should embody the fullness of who they should be in God. They should have submitted their heart, will, and life to the Lord so that they can clearly hear him regarding how they should love. The love of God should be the very thing that governs his heart, mind, actions, and life. They should want personal growth and development because of their devotion to God, not solely because they are interested in you.

What are your thoughts regarding yourself and regarding your potential mate as you consider this revelation? How can each of you grow in the true love of God?

13. As you consider the qualities of a godly mate, complete the following activation:

   A. Journal your thoughts on the attributes above. Which is most important to you?
   B. Ask God for his standard for you and for your godly mate and the purpose for which they are to have these standards.
   C. Ask God for revelation on the standards you are to have to be equally yoked with your mate.
   D. Ask God to give you three to five goals to work on to prepare for dating and for marriage.
   E. As you would date and court, share this chapter with your mate. Work together to set goals to SHIFT together in greater character and fortification as a godly person and as a godly couple.

14. Search with God what are the standards you need to date in a safe, godly, and healthy manner.

15. Search with God what are the standards you need to court in a safe, godly, and healthy manner.

16. Search with God what are the standards you need to have in a healthy, evolving marriage.

17. Journal the reason God gave you these standards and the reason they are important to your life and destiny.

18. Does your standard align with God's Word, and does it support his truth?

    A. Is your standard playing it safe rather than truly embodying the high moral status that God is calling you to?
    B. Does your standard embody purity in mind, body, soul, and spirit and not just the outward appearance?
    C. Is your standard deemed admirable by God?
    D. Is your standard based on the world's approval?
    E. Does your standard require you to operate in the excellency of God?

19. Study these scriptures regarding godly stewardship and journal what you learn.

    Luke 16:10 *One who is faithful in a very little is also faithful in much, and one who is dishonest in a very little is also dishonest in much.*

2Timothy 2:15 *Do your best to present yourself to God as one approved, a worker who has no need to be ashamed, rightly handling the word of truth.*

Romans 12:1 *I appeal to you therefore, brothers, by the mercies of God, to present your bodies as a living sacrifice, holy and acceptable to God, which is your spiritual worship.*

Luke 14:28 *For which of you, desiring to build a tower, does not first sit down and count the cost, whether he has enough to complete it?*

2Timothy 2:15 *Study to shew thyself approved unto God, a workman that needeth not to be ashamed, rightly dividing the word of truth.*

Luke 21:3 *Watch therefore, and pray always that you maybe counted worthy to escape all these things that will come to pass, and to stand before the Son of Man.*

20. A person of God who is not presently faithful over their personal growth, healing, and relationship with God will likely not be able to be a good steward over their relationship with you. It is important to govern yourself accordingly when you meet someone and realize that they are not yet in a place of maturity to bear the cost of a relationship with you.

    - Is the person willing and able to be with someone who is called by God?

- Does that person's purpose align with your purpose?
- Is the person willing to cover you in prayer and intercession?
- Is the person able to respect and honor the standard of purity God has set for your life?
- Is the person willing to display maturity and proper stewardship in their finances, time, and over their personal life?
- Is the person interested in learning who God has called them to be or are they only concerned about what you can be for them?
- Does the person love the idea of having a mate but lack foundation on how to love you like Christ loves the church and desires you to be loved?

These are all questions to consider. If you are considering someone, spend time journaling regarding these areas.

21. ***Philippians 1:9-10** says "And this is my prayer: that your love may abound more and more in knowledge and depth of insight, so that you may be able to test and prove what is best and may be pure and blameless for the day of Christ.*

For us to truly be in a place where we live from the overflow of godly wisdom and love, we must spend time with the Holy Spirit seeking clarity and an impartation of what he deems best for us. We want to remain blameless in this process.

Blameless is defined as:

Spotless	Moral
Exemplary	Upright
Innocent	Sinless
Pure	

Standard means moral excellence and a measurement of value, as well as a model of authority:

- A level of quality or attainment.
- An idea or thing used as a measure, norm, or model in comparative evaluations.
- A tree or shrub that grows to full height (take note that a godly man should be fully grown in order to be the standard).

Isaiah 59:19 *So shall they fear the name of the LORD from the west, and his glory from the rising of the sun. When the enemy shall come in like a flood, the Spirit of the LORD shall lift a standard against him.*

- Scripture shows us that it is the standard of God that protects us from the flood of the enemy. When we don't have standards, we are susceptible to compromise, settling, attack, and destiny killing spirits.

- The standards you have for yourself as a woman assist in fortifying you in God's truth while hiding you from those who desire to snatch you out of the will of God. It also keeps you from operating out of a fantasy where you are expecting a certain man but have not yet allowed God to birth you into that type of woman.

  Journal how you would explain the need for having standards to someone who does not know what they want in a relationship and what they deserve from a relationship.

22. What ways can you grow to trust God for the standards he has given you for your life and for what he is requiring for you as it relates to a mate?

23. Practice growing in trust with God and living your standards as a lifestyle.

> Know that as you continue learning from this manual, your answers may change or evolve. This is a good thing, as it means you are embodying what God is speaking and are being cultivated by his will and purpose for your life, marriage, and destiny.
>
> ## SHIFT!

GODLY SUBMISSION

The Foundation Of Godly Submission!
Lack of understanding of submission and the divine order of marriage and family opens the door to discord, conflict, resentment, division, and demons. Couples should explore and be sound in their understanding of headship, submission and unconditional love. Study *Genesis 2-6* and *Ephesians 5* Ask God to give you a heart of submission and a love to submit one to another.

1Corinthians 11:3 But I would have you know, that the head of every man is Christ; and the head of the woman is the man; and the head of Christ is God.

Ephesians 5:22-33 Wives, submit yourselves unto your own husbands, as unto the Lord. For the husband is the head of the wife, even as Christ is the head of the church: and he is the saviour of the body. Therefore as the church is subject unto Christ, so let the wives be to their own husbands in every thing.

Husbands, love your wives, even as Christ also loved the church, and gave himself for it; That he might sanctify and cleanse it with the washing of water by the word, That he might present it to himself a glorious church, not having spot, or wrinkle, or any such thing; but that it should be holy and without blemish. So ought men to love their wives as their own bodies. He that loveth his wife loveth himself.

For no man ever yet hated his own flesh; but nourisheth and cherisheth it, even as the Lord the church: For we are members of his body, of his flesh, and of his bones. For this cause shall a man leave his father and mother, and shall be joined unto his wife, and they two shall be one flesh. This is a great mystery: but I speak concerning Christ and the church. Nevertheless, let every one of you in particular so love his wife even as himself; and the wife see that she reverence her husband.

The Amplified Bible *Wives, be subject to your own husbands, as [a service] to the Lord. For the husband is head of the wife, as Christ is head of the church, Himself being the Savior of the body. But as the church is subject to Christ, so also wives should be subject to their husbands in everything [respecting both their position as protector and their responsibility to God as head of the house].*

Husbands, love your wives [seek the highest good for her and surround her with a caring, unselfish love], just as Christ also loved the church and gave Himself up for her, so that He might sanctify the church, having cleansed her by the washing of water with the word [of God], so that [in turn] He might present the church to Himself in glorious splendor, without spot or wrinkle or any such thing; but that she would be holy [set apart for God] and blameless. Even so husbands should and are morally obligated to love their own wives as [being in a sense] their own bodies. He who loves his own wife loves himself.

For no one ever hated his own body, but [instead] he nourishes and protects and cherishes it, just as Christ does the church, because we are members (parts) of His body. FOR THIS REASON, A MAN SHALL LEAVE HIS FATHER AND HIS MOTHER AND SHALL BE JOINED [and be faithfully devoted] TO HIS WIFE, AND THE TWO SHALL BECOME ONE FLESH. This mystery [of two becoming one] is great; but I am speaking with reference to [the relationship of] Christ and the church. However, each man among you [without exception] is to love his wife as his very own self [with behavior worthy of respect and esteem, always seeking the best for her with an attitude of lovingkindness], and the wife [must see to it] that she respects and delights in her husband [that she notices him and prefers him and treats him with loving concern, treasuring him, honoring him, and holding him dear].

The MAN Becomes God's Sacrificial Love to His Wife!

The Amplified Bible states that husbands give up their lives to the highest good so that she - his wife - can be her best self. The husband sacrifices himself unto death – die to self so he can resurrect in Christlikeness in the identity, power, and grace of God. He does this so that he can love his wife properly and provide her with the greatest opportunity to

SHIFT into the best version of herself - the blameless version of herself that allows her - the bride - to be and look like Christ.

JUST PONDER THIS FOR A MOMENT!

LET ME SAY IT ANOTHER WAY!

Husbands love their wives, even as God loves the church and gave himself for it. Jesus came and died for the church. According to that scripture passage, the husband possesses the capacity and capability to love his wife in this manner. The husband is given the responsibility of dying like Christ so he can love, cover, lead, protect, and provide, as God would require for him and his family.

JUST PONDER THIS FOR A MOMENT!

LET ME SAY IT AGAIN ANOTHER WAY!

Even as the husband considers what it truly means to love like Christ loves the church, you husband, are constantly dying DAILY to love your wife like the church. I am taking the time to really drive this revelation into you – husband – and even the wife that reads it - because the church is big on making sure wives know they **MUST** submit, but we do not realize the magnitude of teaching husbands that they **MUST** love their wife like Christ loves the church.

THIS DIMENSION OF LOVE IS:

Selfless	Empowering	Holy
Sacrificial	Enduring	Righteous
Personal	Steadfast	Just
Relational	Faithful	Protective
Caring	Trustworthy	Safe
Passionate	Loyal	Constant
Honoring	Giving	Steadfast
Glorious	Blessed	Sufficient
Compassionate	Expressive	Fulfilling
	Thoughtful	Finite
Gracious	Hopeful	Eternal
Unconditional	Helpful	Sovereign
Relentless	Pure	Supreme

I want the wife to recognize what her husband should be giving to her even as I help the husband to understand his role of leadership unto God, his wife, and the marriage covenant. When a husband subjects himself to God, and dies in submission under the leadership of God, he becomes

Christlike and is **RESURRECTED** into what is needed to look, behave, represent, lead, provide, and govern like Christ. That husband will be able to hear from God what sacrifices, plans, and purposes need to be made to help the marriage and family, successfully produce the glory of God.

MY GOD! SHIFT RIGHT NOW! SHIFT!

The WOMAN Submits to Her Husband as Unto the Lord!

A Husband Loving Himself as the Church Is a Form of Submission!

Submitting in Greek is *hypotassō* and means:
1. to subordinate; reflexively, to obey, to be under obedience (obedient), put under
2. subdue unto, (be, make) subject (to, unto), be (put) in subjection (to, under), submit self unto
3. to arrange under, to subordinate to subject, put in subjection to, subject
4. obey oneself
5. to submit to one's control
6. to yield to one's admonition or advice, to obey, be subject

7. A Greek military term meaning "to arrange [troop divisions] in a military fashion under the command of a leader
8. In non-military use, it was "a voluntary attitude of giving in, cooperating
9. assuming responsibility, and carrying a burden

Wife, per scripture, when you submit to your husband, it is like you would AS UNTO THE LORD. Wife, you are loving, honoring, obeying, trusting, believing in, faithful too, and surrendering to that man like you would the Lord.

Wife, this posture of submission is not conditional. It is unconditional. It is not dependent on whether that man deserves to be submitted to or has proven that he can be trusted to be submitted to. Once you contend that this man is your husband that God chose for you and you say **I DO**, you are humbling yourself into submission unto that husband. This is the reason it is so important to marry **THE ONE**! It is so important to marry a man you can submit to. **IF YOU DO NOT BELIEVE YOU CAN SUBMIT TO HIM, DO NOT MARRY HIM!**

JUST PONDER THIS FOR A MOMENT!

LET ME SAY IT AGAIN ANOTHER WAY!

Wifey, when you say I DO, you are saying:

I am willing to love this man like I love the Lord.
I am willing to obey this man like I comply to the Lord.
I am willing to honor this man like I glorify the Lord.
I am willing to trust and be faithful to this man like I am devoted to the Lord.
I am willing to praise this man like I reverence the Lord.

Per the scripture passage, wife, you possess the capacity and capability to submit to your husband in this manner. Such a posture is not about putting your life in your husband's hands but trusting God and his sovereign word to work his principle of submission into the marriage covenant. As you are obedient to God, you demonstrate that you trust the fruit and blessings of submission to manifest in and through the marital vision.

SUBMISSION IS A TWO-WAY STREET!

Many people dread having to submit in marriage, but submit is twofold:

- ➢ Wives submitting to husbands.
- ➢ Husbands submitting to God.

POWER OF SUBMISSION
✓ Submitting SHIFTS the covenant marriage in alignment with God's purpose for the union where his love and purpose for marriage can flow properly.

- ✓ Submitting SHIFTS each spouse into a posture to be self-sacrificing where they can have the heart of God for their spouse.

- ✓ Submitting SHIFTS each spouse into divine order where they can receive godly vision and clarity for their mate, marriage, and family.

- ✓ Submitting SHIFTS the covenant marriage under the hedge of God where the wars and persecutions against, and within the marriage can be thwarted as each spouse allows God's perfect will for marriage to guide them and be a military force and governance within and around them.

- ✓ Submitting SHIFTS each spouse to where they are under the truth of God where they can lay down and avoid false burdens while viewing marriage as a needed and heartfelt responsibility so that they are able to bear and carry the YOKE OF GOD for the marriage.

- ✓ Dr. Jackie Green contends that submission is divine protection. When I consider this wisdom, I would declare this regarding submission:

- Submission keeps a godly woman protected inside the refuge, counsel, and honor of God.
- Submission keeps a godly man inside the protection of receiving God's comfort, care, and aid in a safe pure manner.

Matthew 11:27-30 *All things are delivered unto me of my Father: and no man knoweth the Son, but the Father; neither knoweth any man the Father, save the Son, and he to whomsoever the Son will reveal him. Come unto me, all ye that labour and are heavy laden, and I will give you rest. Take my yoke upon you, and learn of me; for I am meek and lowly in heart: and ye shall find rest unto your souls. For my yoke is easy, and my burden is light.*

Though marriage is work, it should not be a burden where you dread submission or dread doing the work it takes to further evolve personally and as partners in Christlikeness and in personal and marital vision and destiny. When this occurs, it is an indication that you are not operating in agape love – the love of Jesus Christ.

The principle of submission requires everything about the marriage to flow through love which SHIFTS into building a God designed covenant marriage.

Godly love is an action work. Love is covenant in action.

True agape love makes you want to submit and to be self-sacrificing. This is the reason Jesus Christ could make this statement:

John 4:34 *Jesus saith unto them, My meat is to do the will of him that sent me, and to finish his work.*

Food in Hebrew means literally, or figuratively, victual. *Victual* means food or provision - it is my provision to please him.

<u>*Will*</u> in the Greek is *thelēma* and means:
1. a determination (properly, the thing)
2. i.e. (actively) choice (specially, purpose, decree; abstractly, volition) or (passively) inclination: — desire, pleasure
3. what one wishes or has determined shall be done
4. of the purpose of God to bless mankind through Christ
5. of what God wishes to be done by his commands, precepts
6. will, choice, inclination, desire, pleasure

Jesus hungered to please – to be submitted to God. He understood that this posture was provision for him even as it was provision for God. We discern from the definition that when we posture properly, it SHIFTS forth:

- ✓ A determination to please God.
- ✓ An active choice that decrees it will purposely please God.
- ✓ A pleasure, hunger, and desire to please God.
- ✓ An understanding of the importance of pleasing God.
- ✓ A delight to want to hear and do the commands and precepts of God.

Truth is covenant is for a lifetime and this mindset and standard should be rooted in the foundation of the dating, engagement and marital relationship.

Covenant,

- Is a promise fulfilled and proceeding (continual) prophecy by God and a promise you enter into via godly agreement by the enactment of your will and YES to him as a believer - a son who is now a kingdom heir to his throne.

- An act of being in harmony with God and those he has you in covenant with.

- Is a display of divine faithfulness and loyalty to God and what he has released and is doing in your life.

- Covenant keeps you and the marriage safe and protected in God and in the reigns and principles of what he has said in his word and has ordained for your life as God has promised to bless and protect those who keep his word and live faithfully for him.

- Covenant relationships are give and take. You care for one another's soul and heart and have grace to walk with one another.

- Covenant is self-sacrificing. You sacrifice yourself to God, your spouse, his kingdom, and to your God given will and purpose. You are sacrificing embarrassment, ego, pride, righteous indignation, fear, and control of how you want and expect your spouse, situations and the marriage itself to be.

Covenant **SHOULD NOT** be ghosted, breached, divorced, cut off just because you conflict with someone – in this case – **YOUR SPOUSE!**

- Covenants must be guarded, nurtured, and cultivated.

- Covenant must be honored.

- You must have grace for your covenant partner by yielding space, opportunity, time, and expectation for personal and marital growth. When there is no grace, constant ridicule, rebuke, punishment, and chastisement overrides the opportunity for God to impact and mature his God identity, character, nature, destiny and purpose in your spouse and in the marriage covenant. You essentially snuff the heart and drive out of your spouse to want to try to grow and breed resentment to want to grow with YOU. Your partner expects you to point out their shortcomings, while pretending as if you are helping and even holding them accountable. What you are really doing is lording over them, taking the place of God in their lives, and/or using the opportunity to passive aggressively hit them through covetousness, jealousy, or an unresolved issue you have with them. You could also be operating in pride which causes you to be self-validated by pointing out their flaws in effort to overshadow your own weaknesses or to prove that you know and do it better than they do. These operations cause division and open the door to covenant breaking. Learn to love your partner like God loves. Ask God for a grace and heart for them such that you build them up rather than tear them down.

- **Remember marriage is building. Relationship is building. Every time you tear your partner down; you tear the covenant relationship down.**

- You must cover one another and protect one another.

It is important to learn what reasons God placed your spouse in your life. Examine and know the following:

What reasons God gave you that relationship?
Learn that person.
Learn who you are to that person.
Learn what God requires of you personally and you and that person together as it relates to future maturity and the evolving of God identity, character development, your destinies, and callings.
Learn some applicable and spiritual skills and tools to build that relationship into the purpose to which God gave it.

The marriage and the family itself serves as an altar, such that as you all offer up prayers, sacrifices of servanthood, fellowship, and journeying in covenant destiny with God as a lifestyle, the purpose of your family lineage can unveil and evolve in the earth.

As covenant is built upon God, parents govern the family dynamics through his character, nature, biblical principles, and family vision. This foundation roots the family structure in the righteousness, holiness, healthiness, purposes, kingdom governance, mercy, goodness, blessings, favor, and eternal legacy of God. Legacy enables the marriage and family to withstand carnality, worldliness, demonic oppression, possession, wickedness, witchcraft, idolatry, unhealthy and ungodly cycles and patterns, where the fullness of salvation can be evident in their lives and lineages.

GODLY SUBMISSION ACTIVATION

1. Journal what you learned about submission in this chapter.
2. What did you learn about your posture in godly submission?
3. What did you learn about your partner's posture in godly submission?
4. If you are not married yet, do you see yourself submitting to your partner 10, 30, 60 years from now? Spend time praying and processing this question. Journal the thoughts, emotions, visions, and impressions you are receiving from God. BE HONEST with what is occurring. Do not focus on potential. Focus on reality. Also ask God if it is his will for you submit to this person as a husband or wife. Journal what he says.

5. If you are married, ask God to give you vision for the reason you are to submit now and in the future to your partner. Ask him for three goals personally and as a married couple to strengthen your submission posture according to Ephesians 5.
6. What reasons does God requires the Ephesians 5 mandate in your covenant marriage?
7. Why is submission a vital foundational principle in your covenant marriage?
8. How will submitting God's way help you in your covenant marriage? How will it help your spouse?
9. Set five goals where you can be intentional to live through godly submission?
10. Ask God to give you a heart of submission and a love to submit one to another. Journal on how God desires you to posture in submission through the love and heart posture he is revealing to you.
11. Ask God to give you a love for your partner's voice so you honor the God in them. Practice honoring one another's voice and the God in one another.
12. As you and your partner mature, search out what submission looks like in those times and seasons of your life. Renew your goals and posture of submission to meet the maturity and expansion of who you all have become personally and in your marriage covenant.

> **DECREEING GOD'S KINGDOM COVENANT REIGNS IN YOUR MARRIAGES & FAMILIES AS YOU ALL SUBMIT GOD'S WAY!**

MY HELP MEET

Unequally Yoked In Marriage
Kingdom vision in marriage must breed kingdom agreement and yoking. Marrying a person, we are not equally yoked to or who is not willing to do the work causes demonic spirits to oppress you and the marriage. When we are unequally yoked, there is no foundation for agreement.

Agreed is *yâ'ad* in Hebrew and is a primitive root that means:
1. to fix upon (by agreement or appointment)
2. by implication, to meet (at a stated time), to summon (to trial), to direct (in a certain quarter or position), to engage (for marriage)
3. agree (make an) appoint (-ment, a time), assemble (selves), betroth, gather (selves, together), meet (together), set (a time)

4. to be design, to be fixed

Agreement produces harmony, synchronization, rhythm, momentum, direction, godly timing, godly design, unity, and consistent alignment.

***2Corinthians 6:14** Be ye not unequally yoked together with unbelievers: for what fellowship hath righteousness with unrighteousness? and what communion hath light with darkness?*

<u>*Unequally Yoked* is *heterozygeō* Greek and means:</u>
1. to yoke up differently, i.e. (figuratively) to associate discordantly
2. unequally yoke together with
3. to come under an unequal or different yoke, to be unequally yokedto have fellowship with one who is not an equal
4. *2Cor 6:14*, where the apostle is forbidding Christians to have intercourse with idolaters

<u>*Unbelievers* is *apistos* in Greek and means:</u>
1. (actively) disbelieving, i.e. without Christian faith (specially, a heathen)
2. (passively) untrustworthy (person), or incredible (thing)
3. that believeth not, faithless, incredible thing, infidel, unbeliever(-ing)

<u>*Righteousness* is *dikaiosynē* in Greek and means:</u>
1. equity (of character or act); specially (Christian) justification: — righteousness

2. in a broad sense: state of him who is as he ought to be, righteousness, the condition acceptable to God
3. the doctrine concerning the way in which man may attain a state approved of God
4. integrity, virtue, purity of life, rightness, correctness of thinking feeling, and acting
5. in a narrower sense, justice or the virtue which gives each his due

Unrighteousness is *anomia* in Greek and means:
1. illegality, i.e. violation of law or (genitive case) wickedness
2. iniquity, transgress (-ion of) the law, unrighteousness.
3. the condition of being without law
4. Violating it due to ignorance of it
5. contempt and violation of law, iniquity, wickedness

Spirits Operating Through Failed Vision & Being Unequally Yoke		
Spirit of Deception	Spirits of Disobedience	Spirits of Abandonment
Spirits of Rejection	Spirit of the Vagabond & Wanderer (Displaced from God & in destiny)	Spirits of Carnality
Spirits of Anti-submissiveness	Spirit of the Bastard	Spirits of Mistrust, Doubt, Unbelief
Spirits of Rebellion	Spirits of Unequal Yoking	Spirits of Justifications
Spirit of the Orphan	Spirits of Unrighteousness	Spirits of Entitlement

Spirits & Operations of Permissive Will (our will & desires) Versus God's Perfect will	Spirits of Blindness	Death & Dumb Spirits
Spirits of Witchcraft	Spirits of Idolatry	Spirits of Worldliness

These spirits must be repented for then cast out for deliverance to manifest. There must be a strategy sought regarding whether an equal yoking can occur and what those in the relationship or marriage need to do to align in godly agreement. Many times, this is not possible because one person will come to deliverance or counseling due to frustrations for the unequally yoking occurring while the other person is resistant to addressing the issue and to changing. Intercession has to be done or decisions according to God's will have to be made. As God intervenes or provides grace, intervention eventually occurs. But many times, this is not without extended labor and processing which is the reason the word warns us to avoid being unequally yoked.

Sometimes God will require unequally yoked relationships to end. And generally, when it comes to marriage, people have to remain when there is no biblical or substantial reason to divorce, while allowing the Lord to help them find fulfillment and grace in what is not yoked through him. In recent times, we have experienced people divorcing with no biblical or substantial grounds, repenting, and hoping God forgives and restores them. We are also experiencing people using divorce as an option when marrying those they are not equally yoked to, and hoping the person will change or that they can transform the person during the marriage.

Kingdom Marriage Breeds Covenant & Fellowship
God never meant for man to be alone, neither did he envision families having a single head of household. He created Adam and despite being God who can be everything, God told Adam,

Genesis 2:18 *And the Lord God said, It is not good that the man should be alone; I will make him an help meet for him.*

Help meet is êzer in Hebrew and means:
1. aid: — help help meet
2. help, succour help, succour one who helps

Interestingly the word succour means, "assistance and support in times of hardship and distress."

Synonyms: aid, help, a helping hand, assistance; ministration, comfort, ease, relief, support, guidance, backing, easement, lend a (helping) hand to, be of service to; minister to, care for, comfort, bring comfort to, bring relief to, support, be supportive of, sustain, protect, take care of, look after, attend to, serve, wait on

Let's examine this scripture in other bible versions:

The New International Bible *The Lord God said, "It is not good for the man to be alone. I will make a helper suitable for him."*

English Standard Bible *Then the Lord God said, "It is not good that the man should be alone; I will make him a helper fit for him."*

New Living Bible *Then the Lord God said, "It is not good for the man to be alone. I will make a helper who is just right for him."*

The Holman Christian Standard Bible *Then the Lord God said, "It is not good for the man to be alone. I will make a helper as his complement."*

The Amplified Bible *Now the LORD God said, "It is not good (beneficial) for the man to be alone; I will make him a helper [one who balances him—a counterpart who is] suitable and complementary for him."*

The Amplified Classic Bible *Now the Lord God said, It is not good (sufficient, satisfactory) that the man should be alone; I will make him a helper meet (suitable, adapted, complementary) for him.*

Adapt means, "to make suitable to requirements or conditions; adjust or modify fittingly; to adjust oneself to different conditions, environment, etc."

Adaptability is the resilience and power we see in women as they possess the ability to create and to adapt to different conditions to be a help meet to their husbands but also to fulfill roles and positions where the fulfillment of vision and purpose can manifest with sustaining success.

God made Eve from Adam's rib, which symbolizes that a woman – a wife - is an extension of her man – a husband. They are one flesh that is innocent, pure and covered from shame and the oppressions of the world, people, and demons. As long as they operate as one flesh, and do not allow the enemy to come in and divide them, they are able to cover one another from vulnerabilities, shortcomings, sin, shame, disappointment, disconcertedness, imperfections and deficiencies.

LET'S EXAMINE THIS TRUTH IN SCRIPTURE!

Genesis 2:21-25 And the LORD God caused a deep sleep to fall upon Adam, and he slept: and he took one of his ribs, and closed up the flesh instead thereof; And the rib, which the LORD God had taken from man, made he a woman, and brought her unto the man. And Adam said, This is now bone of my bones, and flesh of my flesh: she shall be called Woman, because she was taken out of Man. **Therefore, shall a man leave his father and his mother, and shall cleave unto his wife: and they shall be one flesh. And they**

were both naked, the man and his wife, and were not ashamed.

MY GOD!

If you do not want help. Do not get married. If you are already married and dread having help, you should not have gotten married.

A help meet discerns where help is needed in their mate, marriage, home, family, and children, then adapts to provide HELP.

A help meet HELPS according to how God has ordained, not in accordance with what they want or think they should give their covenant partner.

As a help meet, it is important to cover your spouse and be who God has graced you and given you vision to be in the marriage. You are a team. You should be able to catch one another's blind spots and cover one another when necessary; such that nothing is lacking. You are an extension of your spouse, and they are an extension of you.

A help meet does not chastise, punish, or whip their spouse like they are a child. You are not their mother. You are not their father. You are their spouse – their covenant partner. You are their help meet. It is your responsibility as a help meet to HELP where needed such that the two of you remain one.

A help meet does not assume the person did not give their best effort. A help meet HELPS so that their mate, the marriage, the children, and the household is sufficient, safe, advancing, and benefiting from the wholeness of being joined together as one.

The spouse does not assume the help meet is usurping them when they are striving to help. The help meet is there to fulfill areas where that spouse needs support, encouragement, reminders, and assistance. This HELPS the marriage, children, and household to operate smoothly and sufficiently.

This revelation is so vital as so many couples conflict due to not understanding the concept and importance of a help meet. Spirits of strife, inferiority, inadequacy, discord, rivalry, division, and divorce operate in and around these couples as they treat one another more like enemies than covenant partners. They reject help while contending that they are viewed as weak and incompetent. The more they

uncover and expose one another through misunderstandings and mishandlings, the more the spirits oppress their communication and ability to trust and receive help from one another.

PROCESS THAT REVELATION FOR A MOMENT!

MY GOD! LET'S SHIFT FURTHER!!!!!!

<u>The Help Meet Versus The Parent:</u>

YOU ARE A SPOUSE, NOT A PARENT.

Before reading this section, go to page 196 to 201 and study "*Build A Mate Syndrome.*" Also study "*Arrested Development*" on page 216 to 217.

Help Meet does not mean **PARENT YOUR SPOUSE**. This revelation is important in making sure you posture correctly in submission and in being a help meet to one another.

Parenting roles should only be utilized with children. Your spouse is not a child.

- ✓ You are not your spouse's mother or father. You did not birth them, and you cannot rebirth them.
- ✓ You are not God in your spouse's life.
- ✓ You are not your spouse's savior. Even if they are going to hell, you have no hell or heaven to put them in.
- ✓ You are not your spouse's judge or dictator.
- ✓ Your job is not to chastise them and keep them in line.
- ✓ Your job is not to punish them when they do something wrong or when they sin.

Even when you speak truth to your spouse, you are speaking to an adult as marriage is not for children but GROWN FOLK!

You should have married a grown man or woman and therefore you should engage your spouse as a grown man or woman.

Even if your spouse has a little girl or little boy spirit, it is not your responsibility to parent or soul tie with this area of their personality. If you do, this is the part of their identity that will be strengthened in the marriage. This is the part of their identity that will respond to you and require you to feed its voids, traumas, immaturity, and need for validation. Hopefully, in dating you can see if a little girl or little boy is in operation and can encourage your partner to seek help, while also deciding if you all are capable of maturing in a healthy adult relationship as they heal.

If you recognize that you or your spouse have a little girl or little boy spirit, you all need to get counseling, deliverance, and/or inner healing to heal these areas of their identity, while praying for this part of their personality to be healed and grow up to the full age they currently are. Support and encourage one another to get help and to heal. You also want to engage, empower, and strengthen, the woman or man that is in each of – the husband and the wife that you are to one another. Be intentional to act like adults while seeking healing for the child within.

Allowing a little girl or little boy personality into the relationship is like committing adultery against one another. You are allowing a child into the covenant to make adult decisions and to fulfil responsibilities and roles that only a married adult should be making. You are also forcing your spouse to parent you which is not a part of a divine kingdom marriage covenant.

When a spouse operates more like a mother or father than a spouse, they are out of order.

> **SPOUSE, YOU ARE OUT OF ORDER WHEN YOU PARENT RATHER THAN ENGAGE LIKE A HUSBAND OR WIFE.**

Such a posture causes the covenant marriage to be unequally yoked and inordinate. It causes you to treat the spouse in ways that are more micromanaging, controlling, dictating, and punishing. You feel the need to train and educate them, while instilling consequences and reprimands to further assist your spouse with doing what you want them to do. You are striving to build them in your own strength and design rather than in the grace, strength, will, and likeness of God. Even when children grow up, they still engage and rely on their parents from a child's posture. If you build your covenant marriage through this well, this is the well that will keep on evolving even as your spouse grows up and your marriage evolves.

Spouses who are parented often rebel because even with a little girl or boy personality, they recognize they are adults and the autonomy they have as an adult. They are resentful and appalled at how they are treated and respond accordingly. This causes a lot of unnecessary conflicts that are rooted in power and control – both parties trying to overpower and control the other one. Couples spend years in these types of wars which result in them tolerating one another, experiencing inconsistent personal and marital growth, and dreading being married. Resist being the child and resist being the parent. Take your role as husband and wife and **LIVE THERE**.

As a help meet, your job is to help your spouse and to cover them in those areas they lack. This help has to come through your role as a marriage partner – a husband or a wife. It has to come through the characteristics of a godly spouse. You must know these characteristics so you can build yourself and your spouse in them. You all also need to hold one another accountable to these adult roles and characteristics.

Qualities of a Godly Husband

A woman should seek a man who is wise, thus Book of Proverbs gives us the characteristics of wise men.
1. A wise husband is kind and compassionate (12:10).
2. A wise husband is honest (29:24).
3. A wise husband is hard-working (12:11; 27:23-27).
4. A wise husband is truthful (12:17,19).
5. A wise husband exercises self-control (12:15; 16:32).
6. A wise husband has a gentle tongue (12:18; 15:1-2,4).
7. A wise husband is generous (14:21; 28:27).
8. A wise husband is willing to be corrected (even by his wife) and listens to counsel (12:15; 15:12,31-32; 28:13; 29:1).
9. A wise husband is a man of integrity (19:1; 20:7).
10. A wise husband is faithful and reliable (17:17; 29:3; contrast 25:19; 31:3).
11. A wise husband is forgiving (19:11).
12. A wise husband is willing to admit he is wrong (28:13).
13. A wise husband is humble (15:25,33; 16:18-19; 18:12; 29:23).
14. A wise husband is not contentious, but a peacemaker (17:1; 18:1,19).
15. A wise husband has control of his temper (14:29; 16:32; 17:27; 29:11).
16. A wise husband is a man who avoids excesses (20:1; 23:20-21, 29-35; 31:3-9).
17. A wise husband has a concern for others, especially the poor and the oppressed (29:7).
18. A wise husband can keep a confidence (17:9; 26:20).
19. A wise husband fears God and is obedient to His Word (13:13; 14:26; 16:20; 28:25; 31:30).
20. A wise husband is not a jealous man (27:4).
21. A The wise husband has a positive outlook on life (15:15; 17:22; 18:14).

www.GodlyWoman.Co

A Biblical Wife
Who is she?
She strives to live her life according to the bible.

She respects her husband
"and the wife see that she reverence her husband."
Ephesians 5:33

She is polite and careful she keeps herself for her husband only.
" To be discreet, chaste, keepers at home, good, obedient to their own husbands, that the word of God be not blasphemed."
Titus 2:5

She brings virtue and honour to her husband
" A virtuous woman is a crown to her husband."
Proverbs 12:4

She has the favour of God.
" Whoso findeth a wife findeth a good thing and obtaineth favour of the Lord."
Proverbs 18:22

She submits to her husband as to the Lord.
"Wives, submit yourselves unto your own husbands, as unto the Lord."
Ephesians 5:22

She is her husbands helpmeet, she supports her husband
"I will make him an helpmeet for him."
Genesis 2:18

She takes care of her home, she blesses her home and family
" Every wise woman buildeth her house:"
Proverbs 14:1

She is made in the image of God.
"So God created man in His own image, in the image of God created he him; male and female created he them."
Genesis 1:27

Faith, Lifestyle and Tea@TeawithMe101 Natalie M.

I love how correction is defined as counsel and not punishment or chastisement. Godly counsel is given without disregarding or overriding the freewill of your

spouse. It is given from a posture of building up and focusing your spouse on the benefits of changing and how such changes could improve them, you, the marriage and family.

***Jeremiah 31:3** The LORD hath appeared of old unto me, saying, Yea, I have loved thee with an everlasting love: therefore with lovingkindness have I drawn thee.*

Lovingkindness means to provide reproof and correction but it is done with grace, mercy, favor, and goodness. These are the actual Hebrew definitions of *lovingkindness* which is interesting because we should be engaging our spouse as the good thing – the favored one – that God has given us. We should have such a delight for them that grace and mercy should be conscious, constant, and everlasting.

PROCESS THAT REVELATION FOR A MOMENT!

> Want To Draw Your Spouse to You Rather Than Push Them Away.

When we punish and chastise ADULTS or in this case your spouse from a parenting position, it instills shame, guilt, and condemnation. It belittles and degrades them. It tears down rather than builds up. The tearing down of whatever is a sin, barrier, weakness, etc., needs to be done in intercessory prayer and with you all working together to heal and mature in the areas that need work not through punishment. When postured accordingly, you help your spouse be responsible for who they are as your covenant husband or wife.

SHIFT RIGHT NOW!

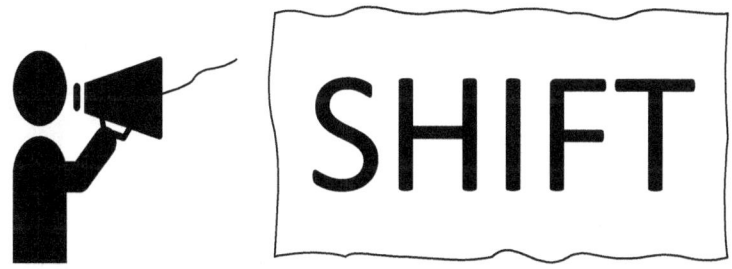

SIDEBAR REVELATION: When chastising children, you should NOT be tearing them down and belittling them as this is abuse. You are chastising to pull out of them what is already in them through God identity or instilling what is needed to help God identity evolve and mature in them.

HELP MEET ACTIVATION!

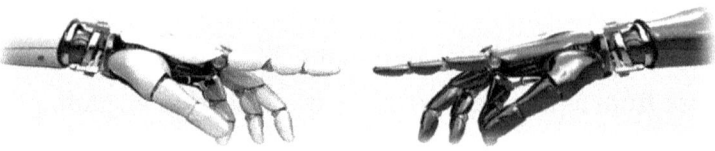

Men
1. Is the woman you are dating, engaged to, married too, adaptable?
2. Can she adjust to various times, seasons, and conditions of life and circumstances?
3. Can she adapt to who you are as a man, a husband, and the vision that God is giving you all for your marriage?
4. If dating or engaged, are you able to view and receive your partner as a help meet? Explain your answer and work on your relationship in this area.
5. If you are married, how can you implement this revelation into your covenant to receive the blessing of your help meet?

Women
1. Does the man you are dating, engaged to, married to know they NEED a woman - help meet?
2. Does the man you are dating, engaged to, married to know what a help meet is according to the Bible?
3. Does the man you are dating, engaged to, married to know your ability to be adaptable is not you trying to be a man, but is an innate quality God gave you to help him fulfill God's divine will and purpose for his life,

your life, the marriage, and as you all reign in dominion in the earth?
4. Answer these questions in detail and truth, while working on them with your partner.
5. Woman and Man make sure you can clearly answer these questions before entering marriage. If you are already engaged or married, examine these questions and seek to establish biblical truth into the foundation of your marriage. Uproot any other faulty or erred ideologies in your marriage foundation.

Couples
1. Identify any unhealthy, imbalanced, unequally yoked, or inordinate roles (*Study* page 212 to 213) in your relationship. Do you or your spouse need deliverance from arrested development - the little girl or little boy spirit? Journal, pray, and share with one another on this topic. Seek deliverance and inner healing if necessary. Set four goals you can implement where you engage as ADULTS – husband and wife – versus parents and children.

> **I WILL LET MY MATE HELP ME~SHIFT!**

GODLY VISION FOR MARRIAGE

God created marriage and family - His perfect design started in the garden when he created Adam, formed Eve from his rib, and gave them dominion in heaven and earth.

God's design and original intent for marriage and family before the foundation of the earth was to bring Him glory and honor throughout generations.
Marriage is a prototype of Christ and His Church.
Marriage is for the purposes of procreation and multiplication, as God replicates himself throughout generations.
Marriage possesses vision of having dominion in the earth such that God's identity, will, and purpose reigns, rules, governs through the sovereignty of who he is as GOD.
Marriage establishes and demonstrates the unconditional agape love and kingdom principles which is the biblical Word of God.

Marriage is not just a human contract. It is a divine covenant. God designed marriage to reflect His love, unity, and faithfulness. In *Ephesians 5*, marriage symbolizes

Christ's relationship with the Church, built on love, sacrifice, and mutual respect. Marriage is a partnership where the husband and wife grow together in faith, honor God, and serve one another. When we follow His design, marriage becomes more than a commitment. It becomes a testimony of His grace.

Marriage should begin, be built, and cultivated in kingdom purpose and vision. God gave Adam and Eve vision for their marriage.

Genesis 1:27-31 *So God created man in his own image, in the image of God created he him; male and female created he them. And God blessed them, and God said unto them, Be fruitful, and multiply, and replenish the earth, and subdue it: and have dominion over the fish of the sea, and over the fowl of the air, and over every living thing that moveth upon the earth.*

And God said, Behold, I have given you every herb bearing seed, which is upon the face of all the earth, and every tree, in the which is the fruit of a tree yielding seed; to you it shall be for meat. And to every beast of the earth, and to every fowl of the air, and to every thing that creepeth upon the earth, wherein there is life, I have given every green herb for meat: and it was so. And God saw every thing that he had made, and, behold, it was very good. And the evening and the morning were the sixth day.

Genesis 2:15-18 And the Lord God took the man, and put him into the garden of Eden to dress it and to keep it. And the Lord God commanded the man, saying, Of every tree of the garden thou mayest freely eat: But of the tree of the knowledge of good and evil, thou shalt not eat of it: for in the day that thou eatest thereof thou shalt surely die. And the Lord God took the man, and put him into the garden of Eden to dress it and to keep it. And the Lord God commanded the man, saying, Of every tree of the garden thou mayest freely eat: But of the tree of the knowledge of good and evil, thou shalt not eat of it: for in the day that thou eatest thereof thou shalt surely die. And the Lord God said, It is not good that the man should be alone; I will make him an help meet for him.

Verse 21-25 And the Lord God caused a deep sleep to fall upon Adam, and he slept: and he took one of his ribs, and closed up the flesh instead thereof; And the rib, which the Lord God had taken from man, made he a woman, and brought her unto the man. And Adam said, This is now bone of my bones, and flesh of my flesh: she shall be called Woman, because she was taken out of Man. Therefore shall a man leave his father and his mother, and shall cleave unto his wife: and they shall be one flesh. And they were both naked, the man and his wife, and were not ashamed.

It is important to have kingdom vision for marriage beyond your personal desires to be married and your personal desires of what you want in a mate. There must be kingdom vision regarding:

Who you are in God.
Who he is in you.
What type of mate God says is suitable for you and is compatible to who you are.
What type of mate God says can evolve in the character, nature, identity, destiny, will, and purpose of the Lord.

➤ When there is no vision, the people perish.

➤ When there is no vision, marriages and families perish.

➤ When there is no vision, we are drawn away by our own lust and enticements.

➤ When there is no vision, demons and people can oppress and mislead us.

➤ You cannot adequately stand together in spiritual war and **PREVAIL** against the wiles of the enemy if you do not have vision.

> *Ephesians 4:9-12 Two are better than one; because they have a good reward for their labour. For if they fall, the one will lift up his fellow: but woe to him that is alone when he falleth; for he hath not another to help him up. Again, if two lie together,*

then they have heat: but how can one be warm alone? And if one prevail against him, two shall withstand him; and a threefold cord is not quickly broken

> When there is no vision, people disregard or abandon the need to operate in self-control, boundaries, godly principles and standards.

Psalm 16:11 *Thou wilt shew me the path of life: in thy presence is fulness of joy; at thy right hand there are pleasures for evermore.*

Proverbs 29:18 *Where there is no vision, the people perish: but he that keepeth the law, happy is he.*

New Living Bible *Where there is no revelation, people cast off restraint; but blessed is the one who heeds wisdom's instruction.*

Vision in Greek is *ḥâzôn* and means: a sight (mentally), i.e. a dream, revelation, or oracle: — vision.

Vision
- vision (in ecstatic state)
- vision (in night)
- vision, oracle
- prophecy (divine communication)
- vision (as title of book of prophecy)

People Often Get Married Because:

They want to fulfill this desire in their lives.
Feel pressured by the person they are dating, family and friends, or society.
They partner with potential rather than reality.
They lack vision so they get married just in case the person is the right one.
They hope to be able to change the person into what they desire in a mate – fix them, rescue them, or save them from their own destruction or challenges.
They do not want to be alone.
They want to have children and a family, so they settle for whoever comes along.
The person is decent, so they settle for what they believe is available to them.
They want the fantasy – the fairy tale of being married.

None of these are reasons to get married. They are God's permissive will rather than His perfect will.

Many times, we equate the fruit of our permissive will as God blessing us. God's permissive will entails our plans – your plans - that God may bless through his Grace or that may provide fruit because of the goals, plans, and principles you utilize to ensure success, but this is your own will at work. God is just honoring your will - what you permit in your own life. This is not his perfect will.

God's perfect will entails what he has ordained for you to do, be, receive, and achieve before the foundation of the earth. You must seek him for his perfect will and submit in obedience to what he has ordained for your life.

God can bless our permissive will as he is a God who will work all things for our good, but these plans come with unnecessary trials and tribulations that he did not desire for us to experience. These plans cause us hardships and challenges rooted in our own choices and freewill or that of others.

When people come to counseling disgruntled about their marriage, the first question I ask is, *"Did God tell you that this was your mate?* When they say NO, I share with them how this is God's permissive will at work. God honors marriage so he tries to work with couples, but they can only receive a measure of blessings in permissive will marriages and sometimes, the covenant has to be totally broken because the marriage is too unhealthy to be salvaged. This is very unfortunate. Often this displays lack godly vision for marriage, a rush to marry, or a marriage that is based on potential rather than reality.

I am amazed at the people who say God told me not to marry them, but I did it anyway. WOW! These people had truth of a perishing vision but rejected it.

I will state that I have seen God honor permissive will marriages as people endeavor to work on building a healthy or decent marriage. I therefore do not want to give the impression that permissive marriages are doomed. I will state that it is better to marry according to God's perfect will, which is in accordance with the mate he has chosen for you. As you seek God, he will give you precise vision for this person and how they are in alignment with your identity, calling, purpose, and destiny.

GOD'S PERFECT WILL REVEALS DIVINE VISION!

God is never requiring us to settle when it comes to choosing a marriage partner. This does not mean your partner will be perfect or won't have challenges. But you and that person will have the grace, capacity, and ability to grow and evolve with one another and in that covenant marriage.

God is never requiring us to fix, or to save someone by marrying them. Jesus Christ is the only savior, and he has already redeemed the ENTIRE world – EVERYONE in the world. Every person has an opportunity to be saved – redeemed through him.

The Bible mentions Prophet Hosea being instructed by God to marry a woman named Gomer, who was a prostitute. This relationship is not a prototype for marriage. It is however, a symbolic act of God's covenant with Israel, highlighting their unfaithfulness and God's unwavering love and forgiveness, even towards those who had strayed. It is also a foreshadowing of Jesus Christ and his ability to be the perfect savior. Prophet Hosea had vision for this marriage. He was not blind to his suffering. He understood the purpose for it – that it was a prophetic sign among Israel. He was operating in obedience to his calling, his purpose, and his destiny.

In my twenty-six years of counseling and ministry, I have never heard God say he was calling anyone to this type of marriage. I have never heard him tell a person they are in a horrible marriage for this reason. I have continuously heard God say, this is not his will and that this is the person's free will at work. We represent Jesus Christ through the salvation that his blood, cross, and resurrection power has brought to our lives. His works SHIFTED us to blessings, restoration, and restitution of the life we should have had before the fall to sin in the garden. If you are not seeking to fulfill this realization in your life, marriage and destiny, you are in your own will.

SHIFT RIGHT NOW!

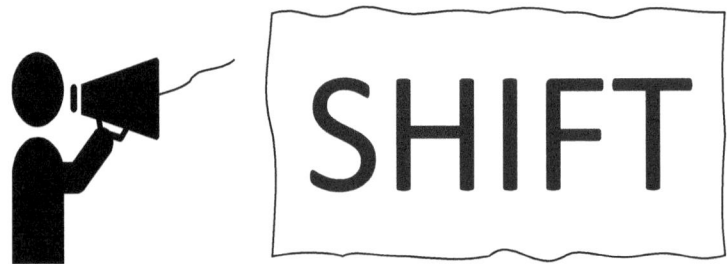

When you have vision, you have eyesight, power of sight, faculty of sight, ability to see, power of seeing, the power of observation, perception, visual perception, eyes, field of vision, view, perspective.

<u>Perish</u> in Hebrew is *pâra'* and means:
1. to loosen; by implication, to expose, dismiss

2. figuratively, absolve, go back, let, (make) naked, set at nought, perish, refuse, uncover, neglect, to loosen
3. (Hiphil) to cause to refrain, to show lack of restraint, to let loose restraints

Ephesians 1:18 *The eyes of your understanding being enlightened (illuminated); that ye may know what is the hope of his calling (the invitation to be, do, have, experience what God release through salvation), and what the riches of the glory of his inheritance in the saints.*

Without vision you fail to receive and honor the rich glory of the reason God put someone in your life.

Habakkuk 2:2-3 *And the LORD answered me, and said, Write the vision, and make it plain upon tables, that he may run that readeth it. For the vision is yet for an appointed time, but at the end it shall speak, and not lie: though it tarry, wait for it; because it will surely come, it will not tarry.*

If you do not have vision, you do not have a clear path to operate in.

You also cannot run properly or run in the proper direction God is desiring to take you.

You cannot discern times and seasons regarding what is occurring or is to occur in your life and in that relationship.

You cannot discern if someone:

Is godly
Sent by him
Is in the proper time and season of your life
Is your God ordained covenant partner

Please note that God has to give relationship vision to you and your mate.

Please know that God knows who you are, who he is in you, and what type of mate is essential to your life and destiny.

Both of you should have vision for what God is speaking and should be able to confirm with one another, what God is saying and where you are going.

Sometimes, one person in the relationship may receive this vision first. Yet I will contend that godly men, should be seeking God for vision for who their mate is and how to find them. I say this because it is a man's responsibility to have godly vision. It is the man's responsibility to seek God for godly vision for:

His life
His destiny
His mate – wife
His family
His children
His community
His sphere of influence

God has created and placed the man as the head of the woman, the family, the land, the community, the region, and the nation.

Genesis 1:27-31 *So God created man in his own image, in the image of God created he him; male and female created he them. And God blessed them, and God said unto them, Be fruitful, and multiply, and replenish the earth, and subdue it: and have dominion over the fish of the sea, and over the fowl of the air, and over every living thing that moveth upon the earth.*

And God said, Behold, I have given you every herb bearing seed, which is upon the face of all the earth, and every tree, in the which is the fruit of a tree yielding seed; to you it shall be for meat. And to every beast of the earth, and to every fowl of the air, and to every thing that creepeth upon the earth, wherein there is life, I have given every green herb for meat: and it was so. And God saw every thing that he had made, and, behold, it was very good. And the evening and the morning were the sixth day.

Genesis 2:15 *So the LORD God took the man [He had made] and settled him in the Garden of Eden to cultivate and keep it.*

1Corinthians 11:3 *But I would have you know, that the head of every man is Christ; and the head of the woman is the man; and the head of Christ is God.*

Ephesians 5:22-33 *Wives, submit yourselves unto your own husbands, as unto the Lord. For the husband is the head of the wife, even as Christ is the head of the church: and he is the saviour of the body. Therefore as the church is subject unto Christ, so let the wives be to their own husbands in every thing.*

Husbands, love your wives, even as Christ also loved the church, and gave himself for it; That he might sanctify and cleanse it with the washing of water by the word, That he might present it to himself a glorious church, not having spot, or wrinkle, or any such thing; but that it should be holy and without blemish. So ought men to love their wives as their own bodies. He that loveth his wife loveth himself.

For no man ever yet hated his own flesh; but nourisheth and cherisheth it, even as the Lord the church: For we are members of his body, of his flesh, and of his bones. For this cause shall a man leave his father and mother, and shall be joined unto his wife, and they two shall be one flesh. This is a great mystery: but I speak concerning Christ and the church. Nevertheless let every one of you in particular so love his wife even as himself; and the wife see that she reverence her husband.

Though God will give a woman standards and vision for her life, the mate she is to marry, and what her marriage is to be like, ideally, the husband receives vision from God for himself, his wife, the marriage, and the family. The wife is responsible for knowing if God wants **HER TO**

SUBMIT TO THAT MAN - FOR HIM TO BE HER HUSBAND!

> **DOES THE MAN ALIGN TO THE STANDARDS GOD HAS GIVEN?**
>
> **CAN YOU SEE HIM IN THE VISION GOD HAS GIVEN YOU FOR A HUSBAND?**

As she decides that he is the one for her and whether he aligns to the vision God has given her for **HER**, she **SHIFTS** into wife posture by honoring and helping him fulfill the vision he has received for the marriage, family, and their destiny purpose. Her vision is absorbed in the enlightenment of what God is revealing to the husband she is submitting to.

This is the reason it is important for a woman to feel safe and confident that she is marrying someone she can submit to.

The Man Must Demonstrate That He Truly:
Has God as the head of his life.
Lives for God.
Prays and communes with God.
Can hear from God.
Studies God's word.
Is obedient to God.
Can receive vision from God.

Can honor and live through Godly vision.
Can receive proceeding words from God as he legislates goals and strategies in bringing God's word and vision to pass.
Can honor his wife.
Can receive her as a help meet.
Can regard the vision and voice of God in her.
Can love his wife like God loves the church.
Can provide for his wife and family.
Is consistently evolving in Christlikeness, destiny, kingdom covenant, and the will and purposes of God for his life and the marriage covenant.

If a man cannot demonstrate this in friendship and dating, then he may be displaying that he does not have capacity to demonstrate this in marriage. The potential has to be there even as there needs to be the ability to self-actualize into the reality of these attributes. Hoping, wishing, or recognizing that he could evolve in this manner is not capacity. This is fantasy or wishful thinking. Capacity is reality. Capacity means that a man has the factual potential or actual ability to perform in these godly characteristics. He possesses the quality or state to fulfill these actions. He is already possessing some measure of what needs to be actualized even if the full potential requires processing or maturity for it to manifest.

> **CAPACITY IS SELF-ACTUALIZED POTENTIAL NOT HOPEFUL POTENTIAL. IT IS EVIDENCE OF QUALITIES ALREADY MANIFESTING IN THE PERSON.**

When a man does not have vision for marriage and family, particularly with the person to whom he desires to marry, they risk building on faulty foundation and erroring in leading the family and the family lineage. This opens the door to division, discord, and divorce, which are covenant breaking spirits. A lack of vision also opens the door to generational curses of covenant breaking spirits operating from their generational line.

Psalm 127:1 *Except the Lord build the house, they labour in vain that build it: except the Lord keep the city, the watchman waketh but in vain.*

Hebrews 3:4 *For every house is builded by some man; but he that built all things is God.*

Matthew 7:24-27 *Therefore whosoever heareth these sayings of mine, and doeth them, I will liken him unto a wise man, which built his house upon a rock: And the rain descended, and the floods came, and the winds blew, and beat upon that house; and it fell not: for it was founded upon a rock. And every one that heareth these sayings of mine, and doeth them not, shall be likened unto a foolish man, which built his house upon the sand: And the rain descended, and the floods came, and the winds blew, and* *beat upon that house; and it fell: and great was the fall of it.*

***Matthew 6:33** But seek first the kingdom of God and His righteousness, and all these things will be added unto you.*

***Psalm 112:1** Hallelujah! Blessed is the man who fears the LORD, who greatly delights in His commandments.*

***Proverbs 14:26** He who fears the LORD is secure in confidence, and his children shall have a place of refuge.*

The wife should be able to come into the marriage vision and completely submit herself to God's mandate for her within the vision. Her ability to submit confirms that she trusts God and her husband for her life and destiny. **WOMAN** if you do not feel confident that you can submit to that man, **DO NOT GET MARRIED!**

JUST PONDER THIS TRUTH FOR A MOMENT!

As you consider ***Genesis 1:27-28***, you must consider the identity of your marriage. God distinguished identity in the man and the woman and then he made them one and gave them vision for themselves and for their covenant. He then blessed them and told them to multiply that which he had already imparted. Anything that is produced in a marriage should directly reflect God's image. Just as each of us have a personal and unique identity of God with different characteristics, there is a distinct identity in each and every one of our marriages and that identity is the image of God. Anything that seeks to disrupt, distort, or disengage YOU in displaying the image of God in your marriage, is a destiny and covenant breaking spirit.

LEAVING & CLEAVING

Revelation From My Manual, *"Kingdom Wellness Counseling & Mentoring, Volume I."*

According to Abraham Maslow, we all have basic needs that must be met in order for us to develop properly into healthy functioning individuals who can self-actualized in life. Self-actualization is the attainment of a person's complete potential or capability through creativity, independence, spontaneity, and achievements, as they seek to conquer their life's destiny.

Maslow believes we must develop and receive these basic needs before we can become self-actualized. Though I do not agree with how some people and/or societies meet these needs as my belief standards are based on biblical principles, I do agree that most of these needs are essential to people having a healthy identity. People need to eat, drink, have shelter, sleep, have sex if they are married, feel safe, have a support system, and a sense of belonging, etc.

Diagram 15.1 Maslow's Expanded Needs Hierarchy

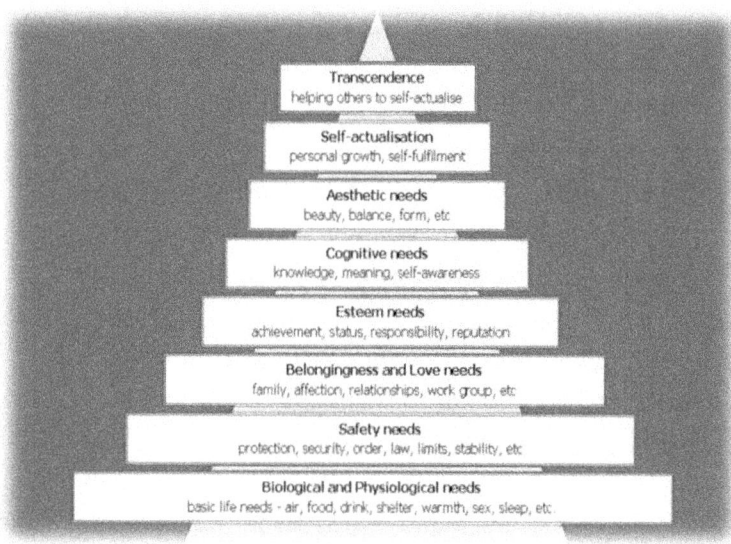

I shared the revelation regarding Maslow's hierarchy of needs because as we SHIFT into being self-actualized, we have an innate need to maintain self-actualization once we become adults, start to independently care for ourselves, and as we SHIFT into marriage and building our own families. When our needs are not met according to God's design, we tend to experience stress, anxiety, fight, flight, or freeze where we are striving to protect ourselves from our needs not being fulfilled.

- **Fight** – Become defensive and combative; has a victim mentality and often feels like it is them against the world.
- **Flight** – Causes them to run, have difficulty sitting still, living and being in one place for a long period of time, run in the face of adversity. They sabotage relationships, life progress, and success due to constant

running and never settling and remaining to deal with life challenges, obstacles, conflicts, or completing anything.
- **Freeze** – Tense and freeze up where they do not handle or face adversity. They stiffen, harden, and become stuck in shock when it comes to trials as they are reliving old traumas during those challenging times.

People that respond via "*fight, flight, or freeze*" have a challenging time asking for help, accepting help, developing meaningful relationships.

  o They will not even know the reason they sabotage their own happiness and fulfillment.
  o They will become defensive when others inquire about their behavior.
  o They feel ashamed, guilty, and condemned regarding their trauma, yet are prideful when encouraged to face truth and accountability about their actions and need for healing.

Trauma is healed by dealing with root issues. This often can require a process of inner healing with a counselor before deliverance should be done, or can be effective and sustained.

Leave and cleave properly so that you and your partner will feel secure in your needs being met in the relationship. Heal from any traumas related to neglect, abuse, and unmet needs as these issues will also surface in the marriage and be a factor in healthy cleaving and leaving.

Genesis 2:21-25 *And the LORD God caused a deep sleep to fall upon Adam, and he slept: and he took one of his ribs, and closed up the flesh instead thereof; And the rib, which the LORD God had taken from man, made he a woman, and brought her unto the man. And Adam said, This is now bone of my bones, and flesh of my flesh: she shall be called Woman, because she was taken out of Man.* ***Therefore shall a man leave his father and his mother, and shall cleave unto his wife: and they shall be one flesh. And they were both naked, the man and his wife, and were not ashamed.***

Leave (Hebrew word *Azab*) means *"to loosen, relinquish, permit, refuse, commit self, fail, forsake, fortify, depart from."*

Cleave (Hebrew word *dâbaq*) is a strong word that has the literal sense of two being held together by force, as when one person captures another. It has a figurative sense of being *"glued to"* through positive family care. Cleave also means *"to glue, to adhere, to join, to stick."*

A man – husband - must leave his father and mother and join, stick to, knit to, glue to his wife so they can become one flesh. When they become one, two whole people become one, while becoming an extension of one another.

They become their own family within their family lineages for the purpose of expanding their family into a greater dimension and purpose of God. The husband must seek God for vision so that he can know what God's purpose is for his marriage and family.

The husband cleaves such that he makes his wife and his children a priority over who he used to be to his parents and other family members. This enables him to be properly aligned where God is his head, he is the head of his household, and his wife is his help meet.

When leaving and cleaving is not properly done, the husband tends to give his parents and other family members the place where God and his wife should be. This causes his home and marriage to be misaligned, thus opening the doors to confusion, strife, division, trauma, and sometimes divorce.

When the wife is properly cleaved to, she feels safe, protected, valued, honored, and provided for. This gives her the confidence and security she needs to properly leave her parents and family, while cleaving and submitting to her husband. This also enables her to take her place sufficiently as a help meet where she willingly wants to care for her husband and her family. Proper cleaving of her husband also helps the wife to cleave properly. The wife will reject putting her parents, family members, and friends, in the position of her husband. But when leaving and cleaving is not done properly, she will seek to be comforted emotionally as she is seeking to fulfill her needs for protection, value, honor, and provision.

Wisdom Key From Apostle Dr. Jackie Green's manual, *"Kingdom Marriages."*

> YOU ARE READY FOR MARRIAGE WHEN YOU ARE READY TO LET GO OF ALL OTHERS AND CLEAVE TO THAT SPECIAL PERSON.

In other words, you must be ready to give that special person priority in terms of needs and ministering to them. You no longer cleave to mamma, daddy, siblings or even your children. They become secondary. Even if you were previously married and now have children, when you remarry, your spouse comes first. This is where many "blended marriages" struggle. If you are not willing to put your children in proper perspective, you should wait on getting married. Your wedding vow is not to your children.

WOW! DECREEING YOU CLEAVE PROPERLY!

Deuteronomy 30:19-20 *I call heaven and earth to record this day against you, that I have set before you life and death, blessing and cursing: therefore choose life, that both thou and thy seed may live: That thou mayest love the Lord thy God, and that thou mayest obey his voice, and that thou mayest cleave unto him: for he is thy life, and the length of thy days: that thou mayest dwell in the land which the Lord sware unto thy fathers, to Abraham, to Isaac, and to Jacob, to give them.*

When we do not cleave to God and leave and cleave in marriage, it opens the door for us to cleave to Satan.

Luke 22:1-6 The Amplified Bible *Now the Festival of Unleavened Bread, which is called the Passover, was approaching. The chief priests and the scribes were looking for a way to put Him to death; for they were afraid of the people [who listened devotedly to His teaching, and who respected His spiritual wisdom]. Then Satan entered Judas, the one called Iscariot, who was one of the twelve [disciples]. And he went away and discussed with the chief priests and officers how he might betray Him and hand Him over to them. They were delighted and agreed with him to give him money. So, he consented and began looking for a good opportunity to betray Jesus to them [at a time when He was] separated from the crowd [because the people might riot or stop them from seizing Him].*

Verse 2 says Satan entered Judas....that word *entered* is the same as *cleave* in the Old Testament where a man shall leave his wife and the two become one... (**Study this revelation and ask God for more insight**).

<u>*Enter* in Greek is *eiserchomai* and also means:</u>
1. to enter (literally or figuratively)
2. of Satan taking possession of the body of a person
3. of entrance into any condition, state of things, society, employment
4. to arise, come into existence or mind, begin to be

Satan possessed Judas and he went and communed with those who wanted to betray Jesus. They were glad to have him among them. The *King James Bible Version* says they made covenant to give him money to betray Jesus.

Covenant is like a marriage - it is a bond, agreement, union. This is the reason the Bible says Satan "entered" Judas. When covenant occurs, you and that person cleave and become one soul - one in likeness of what you are covenanting with.

Judas promised to fulfill his covenant, thus strategizing on the proper way to betray Jesus. He made sure he did not do his dirty deeds among a multitude who would take up for Jesus - who would probably stop his plan and even kill him for his treacherous acts. He did it subtly with a kiss – intimacy with Jesus - and among a small group so he would have less contention in fulfilling his destiny as the deliverer of Jesus into crucifixion.

When you are married and do not properly leave and cleave, it exposes you to cleave to oppressions and behaviors that hinder and destroy the marriage covenant rather than strengthen it. Others can come in and draw you away from your spouse. They can have you become a destiny killing spirit against your spouse, your marriage, and all God desires for you through that marriage. It is so important to make sure you guard yourself, your spouse, and the marriage covenant. This is done by obeying God's biblical word about marriage and the personal vision he gives you and your spouse. This also SHIFTS you into a godly heart to cover your spouse rather than exposing them. It will give you the wisdom to seek God regarding who your marriage confidants should be such that they help to deliver, heal, and build you and your marriage, rather than be an open door for division, discord, betrayal, and destruction.

As you posture to leave and cleave be mindful that you MUST SHIFT all the way out of singleness into your role and position as a husband or a wife. This can be challenging if you have been single for a long time and if you really enjoyed your independence as a single person. It is important to be mindful that you cannot hold on to old mindsets, personality types, and behaviors as it relates to singleness.

- YOU ARE NO LONGER SINGLE! **YOU ARE MARRIED!**
- YOU ARE NO LONGER ONE PERSON! **YOU ARE TWO BECOMING ONE!**
- YOU ARE NOT LONGER JUST A MAN OR A WOMAN! **YOU ARE NOW A HUSBAND OR A WIFE!**

You cannot justify your actions by saying I did this in singleness, it is not unhealthy it is just what I am accustomed to from singleness, this what I enjoyed in singleness, this is what I enjoyed in previous relationships. Your role and position in life has **SHIFTED**! You must **SHIFT** to embody your new role and position of marriage identity. **Your life will be just as fulfilled as it was in singleness, the more you embrace the fullness of marriage and all it entails. The more you hold on to singleness, the harder embracing marriage will be.**

Your actions impact your spouse. You MUST consider them and be intentional to let go of singleness and everything that was comfortable, easy, mindless, selfish, just yours, and SHIFT fully into becoming one with your spouse and the vision God has given you all as a marriage UNION. Be mindful that:

- Marriage is a process of constantly merging two worlds, so **ALL** decisions have to be made together.
- There is a reprogramming period where you have to understand that your life is not your own.
- Watch for times and triggers that cause you to slip back into singleness in action, yet marriage in theory.
- Learn each other's patterns. Invite your spouse into your routine or change your routine to include them.

Leave & Cleave Activation:
1. Journal what you learned from this chapter.
2. Journal the relationship cycles and patterns in your family, especially the marital cycles and patterns in your family. Process and journal if they are godly. Pray and journal with God how your marriage represents him and breaks these cycles and patterns in your family line.
3. Journal what would be difficult about you leaving and cleaving and changing your routine.
4. Journal who in your family or circle would have a problem with your life change of leaving and cleaving. Pray and journal with God what you need to do to align with him while engaging in the relationship in a healthy way.
5. Process this revelation with your partner. Journal four goals you all can implement to leave and cleave God's way.

BALANCING RELATIONSHIPS WITH IN-LAWS

A GOD DESIGNED COMMUNITY IS ESSENTIAL IN MARRIAGE!

As you leave and cleave, everyone cannot be privy to your marriage. Discerning who has godly vision for your marriage is vital to your success as everyone ***should NOT be speaking into your marriage.*** Allowing people to be a voice and participant in your marriage covenant is dangerous. Especially people who do not have a godly understanding of marriage, the purpose to which God has called you to marriage and to marry your spouse, has worldly, fantasy, self-absorbed, misunderstood mindsets and ideologies about marriage; persons who easily offended, holds grudges, ghost, and quit when things become difficult or do not go their way.

It is essential and healthy to have a very small inner circle that upholds marriage as honorable, can hold you accountable to biblical truths regarding marriage, has you and your spouse's best interest in mind and heart as it relates to what God says about each of you, and desires for you to have a fulfilled marriage.

Wisdom Key From Apostle Dr. Jackie Green's manual, "*Kingdom Marriages.*"

> **YOU ARE READY FOR MARRIAGE WHEN YOU ARE READY TO SHARE EVERYTHING WITH YOUR SPOUSE.**

Your body is not your own, your money is not your own, your time is not your own, and even your debts and bills are to be shared. You get to share the not so good side of that marriage partner even the "inlaws and outlaws." Yes, you are not marrying the family, but you are marrying into the family. It is wrong to ask your spouse to disconnect from their family. You are to leave and cleave to one another as a priority, but family is part of our "kingdom ministry." Keep them as a ministry but do not let them meddle and you will not have any mess.

This revelation that Apostle Green shares enables you to have a balanced perspective as you leave and cleave.

DISCLAIMER! I want to first be clear that neglect, ANY FORM OF ABUSE, control, narcissism, mental illness, suicidal ideation, terrorism, witchcraft, occultism, murder, are areas of a marriage that should not be hidden or taken lightly. These are areas of your marriage that you need to seek professional and ministerial guidance, help, and intervention. It is important to choose marital confidants at the beginning of your marriage who understand that this type of behavior is never okay. These confidants can walk with you on your marriage journey and help you navigate in divine truth and safety. Those you choose need to be wise in helping you to discern what is godly covering of your spouse and their shortcomings and what is ungodly, risky, harmful, and dangerous to your wellbeing and to that of your children. You may also need to choose wise mature family members and friends that can help you make responsible safe decisions. Please do not choose impulsive loved ones that will escalate the challenges that are occurring in your marriage. Such people can put your life in danger and even make impulsive decisions that put themselves and you in legal binding. Love your spouse enough not to let him or her destroy you, themselves, or any children you all may have. Keeping these areas a secret can cost you years of unnecessary trauma, and even your life. **DO NOT DO IT! SEEK WISDOM SO YOU CAN BE HELPED!**

With that being said, the wisdom keys below are for healthy and striving kingdom marriages.

Covenant Activation for Balanced Relationships with In-laws:

- *Put Your Marriage First* – Use this revelation already discussed to process with God and your mate who your supports should be and why God chose them. Set goals regarding how you all can cover one another according to the grace and mercy God wants you all to have for one another; and goals you all need to set when intervention, even professional help is needed in your relationship.

- *Implement Healthy Boundaries for Engaging In-laws & Stick to Them* – Set written boundaries together for how you all will handle criticism, misguided advice, challenges, fellowships, events, Holidays, as it relates to in-laws and outsiders. Stick to the goals you implement and only change them as you update them together. Do not feel the need to explain yourself or defend your boundaries and choices. Have a clear marriage vision so that you and your spouse can use it to rest in the truth of why God put you all together. Allow the unfolding of the vision to speak for itself and defend you all rather than trying to prove who you and your spouse are personally and to one another.

- **Engage In-laws from What They Can Give & Who They Can Be** – Having a lot of expectations regarding who family members should and should not be to you all personally and as a couple can put family members in positions in your life that God did not intend. It can also cause you and your spouse to be more to family members than you should be and choose family members over one another. Discuss and journal false obligations and family cultures that would infringe on your biblical principles, your personal destinies, and the marital vision God has given you all. Consider their salvation or lack of, their personal maturity, and how you and your spouse are continuing to evolve personally and maritally with God. Be realistic about who your family members can and should be to you all, journal this revelation and engage them from this posture.

Journal ways to engage and support in-laws without compromising your beliefs, one another, and who you all are in God. Trust God with your family members and trust him to send others to water what you can plant in them, and the prayers you are praying for them. He will bless and transform them as you are obedient to the things he has given you control over. Ask God for spiritual family that can support and journey with you all in your personal destinies and marriage covenant.

- Do not hide family secrets and issues from one another. **BE HONEST** and **OPENLY DISCUSS** your past family history and be open about the cycles, patterns, sins, and trespasses you have experienced with your family and that you know about your family. Have these discussions often especially when a memory is triggered or you see things attempting to manifest in your life and marriage. Discuss and journal ways to intercede and handle these challenges. Remember you, your spouse, and your marriage serve as curse breakers. You possess the key to close unhealthy doors and open godly ones in your life, marriage, and family line.

- Sometimes boundaries may include the need to set timelines for when to visit, what season to visit, and how long to be around family members when you visit. Discern what is sufficient where familiarity will not ensue that would cause conflicts between you all and in-laws or one another because you stay too long at family functions. Or where you all attend events that are centered around conflict, trauma, drama, unhealthy interactions, cultural or traditional functions, that put you in positions that cause unnecessary or increased stress, anxiety, trauma, hardship, etc.

Pray together before you insert yourself into situations so you can have God's wisdom, plan, and posture for these experiences. Set boundaries and support and make one another accountable to them. Update your goals as you grow together in marriage and with family.

GODLY VISION MARRIAGE ACTIVATION

JOURNAL YOUR INSIGHTS TO THIS ACTIVATION

1. Before completing this activation, make sure you have already completed the chapter activation entitled, "*God's Vision For A Mate.*" It will be important to know your destiny, calling, purpose, and God's standards for your life and a mate before completing this activation. That revelation is in the "*God's Vision For A Mate*" chapter.

2. Women and Men, journal what you learned from the previous chapter entitled, "*Godly Vision For Marriage.*" Ask God to reveal ALL pertinent revelation you need to know. Journal what he reveals.

3. Men and Women, journal what you desire in marriage and then ask God what he desires for you in a marriage covenant.

4. Men and Women, journal the purpose God wants you to be married. How will or does it impact where you currently are in life, your destiny, your purpose, and your generational line?

5. Men, seek God for vision for your life, your marriage and family, journal what he shares. Journal goals for bringing God's vision to pass. If you are single, use it to pursue a mate. Share this revelation with your partner. Work together to set present and future goals bring what God is saying to pass.

6. Women, seek God for vision for your life, your marriage and family, journal what he shares. Journal goals for bringing God's vision to pass. If you are single, use it to identify if the man that is pursuing you is God's mate for you. Share this revelation with your partner. Work together to set present and future goals to bring what God is saying to pass.

7. Men, search out and journal with God what type of help meet you need/have and whether the good thing you have found fits the vision God has given you. Journal what you and your good thing need to work on to fulfill the role of help meet in the vision God has given you all, and for you to lead properly as the head of your household and marriage.

8. Women, search out and journal with God who you need to be as a help meet to the man that is/or pursuing you as a wife. Journal what you and your favored husband

need to work on for you to fulfill the role of help meet in the vision God has given you all and for him to lead you properly as the head of the household and marriage.

9. Men and Women, journal the strengths you bring to the marriage covenant.

10. Men and Women, journal the weaknesses you bring to the marriage covenant. Be honest so you can posture to hear God for transformations and applicable tools to be strengthened and sound in these areas.

11. Men and Women, what areas do you need to improve in regarding your character, integrity, identity, and confidence.

12. Men and Women, seek godly counsel regarding the marriage vision God has given you. Such people need to be able to:

    a. Pray and confirm what God is speaking.
    b. Provide further clarity regarding the purpose of your marriage, who your mate is, and how you all will impact the earth for his glory.
    c. Provide wisdom keys for a healthy marriage and for fulfilling your purpose personally and as a married couple.
    d. Mentor and counsel you both as you prepare, birth, and build a solid foundation for your marriage and as you journey together in marriage covenant.

    e. Hold you accountable to what God is speaking, while providing proceeding strategies, goals, wisdom, counsel, support as you achieve what God is speaking for your marriage covenant.
    f. Hold you all accountable to the institution of a godly marriage and treating one another as God requires.

13. Men and Women, pray and ask God what are the destiny killing spirits and covenant breaking spirits that would come for your marriage covenant. Journal what he shares regarding your personal life, your generational line, your destiny and calling, and that of your partner.

14. Build yourself in the truth that in order to combat spiritual wickedness and attacks against your marriage you must have a vision of one.

15. What are some practical check-ins and accountability tools you and your partner can implement to stay up to date with your vision plan where you all remain aligned to what God desires for your marriage.

WISDOM KEYS FOR MARRIED COUPLES

1. **Unconditional Love:** Love one another earnestly from a pure heart. (1Peter 1:22)

2. **Effective Communication:** Let your speech always be gracious, seasoned with salt, so that you may know how you ought to answer each person. (Colossians 4:6)

3. **Mutual Respect:** Submitting to one another in the fear of God. Ephesians 5:21

4. **Shared Spiritual Growth:** Two are better than one, because they have a good return for their labor. (Ecclesiastes 4:9)

5. **Forgiveness:** Be kind and compassionate to one another, forgiving each other, just as in Christ God forgave you. (Ephesians 4:32)

6. **Shared Responsibilities:** Therefore, a man shall leave his father and mother and hold fast to his wife, and the two shall become one flesh. (Genesis 2:24)

7. **Intimacy:** Do not deprive one another, except with consent for a time, that you may devote yourselves to prayer; but come together again so that Satan does not tempt you because of your lack of self-control. (1 Corinthians 7:5)

8. **Conflict Resolution:** Do not sleep on issues or differences: "Be angry, and do not sin:" do not let the sun go down on your wrath, nor give place to the devil. (Ephesians 4:26-27)

9. **Acquire Financial Wisdom:** Do not store up for yourselves treasures on earth, where moths and rust destroy, and where thieves break in and steal. (Matthew 6:19)

10. **Celebrate Together:** Rejoice always, pray continually, give thanks in all circumstances; for this is God's will for you in Christ Jesus. (1Thessalonians 5:16-18)

BALANCING MARRIAGE & DESTINY

From Dr. Taquetta Baker's *"Sustaining The Vision Workbook."*

__Relationship Activation:__ As you and your partner consider these nuggets, set goals to apply them to your relationship.

Make weekly time for your marriage and family. Schedule it on your calendar and make it a priority. Ensure you schedule time for just your spouse alone, as well as the entire family. Remember to never stop dating your spouse! It is also important to confirm on a regular basis that the scheduled time works for the family and change it as needed but do all you can to not cancel it.

Resist adding events to your calendar that are not a part of what God is requiring of you in the present season you are in. Make sure you communicate and share your calendar with your spouse and family to ensure that their needs are covered during these times and/or adjustments can be made.

Resist enabling people and having meetings where people just want to waste time but are not about true change.

Trust your team and promote accountability. If they cannot be accountable, then replace them with someone who can. A lot of times, we keep people in positions to avoid conflict, but this is at the expense of you having to step in and do it. Replace them with someone that can be accountable, so you do not have to spend your time fulfilling duties that others can do.

Pace yourself in your ministry vision. Be cognizant to hear God concerning what you need to be working on in any given season, so you will not stretch yourself too thin.

Be disciplined in scheduling meetings and completing ministry duties when other family members are busy so you all can be working at the same time, as opposed to hitting and missing one another. If there is a time that this cannot be accomplished, it is important that you communicate this to your family and be disciplined with the scheduled time.

Invite and implement your family into your ministry endeavors and what God is doing in your life. Often, we are selfish and protective in this area without realizing that it can cause family members to be jealous of your relationship with God and your ministry. It can also cause wounds and conflicts where there are demands to choose between the two. Ask your family for feedback on your ministry endeavors and be open to hearing them. This will help them feel a part of this portion of your life versus separating the two. Remember your family is your primary ministry!

Every marriage and family are different. It is okay to consider suggestions from others, but it is best to search

God for a vision plan for your marriage and family. What works for others may not work for your marriage and family. Consult with your spouse and family concerning the plan and give them the opportunity to change and add to the plan. The vision plan can include how you desire your relationships to be, desires of spending time together, commitments to supporting one another's life events, activities and outings you all can plan and do together, and etc. Revisit the plan every few months to make sure it still works for your current family dynamics and adjust it accordingly.

Do not try to fit ministry duties and obligations that may not fit inside the dynamics of your marriage and family that season. Take time to evaluate what season you are in with God and share what God has said with your spouse and family. Then together you all explore with God what will be needed to complete the will of God, while also remaining committed to the family needs and desires.

Text, call, and email to express affirmations of love, appreciation, support, and encouragement. Ensure that you are communicating in a fashion that fits each family members' needs. While your child may receive from a text message, your spouse may prefer a call, so they can hear your voice. Know what each family member needs and desires and engage them accordingly. Also, make sure they are aware of your needs and desires, so they can bring fulfillment to your life.

Consistently check on your spouse and families' well-being. Show concern for their soul with such fervor as you would those under your ministry. At no point should your family feel as if they lack priority in your life.

Plan family vacations that are not centered around ministry. It is important that you spend time connecting and making memories with your family to ensure continued balance for both you and your family. It can be as simple as a weekend trip, or a 7-day trip. The key is you are making time to focus on them. Consider and plan separate trips for just you and your spouse, and then one with the entire family at least once a year.

Speak into your family and make sure their spiritual needs are met. They need to see and know that you care about their spiritual growth just as much and more than those you are assigned to in the Kingdom.

What areas do you need to improve in relations to balancing marriage, children, family, dating, and friendships?

What are the biggest challenges you have with taking personal time to be with family and friends?

Use the suggestions above to write a vision plan that you and your family can realistically implement into your daily lives.

BUILDING FINANCIAL MATURITY

Learn & Build Financial Maturity: Couples need to be honest about finances at the beginning of their relationship and then work on resolving as much personal debt as possible. Couples then need to create a plan for working on any debt that is left over. Even though both parties must understand that when they agree to marry, they do it for the good and the bad and thus can very well accumulate one another's debt, this decision and plan needs to be agreed upon together. If you do not have peace and resolve regarding debt that you did not accumulate, do not agree to bear the weight of that debt. This will help avoid conflict in the future. As many partners will claim they are okay bearing financial burdens of their spouse yet, become resentful as other challenges or realizations present themselves in the relationship. Only agree to what is truly your present belief and mindset, then allow yourself to grow in this area with God and your partner as the relationship progresses. Set goals during dating and engagement to dissolve as much personal debt as possible. Be honoring and just to your mate by accepting as much responsibility to resolve debt accumulated before marriage even as you set goals together to resolve joint debt ventures.

Please understand that financial matters can weigh heavy on marriage and families and can cause great stress, anxiety, hardship, conflict, resentment, division, and divorce. As you are dating and married, endeavor to mature personally and together in the following areas.

1. Financial maturity
2. Financial transparency
3. How to manage finances as a couple
4. Saving together
5. Building together
6. Planning together
7. Financial accountability
8. Handling financial responsibilities as a couple
9. Bank accounts
10. Saving for emergencies

<u>Financial Covenant Activation:</u>

1. Study scriptures on kingdom stewardship – what does the Bible say about finances, being a cheerful giver, tithes, offerings, stewarding properly over finances, the warnings and consequences of unwise money management and the potential evils when money is valued over God and one's walk with him. Journal the scriptures and insights that God speaks to you all personally and together in this area.

2. Study scriptures on God blessing the works of your hands, witty ideas, entrepreneurship, pioneering ventures, trusting him as you advance in your personal

and marital destinies and callings. Journal any promises and prophecies God has spoken over you all personally and as a couple. Pray and journal insights he gives you all on how to achieve your purpose and callings. Attend training if necessary to equip yourselves. Support and hold one another accountable to these goals. Keep a journal of promises and prophecies as you journey with God throughout life. Be obedient to what he says and support one another in your faith and work's stance. Get help from experts, coaches, and mentors, who can help you all with these ventures. Discern times and seasons for these ventures such that you do not place undue hardship on your marriage and one another.

3. Discuss and journal concerning personal and joint bills, debt, financial prosperity, financial streams, land and real estate, offshore accounts, stocks, bonds, crypto, inheritances, frugal behavior, etc.

4. Discuss and set goals regarding budgeting, money management, etc.

5. Discuss and learn to understand one another's money personality. This is done by discussing one another's upbringing, personal and generational struggles and strongholds related to poverty, poverty mindsets, money habits, mindsets and behaviors about money and where they stem from, work ethics, financial integrity, risk taking behaviors and patterns, how bills are paid, saving money, planning for the future, investing, etc.

Address strengths, weaknesses, concerns, and how to improve personally and together as a couple.

6. Discuss how and who will manage the finances, incomes and financial streams coming into the home, job security, who will pay what, what is the expectation for the wife regarding work, saving for children, childbearing and working, stay at home father being a factor in the marriage. Discuss and journal plans for joint and separate accounts and what will work best for your marriage in this area.

7. Agree to a budget and savings plan. Update this as needed throughout your marriage. Be honoring to one another's financial personalities. Address any growth and kingdom stewardship that is needed in one another's financial personalities.

8. Put goals in place to process and navigate conflict surrounding finances. When processing:

    a. Listen to one another and allow one another space and opportunity to share before interjecting.
    b. Commit to being resolution focused even as you share your concerns with one another.
    c. Make plans that help you all support one another, be accountable to one another, and allow each of you to be active in the healthy change that needs to take place in your finances.
    d. Set weekly short-term goals that allow for check-ins and immediate interventions. Also,

set monthly or quarterly goals that can be achieved through these short-term goals. Celebrate personal and financial successes no matter how small they are. Empower one another, pray for another, aide one another, and build one another in what is needed to achieve the goals.

   e. Be mindful of your anger and challenges with constant failures, let downs, and weaknesses in this area. Be honest about where you all are and seek your supports who can sit with you all and help to process in a respectable but honest manner that can breed goals to SHIFT you towards resolution.

9. Set future financial goals and strategies concerning where you all want to be in one year, three years, five years, ten years, in relationship to finances and prosperity. Set a prayer plan to intercede for breakthrough and financial integrity concerning these future goals. Set present and future goals to work on personally and together that would help you all achieve your goals. Update your goals and plans as you evolve in life and marriage.

10. Prioritize financial literacy and God's vision for you all to prosper. Study to educate yourselves in the areas of finance; take webinars, trainings and courses together; obtain a trustworthy accountant, financial advisor, and lawyer to assist with success in these areas.

FREEDOM FROM IMPURE ENTANGLEMENTS

This chapter is from my manual, *"The Power Of Purity."* I chose to put this chapter in this book because you need to know how entanglements can occur in your personal life, as you would pursue dating, enter engagement and when evolving in marriage. Engaging in these unhealthy relationship patterns can cause lots of problems in relationships and can even cause divorce.

Study this chapter personally and with your partner. Close doors and get delivered from any of these relationship mindsets and behaviors.

Open Doors - An open door insinuates freedom of access. An open door is a recognized right of admittance where anything or anyone can come in.

When we consider opening a door, personally or relationally, we are stating that our lives are vulnerable to anything and anyone. We do not have any locks, barriers, boundaries, principles or policies in place to keep out what needs to remain out, nor to keep in what needs to stay in.

Entanglement - *complicate; to enmesh; to twist or interweave in such a manner as not to be easily separated; to make tangled, confused, and intricate.*

Entanglements are when a person becomes entangled with another person in a way that they become bonded and intertwined in one another's life. Psychology calls this a codependent relationship. Once entangled, it can be difficult to get free. Often what bonded them together has tied their souls together. They become codependent on one another and the relationship that causes them to find it difficult to live, or view life without each other. They become absorbed in each other's lives no  matter how unhealthy their interactions are. They tend to entangle themselves in a deeper web of pain and trauma before making the decision to break free from one another. Usually, the breakup is painful because it takes difficult decisions, focus, and hard work to untangle what has been tangled. People dread the pain and torment they experience in their hearts, minds, and souls, so often they return to the relationship and further entangle themselves rather than staying the course until they are fully free.

Synonyms For Entanglement

Imbroglio	Complexity	Entrapment	Mesh	Tangle
Liaison	Confusion	Intricacy	Mess	Tie-up
Affair	Difficulty	Involvement	Mix-up	Toil
Association	Embarrassment	Jumble	Muddle	Trap
Cobweb	Embroilment	Knot	Snare	Web
Enmeshment	Ensnarement	Soul tied	Imprison	Bondage

There is nothing good about being in an entanglement. It is like being stuck in a cobweb or a stronghold of ropes that a person cannot get out of. The Bible warns us of entanglements:

Psalm 35:8 *Let destruction come on him unawares. Let his net that he has hidden catch himself. Let him fall into that destruction.*

Galatians 5:1 *Stand fast therefore in the liberty wherewith Christ hath made us free, and be not entangled again with the yoke of bondage.*

2Timothy 2:4 *No soldier on duty entangles himself in the affairs of life, that he may please him who enrolled him as a soldier.*

2Peter 2:20 *For if after they have escaped the pollutions of the world through the knowledge of the Lord and Saviour Jesus Christ, they are again entangled therein, and overcome, the latter end is worse with them than the beginning.*

The Bible views entanglement as a *snare, entrapment, or a trap* that can seem innocent but is usually done through trickery, cunning, or deceitful behavior. A person can become so comfortable with codependent entanglements that they become part of their identity; thus, they are unaware of their behavior or deem that their behavior is normal and necessary.

This is the reason standards are important. They are levees – barriers – that keep a person from becoming entangled.

Picture by Robert Ray -NBC News

Let's explore ways open doors can cause impure entanglements in our lives.

<u>Unhealed Trauma</u> – Trauma entails a shocking, appalling, and/or baffling situation or event that threatens the life or integrity of a person. These experiences can include sexual, mental, emotional, or physical abuse, death, violence, traumatic and unforeseen accidents, abandonment, homelessness, natural disasters, war, community violence, or medical issues.

Trauma is the physical, mental, emotional, or spiritual impact of that event. The person is stuck in the shock, awe, and baffling of that experience and becomes trapped in the impact the traumatic event had on their lives.

When trauma is not dealt with, the unresolved pain, fears, stress, distress, anxiety, insecurities and instabilities can impact and alter every area of a person's life.

This is the reason trauma is a stealer – a killer – a destroyer.

John 10:10 *The thief cometh not, but for to steal, and to kill, and to destroy: I am come that they might have life, and that they might have it more abundantly.*

That trauma becomes part of your personality and identity and becomes interwoven in who you are. You think you are cycling, manifesting the same emotions, thoughts, and behaviors while not progressing, progressing slowly, are inconsistent, dysfunctional, unfulfilled, or never enjoying the fullness of life and salvation because of other reasons, however, this is because of the unresolved trauma.

> **TRAUMA CAN CHANGE YOU AND YOUR ORDAINED DESTINY PATHWAY.**

- Trauma can shape our physical, emotional, intellectual, and spiritual development. Especially if you do not receive healing from how it impacted you and now you live through a trauma mindset where what you do, or do not do, is because of what happened to you.

- When trauma occurs early in life, it can alter destiny, identity, and the ways we embrace and engage in life.

- Trauma can impact our success and our ability to survive, thrive, and persevere in life.

- People, especially children, can become imprisoned in their brains when experiencing traumatic experiences. This can cause their brains to SHIFT into states of "fight, flight, or freeze" response. Instead of dealing with stress, anxiety, and challenging situations in a healthy manner, they enter "fight, flight, or freeze" responses that cause them to:

    ✓ **Fight** – Become defensive and combative; they have a victim mentality and often feel like it is them against the world.

    ✓ **Flight** – Causes them to have difficulty sitting still, living, and being in one place for a long period of time, and to run in the face of adversity. They sabotage relationships, life progress, and success due to constantly running and never settling and remaining to deal with life's challenges, obstacles, conflicts, or completing anything.

- ✓ **Freeze** – Tense and freeze up where they do not handle or face adversity. They stiffen, harden, and become stuck in shock when it comes to trials as they are reliving old traumas during those challenging times.

- The people that respond via "fight, flight, or freeze" have a difficult time asking for help, accepting help, or developing meaningful relationships.

    o They have a difficult time understanding the reason they self-sabotage their happiness and fulfillment.

    o They become defensive with others inquiring about their behavior.

    o They feel ashamed, guilty, and condemned regarding their trauma, yet are prideful when encouraged to face truth and accountability about their actions and need for healing.

Any unhealed trauma, especially mother or father wounds, sexual abuse, trafficking, or childhood trauma that has you stuck in fluctuating between acting as a child and an adult, unresolved relationship issues, church hurt, etc., can be open doors to impure entanglements. You are trying to heal trauma and fill voids that can only be healed in a process to wellness with God.

Trauma Bonding – When two people have unresolved trauma in their lives and bond due to the pain, heartache, and hardship; this is trauma bonding.

Dictionary.com defines *bonding* as:
1. something that binds, fastens, confines, or holds together.
2. a cord, rope, band, or ligament.
3. something that binds a person or persons to a certain circumstance or line of behavior
4. an agreement or friendship, that unites individuals or people into a group

The general concept of bonding occurs as the two people grow in relationship with one another by:

Spending time together
Learning one another
Communicating with one another
Living and eating together
Displaying intimacy with one another
Making love together
Having children and raising a family together
Being there for one another
Supporting one another through challenging, stressful, distressful times, and seasons
Towering through and over struggle and adversity together
Celebrating success together
Advancing in success and destiny together
Creating trauma to further bind together

Bonding brings about a sense of security, firm assurance, loyalty, tie, and even a covenant. The bonding can be an unconscious emotional bond that occurs even when they are unaware of it.

When bonding is attached to trauma, especially like or similar trauma, it strengthens the bond. The bond is also strengthened when people endure trauma together, while constant trauma compounds and strengthens the bond. This is generally because they gravitate towards one another due to feeling safe and understood, or due to the experience of the trauma itself. Though unhealthy and inordinate due to the trauma, this concept is realistic and needed as the Bible says:

Galatians 6:2 *Bear ye one another's burdens, and so fulfil the law of Christ.*

<u>Bear is *bastazo* in the Greek and means:</u>
1. to lift, literally or figuratively (endure, declare, sustain, receive, etc.)
2. bear, carry, take up, to take up with the hands, to take up in order to carry or bear
3. to put upon oneself, (something) to be carried, to bear what is burdensome
4. to bear, to carry, to carry on one's person, to sustain, i.e. uphold, support
5. to bear away, carry off, to sustain.

God's law is his word, his standards, and his principles. God's law does not entail what others think, feel, believe, or want. God's law encompasses what he has said in his word, including what is appropriate, acceptable, and lawful according to his word. If the law goes against his word, then we should not do it or expect it of others. This is the reason trauma bonding is ungodly. It fulfills the law of man or demons rather than God. These ungodly laws are rooted in unhealthiness rather than the principles of God.

<u>When we bear (hold) one another up in a godly manner:</u>
- ✓ It should not bind us, trap us, dismantle us.
- ✓ It should not control us, dominate us, intimidate us, manipulate us.
- ✓ It should not cause us or others to be contrary to God's word and purpose.
- ✓ It should not put us under duress or arrest us where we feel obligated to do something we do not want to do.
- ✓ It should not incite enabling the other person in areas where they are fully capable of doing or handling a matter for themselves, but are forcing us to do it, taking advantage of us, or we are obligating ourselves to do it even though we do not want to or it is causing us to defy the law of Christ. There is a torment that accompanies false obligation because our true identity knows we are being used, taken advantage of, not being true to ourselves, to God, or to the other person.
- ✓ It should not bind us to trauma where we are soul tied to others through issues, hardships, and pain.

Ungodly forbearance causes ungodly trauma. Trauma bonding is because of the following:

Like or similar trauma or painful experience
General life pain or a traumatic experience
Drama and conflict within the relationship
Experiences with an abuser or offender that keep a person bound in trauma, especially when the victim develops sympathy and affection for the abuser
Physical and emotional abuse
Stockholm Syndrome, which is an emotional attachment to a captor formed by a hostage as a result of continuous stress, dependence, and a need to cooperate for survival.
Domestic abuse
Child abuse
Incest
Elder abuse
Exploitative employment, such as one involving people who are immigrants that have no documentation
Kidnapping or hostage-taking
Human trafficking
Abusive leaders in authoritative positions
Religious extremism or cults

The relationship has no healthy purpose as it is founded and built on trauma. Trauma bonding can be done by bonding in:

Fear of not having anyone else to relate or to understand one's pain or struggle

Fear of not feeling supported, loved, connected to, close to, or bonded to someone in this way again
Fear of being alone, fear of failing, fear of struggling, fear of not being supported
Passion in which a person has strong, sensual, fleshly, and lustful thoughts and feelings rather than a healthy spiritual connection
Sexual excitement or passion incited from drama and conflict
Abuse
Intimidation
Manipulation
Control
Worry/Stress/Anxiety
False Obligation
Not wanting to take a risk towards a different life or path that may prove healthy and successful

When we are bonded in pain, it increases the pain, as well as the emotional and soul ties of the relationship. Such relationships tend to cause unhealthy dependence on one another and even addictions to one another, the cycles, and the trauma. There is a mindset of anguish at not being able to live or navigate life without each other and that the only way to diminish or lessen the anguish is by remaining in an unhealthy relationship. As the pain and trauma increases, our desire to rescue, fix, and enable one another as we are striving to be God to one another and cure each other's pain increases rather than bearing up in the strength of God's law, the principles of his word regarding deliverance and healing, and regarding what he is telling us personally to do to be made well.

Matthew 11:28-30 *Come unto me, all ye that labour and are heavy laden, and I will give you rest. Take my yoke upon you, and learn of me; for I am meek and lowly in heart: and ye shall find rest unto your souls. For my yoke is easy, and my burden is light.*

Laden means to load up, to overburden with a ceremony or spiritual anxiety, to lade (load oppressively), to load a burden upon, to load one with a burden (or rites or unwarranted precepts).

Jeremiah 29:11 *For I know the plans I have for you," declares the LORD, "plans to prosper you and not to harm you, plans to give you hope and a future.*

Psalm 34:18 *The LORD is close to the brokenhearted and saves those who are crushed in spirit.*

Psalm 147:3 *He heals the brokenhearted and binds up their wounds.*

2Corinthians 1:3-8 *Praise be to the God and Father of our Lord Jesus Christ, the Father of compassion and the God of all comfort, who comforts us in all our troubles, so that we can comfort those in any trouble with the comfort we ourselves receive from God. For just as we share abundantly in the sufferings of Christ, so also our comfort abounds through Christ. If we are distressed, it is for your* *comfort and salvation; if we are comforted, it is for your comfort, which produces in you patient endurance of the same sufferings we suffer. And our hope for you is firm, because we know that just as you share in our sufferings, so also you share in our comfort. We do not want you to be uninformed, brothers and sisters, about the troubles we experienced in the province of Asia. We were under great pressure, far beyond our ability to endure, so that we despaired of life itself.*

The Amplified Bible Verse 3-4 *Blessed be the God and Father of our Lord Jesus Christ, the Father of sympathy (pity and mercy) and the God [Who is the Source] of every comfort (consolation and encouragement), Who comforts (consoles and encourages) us in every trouble (calamity and affliction), so that we may also be able to comfort (console and encourage) those who are in any kind of trouble or distress, with the comfort (consolation and encouragement) with which we ourselves are comforted (consoled and encouraged) by God.*

1Peter 4:12-14 *Beloved, do not be amazed and bewildered at the fiery ordeal which is taking place to test your quality, as though something strange (unusual and alien to you and your position) were befalling you. But insofar as you are sharing Christ's sufferings, rejoice, so that when His glory [full of radiance and splendor] is revealed, you may also rejoice with triumph [exultantly]. If you are censured and suffer abuse [because you bear] the name of Christ, blessed [are you—happy, fortunate,to be envied,with life-joy, and satisfaction in God's favor and salvation, regardless of* *your outward condition], because the Spirit of glory, the Spirit of God, is resting upon you. On their part He is blasphemed, but on your part, He is glorified.*

When we bond over trauma rather than bearing and supporting one another properly while leaning on and working the word of God, we remain rooted in trauma and in the increased anguish our bond produces, rather than processing and SHIFTING out of suffering into wellness with God.

Romans 8:18 *I consider that our present sufferings are not worth comparing with the glory that will be revealed in us.*

When we form a bond, it does not automatically go away when the relationship ends. The bond has to be broken in the soul and spiritual realms even as it has to be broken in the natural realm, otherwise the bond is still there.

Signs Of Trauma Bonding - The main sign that a person has bonded with an abuser is that they try to justify or defend the abuse. They may also:

- Agree with the abusive person's reasons for treating them badly.
- Try to cover for the abusive person.
- Argue with, or distance themselves from people trying to help, such as friends, family members, or neighbors.
- Become defensive or hostile if someone intervenes and attempts to stop the abuse, such as a bystander or police officer.

- Be reluctant or unwilling to take steps to leave the abusive situation or break the bond.

A person bonded with their abuser might say, for example:

- "He is only like that because he loves me so much - you would not understand."
- "She is under a lot of pressure at work; she cannot help it. She will make it up to me later."
- "I will not leave him. He is the love of my life. You are just jealous."
- "It is my fault — I made them angry."

It is worth noting that these feelings of attachment do not necessarily end when the person leaves the harmful situation. A person may still feel loyal or loving towards the person who abused them and feel temptation to return.

- **Breaking A Trauma Bond -** Breaking a trauma bond can be challenging and may take time, but it is possible.

- **Break free from trauma-bonded relationships:** Recognize when you are trauma-bonded and take the necessary steps to end and stay out of the relationship. Get accountability partners that can walk with you closely, so you won't return to bondage. Use your supports as much as needed to stay free.

- **Counseling & Deliverance:** Enter a season of counseling, deliverance, and inner healing to heal and break free from the roots of trauma bonding. Stay in the process until you are completely healed and are displaying sustaining tools and behaviors that keep you free.

- **Focus on the present and future:** Do not remain stuck in what you did or what was done to you. Commit to healing from that and moving forward in wellness and having a better life.

- **Focus on the evidence:** If a person continues to abuse, or takes no steps to get help, make decisions that are best for you. Leave the relationship and trust that if that person gets help, then God can restore the relationship. But do not remain because of potential as it will just further bind and entangle you to trauma.

- **Use scriptures & declarations to empower yourself:** Abuse can lower a person's self-esteem and make you feel like you cannot live without the abusive person or deserve to be abused. Speak life and truth through the scriptures and through what God has said and is saying about you. Get around people who can empower you and breathe life and truth into you.

- **Practice self-care:** Learn to take care of yourself and to make deliverance and healing an active and consistent part of your lifestyle. This way you break free from entanglements quickly and do not yield to unhealthy interactions when you are stressed, weary, or unfulfilled. Practice being balanced with taking time for yourself. Also spend time journaling, soaking in God's presence, praying, studying and meditating on scriptures, engaging in exercise, hobbies, and spending time with trusted friends.

- **Learn to spot abuse:** Learn about abusive and toxic relationships so that you can spot the signs early and reinforce that they are not healthy.

- **Learn healthy relationship skills:** Learn what healthy relationships look like and seek them out.

Sex Trauma Bonding – This is when couples have verbal and/or physical conflict and then engage in make-up sex that is generally very intense and passionate due to the level of conflict and trauma they have caused one another. We see this on TV all the time. It looks pleasurable and fun but the reality of the trauma this does to the soul is far from this false perception that television gives. Some people are not able to enjoy sex without trauma bonding. They have become addicted to this type of sex so they create drama in their relationship interactions so they can engage in make-up sex. Many people stay in these types of toxic relationships for years as they equate the trauma and make-up sex to love. This is unhealthy and ungodly. There can also be spirits of perversion, inordinacy, burning lust, abuse, and offense in operation.

Poor Relationship Boundaries - Not defining, or wanting to define, boundaries that would keep the relationship balanced and healthy is an open door to impure entanglements. Having blurred or weak boundaries to control the narrative of the acquaintanceship, friendship, situationship, relationship, or to enmesh the relationship where each person cannot determine their identity, worth, independence, what they desire, require, or need from the person or the relationship is unhealthy. Having strict boundaries where the other person does not know what the purpose or expectations are in the interactions, or in the relationship are just as dangerous.

Poor, or lack of boundaries, allow people to change the rules or intent of the relationship as they see fit. Poor boundaries can cause each person to become emotional, vulnerable, fearful, or confused in their reaction to everything that is said and done to them. One or each person may become defensive where there are constant conflicts because the lack of boundaries does not allow for a clear understanding of what should occur in the relationship and how the relationship should operate. Poor boundaries strengthen the dependence of the interactions, while enabling the person or both people to keep the other person enthralled and entangled in their web where they are unable to envision a clear path to exit the toxic relationship. While trying to avoid entanglement, setting proper boundaries is foundational to healthy relationships.

Not Regarding Godly Standards – It does not do any good to have godly boundaries if you do not abide by them.

When you do not abide by them, you succumb to snares and traps of entanglements – **PERIOD**!

Not Setting Realistic Standards & Boundaries - Many people are striving to see just how much of the world and their flesh they can hold on to, so they set unrealistic boundaries, do not set boundaries at all, or adhere to the necessary godly boundaries to keep them pure and in alignment with God. They operate in pride where they claim they can handle engaging in acts and behaviors without falling to sin. Please know that this is a trap.

> **NOT SETTING REALISTIC BOUNDARIES & STANDARDS IS A TRAP!**

- ✓ Your flesh is not your friend!
- ✓ The voice of your flesh that lusts for the world and sin is not your friend!
- ✓ Your thoughts and heart are not trustworthy!
- ✓ The world is not your friend!
- ✓ Any friend that encourages you to sin or toe the boundary line with God are not real friends!
- ✓ That person that says you won't go to hell or God will not be displeased with you if you sin is a LIE – they are not your friend!
- ✓ The demons intertwined in your personality that entice you to sin ain't your friends!
- ✓ Your family members that just want you to get "married already and have a baby" do not have God's plan for you.

- ✓ Your hairdresser, best friend, coworker, sister, brother, bro, sis, cousin, etc., who speaks contrary to true godly purity does not love you like God loves you – they do not love you in Godlikeness. They love you based on their perception and standards and their standards are an enemy against God's will and purpose for your life. They are not your friends!
- ✓ Those carnal believers who tell you that you are human – that you have needs – are not your real friends!
- ✓ Those people you listen to on social media websites and apps that feed your lust, perversion, carnality, and worldliness are not your friends!

Every time you compromise your standards and boundaries; you crack the door to compromise in your life. A cracked door is still an open door.

> **A cracked door is still an open door.**
> **Open doors lead to impure entanglements.**

The only way to NOT get entangled with impurity is to know what God desires for you and make it a practice – a lifestyle – to use this as a levee against every contrary voice and standard in your life.

Conflicting Communication – Due to blurred boundaries, communication is often conflicting when intertwined with an impure entanglement. The unhealthy, or challenging, person will change their expectations to meet the moment rather than setting goals and standards that progress the relationship in a healthy manner. They may set goals and standards that when they are not met, where they cannot fix you or you cannot fix them, when they become stressed, or they just become weary of you or the relationship, they will then contend they did not agree to those goals or only agreed to suffice your desires. They will take no responsibility for the challenges in the relationship and will blame you for it being unhealthy. This is the reason having no boundaries is dangerous. These interactions can be draining, distracting, and depleting. Instead of growing from the person in your life, you start to become less than who you are and what you deserve in life.

Grooming – I wanted to discuss grooming because often we speak of grooming in relations to pedophiles, rapist, etc. But a groomer is anyone with an impure, unhealthy, or ungodly intention.

Grooming is when a person builds a relationship, trust, and emotional connection with a person and then uses their position to manipulate, exploit, use, and abuse them.

- ✓ The intention can be covert or overt – intentional or unintentional – it is still grooming.
- ✓ The intention can be something they did not even realize was there as it is rooted in an unhealed or traumatized area of their life, an area where they are not discipled into Christlikeness, or rooted and grounded in God-identity.

When these areas are dormant or not properly submitted to God for a process of deliverance and healing, we can become groomers. We have the best intentions of governing the people and things that God has granted to our hands, but the lack of Christlikeness, healthy identity, godly truth, and the biblical principles needed to make healthy choices lead us to becoming groomers.

This is an area that many need to be delivered from. It is the reason that many have mishandled people and seduced them into emotional and sexual relationships. They have made people trust them, while posturing themselves and others in situations they believe they can handle, and may even believe is of God, only to realize in the moment that their flesh and unhealed areas have more of a pull than the God in them. As that war stirs in them, the need to fill their void, desires, and flesh is what wins. The grooming they did to draw them and that person into that situation causes them both to fall into ungodly behaviors.

This is the reason it is important to know what you can handle according to what God is saying for your standards and abide by them.

- Do not put your purity in the hands of another person.

- Do not expect others to make decisions about your body and your purity that only you and God should be making.

- Do not allow people to talk you into engaging in conversations and acts that tempt your flesh.

- Recognize when you are being groomed, seduced, and encouraged to compromise, then call it what it is. Do not make excuses for their behavior or yours. Call it what it is and hold one another accountable for being delivered and healed.

- When there is a slip up, where you realize that something was said or done to cause you and that person to fall, implement boundaries and accountabilities immediately to not do it again. Do not let that person coerce or trick you into thinking that it will turn out a different way if you all do it again. You are being groomed. If not by them, then by the unhealed, traumatized, seducing, and/or perverted part of them. YOU WILL FALL AGAIN, and they will keep pushing the envelope until you are so entangled in bondage it will be challenging to get out of it. You will crave the bondage.
  - Your thoughts will crave the bondage.
  - Your flesh will crave the bondage.
  - Your heart will crave the bondage.
  - Your soul will crave the bondage.
  - Your imagination will have you fantasizing on the bondage and on the potential of what could happen if you totally surrender to it.
  - Ultimately, you will yield to the bondage. Then, where you were groomed, now you become the groomer. You become a participant in creating opportunities to be

groomed so you can feed what the groomer has awakened in you.

I know this is hard to hear. When I recognized the areas that I had been groomed and became the groomer, I was shaken as well. I was made to recognize that I had what I call, a sneaky spirit. I am a risk taker at heart. This is a good thing when submitted to God. It is a freaky, sneaky, inordinate personality trait when not submitted to God. As God revealed this to me, I had to recognize where people were in their lives and then walk and make decisions that were best for me and my sustaining in purity and not out of my heart for them. Some folks will not be capable of seeing the error of their ways. Thus, they will not be capable of walking in healing with you in this area. You will have to do what is best for you and trust them to God.

Some will be upset because you will reject being a groomer and being groomed.

- ✓ You will reject keeping doors open that need to be closed.
- ✓ You will reject staying entangled in areas that benefit the flesh and not your spirit.
- ✓ You will have to be okay with putting boundaries in place that SHUTS DOORS and totally sacrificing the relationship if needed for the good of your relationship with God.

When a groomer is benefiting from you satisfying them and they are not in a place to seek godly healing, they will not want deliverance.

- ✓ They will be angry and resentful of you pursuing it.
- ✓ Some of them may become emotionally manipulative where it can feel like torment to your mind or even become abusive or passive aggressive.
- ✓ They will make you feel like you are doing something wrong for not wanting to please them anymore.
- ✓ They will withhold in other ways that you could be a blessing to each other's lives as punishment for not giving them what they want.
- ✓ They will use emotional jargon and entanglements to draw you back into their web.
- ✓ Some of them will operate in mentally unstable ways to play on your heart for them.

One thing I recognize now that I did not recognize when I was engaging with groomers is that, when you are dealing with someone who is constantly grooming you, or you are constantly grooming them, this is an indication that this relationship is not safe. There is no way to have your guards down around a groomer. You must consciously be on guard to protect your boundaries and standards.

- What reasons do we remain in relationships of this nature?
- What is healthy about a relationship that causes us to compromise and succumb to sin?
- What is beneficial about a relationship that is really a threat to our purity and walk with God?

This is the reason I say call it what it is – GROOMING – and GET OUT!

Deliverance Activation:
1. Spend time really searching grooming with God and journal ways where you have been groomed and/or where you are a groomer.
2. Spend time asking yourself the questions above concerning relationships you are and have been in.
3. Set goals and standards that protect you from grooming and from being groomed.

Not Being Discipled into Christlikeness - Here are some essential keys to determine if you are discipled into Christlikeness regarding your life and relationships:

1. Do you know and love God for who he is and not just what he does?
2. Can you stand with God and continue to build covenant relationship and destiny with him when life is challenging or when he is not doing what you feel he should do for your life?
3. Are you learning to love the things that God loves and hate the things that God hates and consistently demonstrate that you choose God over anyone and anything?
4. Are you rooted and grounded in consistent prayer, studying your Bible, and demonstrating the Word in your daily life and choices?
5. Are you able to live Christlikeness as a consistent lifestyle, repent and change your ways, and transform into embodying his ways and thoughts?
6. Do you still act like a child, or you are immature in your behavior and how you engage in life and relationships?

7. Does trauma and life experiences dictate and guide your thoughts, behaviors, and life decisions?
8. Do you trust God to help you fulfill your destiny and purpose?
9. Do you trust God to put the mate he desires you to have in your pathway? Do you trust him to send you a mate?
10. Even as God would allow you to date and guide you in learning what and who is important for you and how to remain in your standards, are you able to stand strong in the Lord and the principles and standards he requires for your life?

If you are wavering in five or more of these questions, you are NOT grounded enough in Christlikeness where you can avoid impure entanglements. Work on building a solid foundation before seeking to date or pursue someone as a marriage partner.

1Corinthians 13:11 *When I was a child, I spake as a child, I understood as a child, I thought as a child: but when I became a man, I put away childish things.*

Matthew 22:37 *Jesus said unto him, Thou shalt love the Lord thy God with all thy heart, and with all thy soul, and with all thy mind.*

Deuteronomy 5:33 *Walk in obedience to all that the Lord your God has commanded you, so that you may live and prosper and prolong your days in the land that you will possess.*

1Peter 2:21 For even hereunto were ye called: because Christ also suffered for us, leaving us an example, that ye should follow his steps.

Carnality & Worldly Focused - Being focused on the world and what they have and comparing yourself to the world and others can weaken your ability to stand in God and guard your standards. The world will never love the God in you. It will only love you if you love and abide by the things the world entails. You can never adequately love God if you love and long for the world.

John 17:14-16 I have given them your word and the world has hated them, for they are not of the world any more than I am of the world.

John 15:19 If you belonged to the world, it would love you as its own.

It is important to recognize when you become weary in welldoing and start to become disgruntled, as you become envious of the pleasures of the world. When you start to succumb to the lie that what the world has is better than what God has for you or become impatient in trusting God in the processing and evolving of life, blessings, and wellness regarding you, you risk backsliding or compromising your standards. The world makes everything look lavish and grand. Yet, there are consequences to the world's ways. The world's ways are never going to align or be approved by God. They are rooted in man's ideologies and the demonic assignments of Satan.

1John 5:19 *We know that we are children of God, and that the whole world is under the control of the evil one.*

1John 2:15-17 *Do not love this world nor the things it offers you, for when you love the world, you do not have the love of the Father in you.*

Matthew 16:26 *What good will it be for someone to gain the whole world, yet forfeit their soul? Or what can anyone give in exchange for their soul?*

Matthew 16:24 *Then Jesus said to his disciples, "Whoever wants to be my disciple must deny themselves and take up their cross and follow me."*

2Corinthians 6:14 *Do not be yoked together with unbelievers. For what do righteousness and wickedness have in common? Or what fellowship can light have with darkness?*

To have and live by the true standards of God, you have to reject the world. When your heart begins to wane, seek God for what it is you are desiring from the world and from people. Ask him if it is the season for that matter, his reasons for not releasing it at this time, or how to align further with him so that what you are seeking can be released to your life.

Also make sure it is of God, as we often want things that do not align with God.

2Corinthians 2:11-12 *Beloved, I implore you as aliens and strangers and exiles [in this world] to abstain from the sensual urges (the evil desires, the passions of the flesh, your lower nature) that wage war against the soul. Conduct yourselves properly (honorably, righteously) among the Gentiles, so that, although they may slander you as evildoers, [yet] they may by witnessing your good deeds [come to] glorify God in the day of inspection [when God shall look upon you wanderers as a pastor or shepherd looks over his flock].*

Proverbs 23:17-18 *Let not your heart envy sinners, but continue in the reverent and worshipful fear of the Lord all the day long. For surely there is a latter end [a future and a reward], and your hope and expectation shall not be cut off.*

Psalm 37:1-3 *"Of David. Do not fret because of those who are evil or be envious of those who do wrong; for like the grass they will soon wither, like green plants they will soon die away. Trust in the LORD and do good; dwell in the land and enjoy safe pasture."*

Matthew 5:13-16 *You are the salt of the earth. But if the salt loses its saltiness, how can it be made salty again? It is no longer good for anything, except to be thrown out and trampled underfoot. You are the light of the world. A town built on a hill cannot be hidden. Neither do people light a lamp and put it under a bowl. Instead they put it on its stand, and it gives light to everyone in the house. In the* *same way, let your light shine before others, that they may see your good deeds and glorify your Father in heaven.*

Matthew 6:24 *No man can serve two masters: for either he will hate the one, and love the other; or else he will hold to the one, and despise the other. Ye cannot serve God and mammon.*

Romans 2:12 *Do not conform to the pattern of this world, but be transformed by the renewing of your mind. Then you will be able to test and approve what God's will is—his good, pleasing and perfect will.*

When we envy, it sparks a jealous, lustful drive in us to have what we want and to be angry that we do not have it. The more we brew and feed these thoughts and desires, the more they cause us to yield to rebellion against God and his standards for our life. Our flesh, perceptions, thoughts, and emotions begin to exalt above the truth of God, and we become tormented as our identity wars between what we want and what God wants. (***Study Romans 7***).

Romans 7:23 *But I see another law in my members, warring against the law of my mind, and bringing me into captivity to the law of sin which is in my members.*

It is important to reach out for deliverance, healing, and godly wisdom. Otherwise, the war in yourself to yield to carnality and the world will win, thus choosing compromise over godly standards. Commit to finding wisdom and healing to break free of the snare that is trying to entangle you. I encourage not to try to fight this war without mature, godly help and accountability. So many go into secret shame, guilt, resentment, anger, and pride while thinking they can handle the war by themselves. This war is not a flesh and blood fight. It is seeking to kill, steal, and destroy you. Do not give it any room. Seek support from those who can shift you up – help fortify your levee – your wall of standards - while you fight the good fight of faith with God.

***Ephesians 6:12** For our struggle is not against flesh and blood, but against the rulers, against the authorities, against the powers of this dark world and against the spiritual forces of evil in the heavenly realms.*

Potential Versus Reality – Many people become entangled in impurity because they are misguided by potential and not the reality of the person that comes into their lives. From my manual, *"Crushing Warlock Opposition."*

Potential is:
- Possible, as opposed to actual.
- An idea, concept, intention, or fantasy, more so than a fact.
- Capable of being or becoming.
- Expressing possibility.
- A latent excellence or ability that may or may not be developed.
- Having or showing the capacity to become or develop into something in the future.

- Latent qualities or abilities that may be developed and lead to future success or usefulness.

Reality is:
- The state or quality of being real.
- Resemblance to what is real.
- A real thing or fact; factual.
- The actual truth of what is real; authentic.

There is nothing wrong with potential if the person is demonstrating that they are working towards realization. The person must present that they have the capacity to progress towards realization. You should be able to see the fruit of this in their lives and interactions with you, and the relationship. When there is no true work, and just a lot of talk and empty promises, you may very well be encountering a pretender – potential.

Proverbs 26:24-28 He that hateth dissembleth with his lips, and layeth up deceit within him; When he speaketh fair, believe him not: for there are seven abominations in his heart. Whose hatred is covered by deceit, his wickedness shall be shewed before the whole congregation. Whoso diggeth a pit shall fall therein: and he that rolleth a stone, it will return upon him. A lying tongue hateth those that are afflicted by it; and a flattering mouth worketh ruin.

Proverbs 6:16-19 These six things doth the Lord hate: yea, seven are an abomination unto him: A proud look, a lying tongue, and hands that shed innocent blood, An heart that deviseth wicked imaginations, feet that be swift in running to mischief, A false witness that speaketh lies, and he that soweth discord among brethren.

This person may not even be aware they are a pretender or that those seven abominations are in them ready to work you over. They just keep making promise after promise while encouraging you to trust them and give them a chance. There is minimal, to no fruit to show that they are striving to align with, become, and to do what God says. **Potential will have you making excuses for the lack of productivity in the person's life. The soul tie will have you agreeing to the imprisonment of the false realities of the person's life.**

Many people, especially women, delay ending the relationship because they dread being embarrassed for relenting to potential. Amid their delay, the "fixer spirit" within them SHIFTS into full effect. They literally become a god in the person's life as they go on fasts, consecrations, engage in manipulating intercessory prayers, that I contend is failed bewitchment, while striving to get the person to commit to goals and behaviors that he/she often cannot keep. The person then begins to use their partner's erred actions as ammunition to make them look like the bad person in the relationship. There is some truth to this, as the person's tactics are an effort to lock the person into their web. This results in contention as the warlock behaviors in the man and the witching behaviors in the woman begin to combat against one another and cause codependent abuse that further entangles them with one another.

Regardless of whether they stay together or they breakup, they both lose. The relationship is not rooted in godly acts and principles, so staying together or breaking up results in contentious traumatic and dramatic interactions as they have done nothing but abuse, manipulate, and afflict one another.

- ✓ Some people remain in these relationships for years before they realize what they have succumbed to.

- ✓ Some people are traumatized by a relationship they experienced years ago due to the shock of what they encountered, how they behaved, and how the relationship ended.

Although a person might have potential, it is essential to seek God for vision regarding where a person is now and if they are good stewards over their potential. If they are not committed to stewarding their gifts, calling, career, business, finances, etc., they will not be able to evolve into the person God is setting aside for you. Be okay with facing reality and releasing potential while trusting God to guide you into meeting the person who possesses the real qualities you need and desire for your life.

Build-A-Mate Syndrome – Being absorbed in potential can cause us to strive to build the person into who we think, or want them to be, and/or who we think they should or can be to us. Build according to dictionary.com means *"to construct (especially something complex) by assembling and joining parts or materials: to establish, increase, or* *strengthen (often followed by up): to mold, form, or create."*

Building a mate is a complex process. You are engaged in complex, intricate work and arrangements within your imagination, perception, manipulative or maneuvering ways, and actions. I know you may not have liked that I used the word *"manipulative,"* but any builder will tell you that it takes strategic manipulation, maneuvering, and designing to build properly or according to what is being envisioned.

Building a spouse is comparable to building an idol.

- When you do this, you have decided what that mate should look like, be to you, and have determined how it fits and will operate in your life.

- You have decided when it should respond to you and give or do what you want it to do.

- When you build an idol, you must worship it, keep building it, feed it, and make sacrifices to it for it to be and produce what you want.

We discern these operations in the Israelites while Moses was on Mount Sinai with God. They felt Moses did not come back in time and that his God – their God – was not operating according to their timing, liking, and considerations, so they decided to build themselves a god who would do what they wanted, when they wanted.

Exodus 32:1-6 And when the people saw that Moses delayed to come down out of the mount, the people gathered themselves together unto Aaron, and said unto him, Up, make us gods, which shall go before us; for as for this Moses, the man that brought us up out of the land of Egypt, we wot not what is become of him. And Aaron said unto them, Break off the golden earrings, which are in the ears of your wives, of your sons, and of your daughters, and bring them unto me.

And all the people brake off the golden earrings which were in their ears, and brought them unto Aaron. And he received them at their hand, and fashioned it with a graving tool, after he had made it a molten calf: and they said, These be thy gods, O Israel, which brought thee up out of the land of Egypt. And when Aaron saw it, he built an altar before it; and Aaron made proclamation, and said, Tomorrow is a feast to the LORD. And they rose up early on the morrow, and offered burnt offerings, and brought peace offerings; and the people sat down to eat and to drink and rose up to play.

Operating in build-a-mate is dangerous because we have to become that person's god, parent, and/or fixer.

Let's Ponder That a Moment!

This behavior can also have us operating in witchcraft where we are engaging in crafty words and tactics, wishful ideologies and witchy type prayers, subtle hints to bind, seducing and/or enticing practices and words to draw that person into what we desire. We can also find ourselves using the gifts, callings, and blessings God has given us to shape our idolatrous mate. We see this in the story of the Israelites and the golden calf. This kind of work is not done through healthy wells of communicating our desires, needs, and expectations. They are also not conducted through the ordained purpose to which God gave them to us. Therefore, the more these operations occur, the more they will be needed to build the mate and to fulfill us.

When we operate as God, or the parent, in effort to build a mate, we risk entangling with any parental wounds that person may have. While they are operating as the little girl or boy, we are building them into grown people. Just think, it takes 18 years to raise a child and even then, the child will still need their parents. This means once you start playing the parental role, you never stop playing it. We like to think the person grows up, but part of their personality has bonded to the parent in us and will always want to be parented.

> **Remember what you build, you must maintain.**

If there are trauma wounds, the person will throw tantrums and use manipulating and controlling tactics to keep you bound to them – to keep you mothering/fathering them.

- They will use things they know about the person to guilt and continuously hook them.

- They will create erred, or exaggerated scenarios to make the person feel like they are not treating them fairly.
- They will guilt the person into remaining engaged and bound to them.
- They will make excuses for their actions to make the person feel sorry for them.
- They will promise to work on their behavior even though they do not have the capacity, deliverance, or divine maturity to stay the course to freedom and wellness.

Also, when a natural child grows up, they eventually want to leave home and soar in what they have learned. Often, we wonder why the mates we build leave the nest. They leave because it is innate for a child to want to leave and cleave.

Genesis 2:24 *Therefore shall a man leave his father and his mother and shall cleave unto his wife: and they shall be one flesh.*

Matthew 19:5 *And said, for this cause shall a man leave father and mother, and shall cleave to his wife: and they twain shall be one flesh?*

We expect the mate we have raised to want to finally take their place in our lives. But instead, the innate desire to leave and cleave takes over, and they pursue someone who they can truly bond with as a covenant partner – not a mother or father.

Also, often the builder has been the parent for so long that they do not recognize when the person has grown up. They keep trying to be a parent which causes constant challenges in the relationship. This also causes further codependent entanglements or division. That person who was the child either:

- Resents the builder and breaks the relationship off.
- Rebels against being constantly required to be molded and shaped into what the person desires them to be.
- Cheats because they are looking for a mate and not a parent.
- Leave and cleave with someone they can further evolve in adulting with.

Godly standards help you recognize where you are and where the person is in God and whether you both are naturally, or spiritually children or adults that can handle and evolve in the principles, will, and purposes of God.

Deliverance Activation:
- Ask God what support looks like to the potential mate he has for you.
- Ask God what support looks like for you regarding a potential mate.
- Be mindful to only be and do what God is requiring of you in the relationship. Set boundaries that keep you accountable to God, so you won't end up being momma or daddy in the relationship.

- Set boundaries that keep you accountable to God, so you won't end up being momma or daddy, God, fixer, etc. in the relationship.

Ungodly Soul Tie – Soul ties can be ungodly or godly. You will have to get my, *"Deliverance From Soul Ties"* eBook for a detailed teaching on soul ties. An ungodly soul tie is any **knitting** of ourselves with a person, place, or thing that is not of God or that is not God's will and plan for our lives. God will not have you bound to sin, idolatry, unhealthiness, unfruitfulness, or bondage. He will not have you engage, join to, or remain in a relationship that is a transgression against his word, will, and plan for your life. God will not have you tied to something that is going to deplete you rather than build you in him and in your identity, purpose, and destiny.

1Corinthians 6:16 What? know ye not that he which is joined to an harlot is one body? For two, saith he, shall be one flesh.

Genesis 34:1-3 And Dinah the daughter of Leah, which she bare unto Jacob went out to see the daughters of the land. And when Shechem the son of Hamor the Hivite, prince of the country, saw her, he took her, and lay with her, and defiled her. And his soul clave unto Dinah the daughter of Jacob, and he loved the damsel, and spake kindly unto the damsel. Verse 8 And Hamor communed with them, saying the soul of my son Shechem longeth for your daughter: I pray you give her him to wife. Sexual involvement can form such entangling tentacles of soul ties that it is extremely hard to break off the relationship.

Proverbs 5:20-24 *And why wilt thou, my son, be ravished with a strange woman, and embrace the bosom of a stranger? For the ways of man are before the eyes of the Lord, and he pondereth all his goings. His own iniquities shall take the wicked himself, and he shall be holden with the cords of his sins. He shall die without instruction; and in the greatness of his folly he shall go astray.*

Psalm 1:1 *Blessed is the man that walketh not in the counsel of the ungodly, nor standeth in the way of sinners, nor sitteth in the seat of the scornful*

2Corinthians 6:14-18 *Be ye not unequally yoked together with unbelievers: for what fellowship hath righteousness with unrighteousness? and what communion hath light with darkness? And what concord hath Christ with Belial? or what part hath he that believeth with an infidel? And what agreement hath the temple of God with idols? for ye are the temple of the living God; as God hath said, I will dwell in them, and walk in them; and I will be their God, and they shall be my people. Wherefore come out from among them, and be ye separate, saith the Lord, and touch not the unclean thing; and I will receive you, and will be a Father unto you, and ye shall be my sons and daughters, saith the Lord Almighty.*

Soul ties are about agreements. When you engage in compromise in emotional, sexual, worldly, carnal, or unhealthy entanglements, you come into soulish agreements with that person, place, or thing. Everything about what their life and belief system entails is joined to you and vice versa.

Amos 3:3 Can two walk together, except they be agreed?

The Message Bible *Do two people walk hand in hand if they aren't going to the same place?*

When the agreement is unhealthy, it makes for an ungodly soul tie. Regardless of whether you agree or not, if a soul tie is formed, it must be broken for you to be free of whatever was knitted and transferred through that tie. This is vital as rape, incest, abuse, mind control, religious sects, erred beliefs, and more are soul ties that form without our agreement. In some cases, it is out of ignorance, fear, or lack of knowledge, depending on the circumstance. When they are not broken, whatever the offender deposited lives in us. Some people will end up manifesting the traits of their offender while others live in the false identity of what was deposited.

Deliverance Activation:
Spend time breaking ungodly soul ties by doing the following:

- Spending time before the Lord identifying every ungodly soul tie.
- Confessing and repenting for your role in the soul tie, even if it was just giving into the lies and false identity of your offender.

- Forgiving your soul tie partner and forgiving yourself for engaging in the soul tie.
- Breaking and removing the soul tie. Be sure to call out every person's name you have a soul tie with. Go through these steps, then break and remove each tie.
- Using the blood of Jesus and the fire of God, cleanse yourself of all ungodly deposits, and command any parts of your soul, heart, mind, and identity to be restored back to you.
- Though there are godly soul ties, sometimes we can become too familiar with each other and take one another for granted. This causes us to behave towards each other in ways that can be inordinate, unbecoming, possessive, or dishonoring. To avoid such behaviors, I suggest occasionally breaking any ungodly soul ties that have formed through familiarity, misunderstanding, miscommunication, lack of regard, being more to one another than God has said, becoming lax in the relationship, fleshly, or imbalanced in your interaction then declaring that only the godly soul tie you are to have with that person remains, or is re-established.

Situationships – Dictionary.com defines *situationship* as, "a romantic or sexual relationship that is not considered to be formal or established." Situationships are dangerous because they lead to soul ties and entanglements that cause all kinds of challenges. The boundary lines are blurred and are often crossed. Both people tend to be guarded, while trying to act like the marital and relationship interactions they have do not matter or mean anything. Yet the flesh, heart, mind, and soul cannot be put in a box. No matter how many walls you put up to guard from being hurt, the more you feed emotions, desires, and flesh, the more they grow and break down the false barriers, as deep down, one or more people in the relationship want the situationship to be a real relationship. When there is a person who wants the pleasures of a relationship but not commitment, then betrayal, or the feelings of being betrayed soon follow. The person who wants the relationship will feel used and betrayed when reality has set in, and they truly acknowledge the motives and intent of that other person.

I say this because it requires living in a false reality and false hope to engage and settle in a situationship. The person is living a fantasy of potential, while compromising and being used in situations that fill temporary voids and pleasures. God never meant for his people to live in worldly or manmade obscurity. It leads to darkness, trauma, pain, and bondage. Obscurity is also NOT faith. Faith should be put in God, not man or worldly concepts. Faith should ONLY be put in God. He is the ONLY one who can fulfill the truth of what you need and deserve in life and relationships.

Jeremiah 29:11 *For I know the plans I have for you," declares the Lord, "plans to prosper you and not to harm you, plans to give you hope and a future.*

Psalm 147:11 *The Lord delights in those who fear him, who put their hope in his unfailing love.*

Roman 15:13 *May the God of hope fill you with all joy and peace as you trust in him, so that you may overflow with hope by the power of the Holy Spirit.*

Psalm 62:5-6 *Yes, my soul, find rest in God; my hope comes from him. Truly he is my rock and my salvation; he is my fortress, I will not be shaken.*

Phillipians 1:6 *Being confident of this, that he who began a good work in you will carry it on to completion until the day of Christ Jesus*

False Obligations & Loyalties – Often, when we get into entanglements we start to be snared by false obligations and loyalties that cause us to think we must remain in the relationship when everything about it SCREAMS, "THIS IS NOT GOD!" We try to make it be God and spiritual when God is not in it. Our permissive will overtakes us, and we operate through our human morals that have us doing good things, but not godly things that keep us entangled in relationships. False obligations and loyalty eventually become burdens. We even start to feel the burden and the weight of carrying the other person, or whatever it is that we have taken on as a project. The more we yield to this, the more compromise SHIFTS into the situationship.

False Burdens - Inappropriately bearing one another's burdens where that issue drives one's focus or interactions.

False Obligations - Feeling obligated to remain in the relationship or to do things in the relationship from a posture of false loyalty.

Excessive Caretaking - Overly caring for the person while sacrificing one's own needs, desires, time, responsibilities, and relationships. The person helps to the point of losing self, sacrificing self, or becoming a fixer in the other person's life. They are made to feel neglectful when refusing or not wanting to take care of the person. They feel guilty when not being able to care for the person the way they need or desire, or when not being able to fix the other's problems.

Perfectionistic Behavior – When a person is perfectionistic, they have a need to make people and relationships projects, to fix themselves and others. Also, within the relationship, mistakes are constantly highlighted to cause shame, guilt, compliance, and strengthen the unhealthy entanglement where the perfectionistic person becomes obsessed with making themselves perfect to please the other and/or doing demanding things to perfect the other person. They also tend to remain in entanglement to avoid feeling like a failure when it did not work out.

Deliverance Activation:
Examine if this is a behavior rooted in you from unhealthy family ideologies. Spend time journaling, acknowledging, and healing from family false obligations, loyalties, caretaking roles, perfectionistic behaviors, and every way these erred perceptions have interjected into your relationships and life in general. Set three goals you can work on to weed these entanglements out of your life.

Enabling – Enabling is when one or both parties in the situationship or relationship maintain unhealthy perceptions and behaviors regardless of the consequences of that person's actions.

Fixers – A fixer is when a person takes on another person's burdens or brokenness as a project. Once they "fix" the person, they end the relationship abruptly and move on to the next project. They may also stay in a relationship and break the person in another area of life to create a need for their presence. If they cannot fix the person, they make it out to be the other's fault. They often become offended as they wreak havoc in the relationship, or cause upheaval followed by ending the relationship.

Control & Manipulation – Control and manipulation is when a person uses words, behaviors, information, and situations to make the person dependent, or to cause the person to be one's dependence. The controlling person will punish the person with words or by withholding love, attention, needs, and desires when they cannot control and manipulate them. They will also end the relationship without giving reason to further manipulate and control the person's emotions and actions by inflicting the pain and drama in ending the relationship.

Misconstruing The Concept Of Healthy Love – In such experiences, love is rooted in doing and proving rather than in healthy attributes of what love is. Love rooted in conditions that is centered around manipulation, control, pity, seduction, or sensual lust used to lure the person into compliance is at the forefront of the relationship. Withholding love, sex, and affection to get a person to do as they desire and to control the intimacy of the relationship.

Relationship Dependent – A dependent person does not like being alone. They do not like being without some form of relationship, especially a codependent one. They live through abandonment fears that are often tormenting and agonizing. The person feels insecure and void without a relationship. The person has a need to be fixed and to fix others through relationship. The person that fears abandonment will strive to get the other person to vow to never leave. They will make the other person feel bad for wanting to leave or for considering leaving the unhealthy relationship.

Insecurity & Low Self-esteem – It is so important to be delivered from insecurity and low self-esteem. These people need constant validation through work and support of the other person in the relationship. They have the other person constantly proving that they support them and deem them valuable. They feel "less than" when they are not able to keep abreast of the demands needed to make the person feel validated. They operate in perfectionistic and prideful mindsets and behaviors that are usually a sign of low self-esteem, insecurity, and a need for approval and endorsement. Moreover, they are challenged when not validated in the way or areas to which the person desires. They punish others by withholding love, attention, support, needs, and desires when not validated accordingly. They will also leave the relationship and turn others against the person when not validated as they desire.

People Pleasing – People pleasers have a challenging time saying no. They feel obligated to say yes. They experience shame, guilt, anxiety, and stress when having to say no. The person feels as if they are letting the other person down and as if the other person will be upset with them if they say no. These people want to please others to the point of saying yes, even at the expense of self, others, and the frustrations it brings to their lives. They engage in unhealthy self-sacrificing where they are denying their own needs, thoughts, and feelings to please others.

Ghosting – Ghosting is when someone cuts off all communication without explanation. We are seeing a lot of this due to being able to contact people by messenger, online, communicate on their social media posts, chat rooms, and live videos. Usually, a person will engage in a lot of contact and communication that is intimate and personal. Then, suddenly, they will stop calling, texting, or responding when you call or text. The person may go silent for days, weeks, or forever. When, or if they do return, they may have a lame excuse or act as if it is not a big deal or that the relationship was not serious enough for you to be challenged by them not conversing.

There is no way around the fact that due to the initial constant communication and personal dialog exchanged that an emotional soul tie may have been formed. When that person breaks the tie abruptly, without explanation, it can be confusing and even painful.

The lack of closure, or the reason for ghosting, leaves a person and that relationship in ambiguity. Ambiguity is where doubtfulness or uncertainty of meaning, or intention resides. You are left trying to figure out if anything the person said was truthful and whether the interactions meant anything. Also, when there is no closure, even in small communication, it leaves an opportunity for people to make inferences about themselves, the person that ghosted them, and the relationship. Having and sustaining your standards helps to navigate this ghosting behavior, not take it personal, and/or work through the heart challenges when their actions do impact you. Your standards keep you trusting that standing in what God is saying will remove anything that needs to be shaken from your life. Often, we do not like how they are removed, but in time, we learn to be thankful for the removal of anything that is ungodly or harmful for us.

Hebrews 12:27 And this word, Yet once more, signifieth the removing of those things that are shaken, as of things that are made, that those things which cannot be shaken may remain.

Inordinate Affections – Inordinate affections are when a person/persons engage in inappropriate, improper, unrestrained, immoderate, or unreasonable roles and behaviors in the relationship that cause it to be sensual, lustful, worldly, imbalanced, uncontrolled, unregulated, and/or disorderly. Sexual activities such as tongue kissing, heavy petting, clothes burning, sensual and sexual massages, masturbation, oral sex, sleeping together in the same bed or area, watching pornography, sexting, sending sexual pictures etc., falls under inordinacy and is still SEX. We will discuss this in more depth later in this manual but please know such behaviors lead to impure entanglements.

Colossians 3:5 Mortify therefore your members which are upon the earth; fornication, uncleanness, inordinate affection, evil concupiscence, and covetousness, which is idolatry.

Warlock & Witch Hookings – Warlocks and Witches hook their prey under their prison of seduction and control. Initially, when the hooking occurs, the person hooked in may experience a sense of security, protection, and regard for being in the intimate or secure space of love and validation. But as soon as the person becomes comfortable, vulnerable, susceptible, unguarded in their perceptions and behaviors, or become reliant and relinquishing of their control to the warlock or witch, the person then enters a war between striving to honor the demands, controls, manipulations, and seductions of the warlock/witch and honoring the truth of God's standards, will, and purpose for his or her life. When a person is locked into relationship with a warlock or witch, their lives become the sacrifice upon the altar to which that warlock/witch worships on. The person knows they are losing themselves and can literally feel themselves dying or having no control over their lives but are so locked in that they cannot make sufficient decisions to come from under the hooking spell. They make excuses for being sacrificed and succumb to whatever lies and manipulations the warlock/witch tells them despite the obvious fact that they are imprisoned in the relationship. These relationships will increase in the coming days as witchcraft continues to become the norm in society.

Sometimes these people are literally into witchcraft practices, ancestral worship, mixture of Christianity with New Age, manipulation of the Scriptures for the purposes of intimidation, control, and seduction. And sometimes there is no blatant idolatrous or witchcraft practices. At any rate, it is essential to discern these types of relationships, avoid, and end them when you begin to recognize that you are in one. The longer you stay, the more difficult it is to get out. These relationships can become dangerous and detrimental as these people are only for the good of themselves and the idol gods that they are sacrificing you to. Consider purchasing my book, "Crushing Warlock Opposition," for further insight on this topic.

RELATIONSHIP DESTROYING DEMONS

From my manual entitled, *"Kingdom Keys to Governing Relationships."*

The demonic spirits listed in this chapter drain people and relationships. They are fruit stealers and relationship killers. You and your partner need to study how these demonic spirits operate in and around relationships, be delivered from them, close doors to how they would operate in and around you all and fortify yourselves and your relationship, so you won't give room to them being a part of your lives.

Decree complete deliverance from them personally and generationally. Decree every root is plucked up as you are enlightened concerning their works and break their powers off your life and relationships.

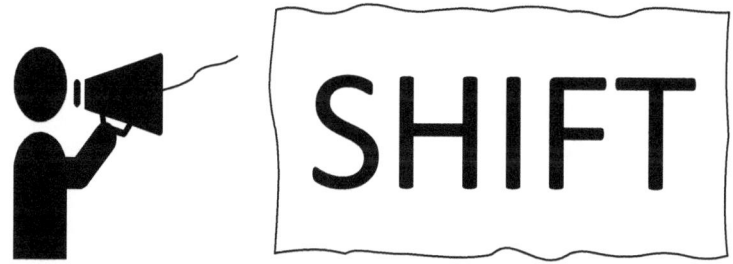

Try just yelling that out as you drive or wherever you are, "**SHIFT**!" I promise you will feel better! Now, let's get down to business and bust up some relationship-destroying demons!

Arrested Development AKA Little Girl/Little Boy Spirit –

If this is an area you or your mate struggle with, I recommend buying my eBook on this topic. It will provide greater insight into how these spirits work and how to be delivered from them. It is important to make sure that you and the person you plan to marry are healed of mother and father wounds, childhood traumas, and that you both have grown up in your personalities, identities, and behaviors. There is nothing more challenging than being married to someone who operates like a child even though they are an adult, or who fluctuates from child to adult depending on what is occurring in their lives and in the relationship. There is also nothing more frustrating than feeling like one is having to be a parent to a spouse who is supposed to walk along side of you as a covenant partner. Once you start parenting a spouse, you never stop parenting them. No matter how grown a child gets, they will always need and want their parents. Remember that! This is not a role you want to cultivate in your relationship. Deal with this before you put a ring on a child and marry them.

When someone is operating in a little girl or little boy spirit, they are stuck in Arrested Development:

Arrested means *"to seize (a person) by legal authority or warrant; take into custody: to check the course of; stop; slow down."*

Development means *"to the act or process of developing; growth; progress."*

Arrested Development is when a person's body grows up, but their mind does not. This results in part, or multiple parts, of one's personality being stuck or imprisoned at the age of trauma or the state that the person stopped developing. As the person operates in arrested development, their personalities fluctuate between child and adult, depending on what is going on in their lives. They literally operate as a child at times, and this is generally during vital times when they need to behave as an adult. They will need deliverance and healing from the trauma that has arrested them at that age, while maturing and learning to operate fully from the age they presently are. I recommend counseling and deliverance for anyone who needs freedom in this area.

Spirit of Victimization - This spirit postures the person as the victim where they generally view themselves as the victim, even when they are wrong. The person usually operates through unresolved wounds where they have been victimized. Repeated offenses prevent their ability to see themselves in any other light or to operate from any other role than the victim. As this spirit uses those wounds as an open door, the person will create drama and experiences to be victimized or to strengthen their victim mentality. They often carry an air that draws offenders and manipulators so that they are continuously bound by victimizing experiences. This air is really the seed and fruit of victimization that has oppressed them where other offending spirits or mentalities can connect and further rape these people of hope and the desire to thrive in life.

Spirit Of Sabotage - This spirit works through people and situations to sabotage relationships. It usually does not want the person to be joyful, loved, or fulfilled in life, or the person is not able to embrace the aspects of life. It seeks to find and open doors to instill fear, suspicion, hopelessness, or drama so that there is a lack of trust in the person or the relationship. It also pursues an opportune time to strike and ruin the relationship. This is a destiny-killing spirit and a relationship-killing spirit. It does not play fairly and is not justified in how it operates. It is seeking to kill anything good and godly. This spirit will set traps and create drama-filled situations so that murder of the relationship can happen.

Spirit Of Passive Aggression - Passive-aggressive spirit is in operation when a person displays a pattern of indirectly expressing their true thoughts and feelings towards someone or a situation. The person is negative or pessimistic when displaying their behavior. They are internally angry but do not initially, or blatantly, display it. The person pretends to be pleasant or unbothered while seething with anger. They engage in other passive or non-overt behavior to demonstrate their anger. This behavior is attempting to punish, retaliate, intimidate, control, and express rage and anger without admitting or acknowledging one's feelings, thoughts, and concerns. The person may deny they are being passive-aggressive when confronted or being held accountable for their actions. They will use jokes, flattery, accolades, gifts, and help in attempting to cover up their indirect aggression. This spirit whips the person with internal psychological and mental warfare, even as it is whipping you with delayed aggression. This spirit will have the person making excuses for their actions and justifying the reason it is okay to whip you. Often this behavior further sabotages the progress of relationships and the ability to resolve conflict in a swift and healthy manner. The spirit in them is dominating and is generally abusive even to the person. It is important to place boundaries in your relationships with passive-aggressive people. Whether they can change or not, do not allow false loyalties and obligations to remain bound to their abuse. Assert your right to be treated with honor and regard. You are not a slave and do not deserve to be constantly whipped by someone who claims to have your best interest at heart.

Spirit Of Leviathan - This spirit is rooted in pride and haughtiness. This spirit interrupts and distorts communication between the speaker and the listener, between God and the person/ministry, and within atmospheres. Its effort is to sow offense, discord, irritation, anger, misunderstanding, faultfinding, ungodly judging, mistrust, and suspicion. God speaks of how Leviathan operates in ***Job 41:26-32***. This spirit was in operation between him and his friends who were striving to understand why God allowed the enemy to bring havoc upon his life. This spirit also distorted Job's views where he could not receive wise counsel from God during this time of trial with the Lord. This spirit will enter when life and relationships are under heavy warfare, experiencing challenges, and/or when they are transitioning to new dimensions in life and in their covenant interaction. It wants to cause an operation of vain haughtiness that distorts communication and creates layers of challenges, where people and the relationship cannot tower or SHIFT forward in life, life situations, and/or in their relationship. Quick repentance and forgiveness are the easiest ways to combat the Leviathan. The unity and love of Christ will dismantle and displace this spirit.

Deaf & Dumb Spirit - This spirit lays like a blanket of clouds over a person's mind so that information cannot get in or be retained. It is a mind-immobilizing spirit where the person feels like they are talking to a mute person. The person is saying they understand, and they are even engaging in dialog at times, but they are not retaining anything to a degree where change will occur. Or it is like talking to a person who is watching a movie. They appear engrossed - they appear to be grasping all that is occurring. They may appear to be staring as if they are listening and comprehending, but nothing is getting past the deaf and dumb helmet that is locked upon their brain. Those oppressed by this spirit will come back and ask the same questions that were just explained or ask for the information to be shared again with the same detail to which it was just downloaded to them. They will be able to share and dialog about what was discussed, however, when proceeding to implement it, the information is zapped out or frozen in their minds. This spirit also causes people to talk themselves out of the information where they are so confused that they do not remember what was said to them or the purpose that it has in their lives. This can be extremely challenging when setting goals, boundaries, and expectations in relationships. The person will constantly receive clear vision but cannot activate it due to a lack of retention. The relationship will feel like you are sharing the same information over and over while doing more teaching and parenting than walking alongside the person.

Spirits Of the Fear of Receiving, Giving Love - This spirit causes panic, extreme anxiety, and paranoia as it relates to being vulnerable, and of being able to receive and give love. The person harbors a fear of being hurt or that the love will be stripped away. This spirit causes them to withhold love for fear of not getting it in return or being taken advantage of. They are constantly fearing the worst and tend to speak a lot of doom and death into the relationship. They are often guarded and on edge. Due to the grip of this spirit, it takes a lot of time and patience to convince them that they are safe and will not be hurt in the relationship. Receiving love can overwhelm them, and spiral them into a panic, where they operate in flight mode. They either run or want to run from the relationship. They do a lot of connecting and disconnecting in the relationship.

Spirit Of Rejection - Rejecting love, fear of not being loved, fear of being hurt. This spirit makes the person feel or believe they are a reject. No matter how much they are told or shown that they are accepted, they are unable to receive it. They self-reject for fear of being rejected. They self-reject, then become passive-aggressive by blaming the other person for rejecting them even though they were self-rejecting due to their fear of being rejected. This rejection creates a bottomless pit in their souls and hearts to where it does not matter how much love, attention, acceptance, and approval they receive, they still feel rejected. They are like bottomless pits that can never be filled. The more they receive, the more they want, and sometimes they become enraged and vindictive if a person attempts to be balanced and healthy in their interactions with themselves.

This spirit will cause people to be jealous and envious of the love, healthy relationships, and success others have. They will strive to connect with these types of people. Sometimes they will strive to live vicariously through others while taking on parts of other's identities to feel loved, accepted, and successful. They will be living through a fantasy, or false reality, in their minds as it relates to this person. They tend to be inordinate and sensual in how they perceive and give love. In friendships, mentorships, or spiritual relationships this will, at times, feel sexual and sensual in nature. The interactions and fellowship become one of a lover more so than the role the person is supposed to have in one's life. In dating and married-type relationships, the person will engage as constantly needy, possessive, moody, and insecure. This spirit causes them to feed off the drive for drama and conflict, then make-up in a passionate manner as this feeds their love for attention and the need for people to perform as a demonstration of love and acceptance. The relationship will be full of inordinate lustful passion due to the person being so overly emotional and needing their emotions and identity constantly fed. When fed, the person tends to respond as intensely loving, sexual, and passionate. This seems great for a time but is draining due to the relationship being centered around continuous drama, and then the need to be habitually validated in their identity and one's approval of them.

Spirit Of Jezebel & Narcissism – It is worth doing a personal study on this spirit as what I will share is only a glimpse of how this spirit operates. This spirit is dominating, rebellious, idolatrous, narcissistic, and operates in witchcraft. This spirit will cause people to control the life and relationships of others. It is a bewitching, tangling, and web spinning-type spirit. Jezebel wants to wear the pants in the relationship. This spirit is not interested in an agreement or walking together in godly covenant and only tends to give and consider the person to gain control over them so that it can release its future needs and desires of governing over the person. This spirit seduces and manipulates its way into setting up rulership and authority in a person's life or relationship. Its aim is to be the main controlling voice in a person's life. This spirit will use their web to connect itself into every area of one's life, to the point they feel helpless without the person, yet entrapped by the person. The Jezebel spirit can operate very cunningly, seductively, and deceptively in the beginning. The person with this spirit will even be very loving at first, but once they have gripped their prey, their true motives and personality manifest.

The study of Jezebel is its own book; however, you can read about this evil queen beginning in ***IKings 16:31***. Jezebel, historically, is a real person but she is also representative of a dynamic that can corrupt a person's character. The characteristics of Jezebel can be in any gender.

- Jezebel is clever, devious, dishonest, and out for personal gain. Jezebel will act like he or she is your new best friend, or the lover you've always wanted. However, they are seducing you into trusting them.

- Jezebel will lavish you with gifts, provide financial support to your life endeavors, and offer to pay for things you need and desire.

- Jezebel is wise by nature. She is also very intelligent and smart. Jezebel will display natural, alluring wisdom and will seek out answers so he or she can gain superiority as the voice to listen to in your life.

- Jezebel watches your life, actions, and interactions so he or she can fill voids, make up for your flaws, and insert suspicion to people or things they feel are competition to her isolating you to herself, so they can use the information to further lure you, or against you, when you reject him or her.

- Jezebel will appear very dependable and insert himself or herself into your life to appear as loyal support, yet he or she is really seeking to control you. They are also aspiring to use the fact that they are your most loyal support later when you try to bring balance to your interactions with her or him. They will demand repayment of what they have done for you and will often want this debt paid by demanding compliance.

- Once Jezebel has you in his or her grasp, they will make everything your fault that you are no longer happy in the relationship. They will punish you by not being what they initially were to you and demand that you perform to receive from them.

- Jezebel will withhold love, attention, encouragement, accolades, time, sex, and support to get you to submit to their controlling ways. This passive-aggressive behavior can be draining, confusing, perverted, and oppressive. You will eventually develop perceptions about yourself that are not true as they play on your identity and self-worth.

- Jezebel can also be verbally, physically, and sexually abusive. This spirit will cause people to have anger and rage outbursts, engage in property destruction, use intimidation, and threats to control others. They will throw tantrums and cause public scenes due to hideous behaviors.

- Jezebel will rally others against you and sow seeds of discord to get others to be suspicious or mistrusting of you. Because they have become intertwined in your life, they will sow seeds of discord where others betray you or give the impression you are betraying others.

The end game is to end your relationships, to punish you, or control you into being subject to their authority.

Many people who operate through the spirit of Jezebel do not know they have this spirit and often do not want to search for themselves when it is pointed out to them. This spirit deceives the person into thinking they are perfect and that everyone else is the problem. This spirit is also very prideful and reprobate. It is not easily penitent, is anti-god, and anti-transformational, especially in relinquishing its place of authority in one's life, in general, and relinquishing the benefits it receives from ruling over people and their relationships.

Spirit Of Ahab – This spirit works with Jezebel. This spirit often marries or is friended by Jezebel and works with Jezebel so it can accomplish its purpose in life and relationships. The spirit of Ahab causes people to fear confrontation and likes it better when it is dominated where others can make decisions for them. This spirit causes the person to be insecure, weak, to live from a failure state, is irresponsible, lacks assertiveness, and unable to rule in areas that he or she should succeed. The person with this spirit is afraid of rejection, tends to expect that bad things will happen, and is passive in putting up with Jezebel or unhealthy behaviors and the actions of others. This spirit causes the person to be clingy, needy, and helpless. They have a need for love and belonging, they fear abandonment and will relinquish their power and authority to others to feel validated, loved, and worthy. They can appear excessively nice but generally have an ulterior motive or because they desire love, attention, and honor. The person will be passive-aggressive in that, when it becomes angry, it will get Jezebel to intervene and punish the person for hurting them or get Jezebel to fulfill his or her desires and to bring joy to their lives. It is also a passively angry, pouting, tantrum-throwing spirit. The person with this spirit may have a little girl or little boy spirit, where at times they will act like a child due to part of their personality being stuck in some childhood or teenage year of their life.

Spirit Of Narcissism – This spirit causes a person to have an inflated, grandiose sense of self-importance. The person tends to be prideful, haughty, overly confident, boastful, self-absorbed, and has a deep sense or need for excessive attention and admiration. They believe they are superior to others and possess extreme brilliance, power, and ability for success. They may be very beautiful, handsome, and seductive. They feel entitled to be treated with high regard and can be aggressive or abusive when they feel they are being treated below their standards. They lack empathy for others, do not have the compassion to be consistent, are unable to care for the hearts, purposes, and lives of others, and can only have relationships if they are centered around them. Most conversations and activities within the relationship are centered around them. They make them seem so important that the other person does not realize that their entire lives are being drawn into a world of narcissism. What they used to like, dislike, the things that were fun, good, bad, etc., no longer matter and are only a distant memory because the narcissist has made them believe that only the things that benefit them are important.

The person with this spirit is NOT CAPABLE of giving and receiving love in a healthy manner; anything they give is for personal gain. Everything is about them, even other people. This can be confusing because such people are very charismatic, alluring, captivating, initially loving, and giving, and they appear to have a caring nature. But somewhere the root of this charm reveals itself and usually baffles and confuses its intended victims. Victims are often left stripped of their own identity because it has been lost or entangled inside the identity of the narcissist. The narcissist tends to passive-aggressively compete with the person they are in the relationship with. This is because they are jealous, envious, and NEED TO MAKE SURE they are always the focus of attention. Therefore, they use negative jabs, belittling comments, verbal abuse, play on words regarding the person's flaws and weaknesses, and subtle suggestions of what the person should change to make the person feel insecure, uneasy, and confused in their identity and self-worth. Their aim is to strip the person of their identity, so that they do not know who they are apart from the narcissist, or so they feel they are no one apart from the narcissist. They use gaslighting behaviors to manipulate, cause doubt and questioning, confuse, dismantle, discombobulate, and drain their victim's identity and strength so they rely on them, and their truth about what the person's life should be, what life is, what occurred during their interactions, conversations, and experiences, and how that person's life should feed theirs. They get bored quickly, so they have a lot of people and projects they are maneuvering to keep their ego fed and empowered. Many victims need time to put their lives back together because the narcissist absorbs their life, so they have to find themselves again.

Spirit Of Abuse – This spirit causes people to be physically, emotionally, and psychologically abusive. This spirit can be accompanied by a personal or generational curse. They tend to be very offensive while using mistreatment, torment, criticism, cursing, exploitation, perversion, and hurt to control, punish, and bind their victims. They treat people as if they are beneath them and worthless. These spirits may have no regard for how they impact others. They also may have no regard for the life and property of others. They tend to be hateful, bitter, unforgiving, resentful, easily angered and enraged, and can explode or strike unwarrantedly.

- Sexual abuse (rape, incest, molestation, sex trafficking, prostitution, sadomasochism),
- Mental abuse (mind control, mind blinding, mind binding, mind games, domination, telepathy),
- Physical abuse (beatings, pushing, shoving, slapping, bruising, cruelty, imprisonment, property destruction),
- Religious abuse (legalism, control, guilt, shame, condemnation, cults, using scriptures to bind people, succumbing to false religious obligation),
- Emotional abuse (hurt, deep hurt, wounds, manipulation of emotions to control the victim, manipulating through crying and mood swings).

Offender Spirit - The person with this spirit may be easily offended. They become upset by the simplest of matters. People around them tend to walk on eggshells because they never know when this person is going to become upset. There can be instances where the offense is true, yet the person will contend they are not offended, while passive-aggressively punishing those who hurt them. These people have a difficult time communicating, resolving conflict, or expressing their thoughts and feelings in a healthy manner. They are usually bitter, pessimistic, and constantly interject negativity into the atmosphere, situations, conversations, and interactions. Some other ways this spirit operates through people are as follows:

- Miscommunication & misperception - where the person continually misunderstands what is being said and communicated to them.
- Unhealed issues of the past where they have been abused, ridiculed, bullied, and truly offended but they are harboring this offense and projecting it upon you when you say something that reminds them of, and takes them back to this offense.
- Triggers - words and actions that remind them of things that happened in the past that take them back to reliving the past offenses. Insecurities, inadequacies, and low self-esteem that have come in through past offenses, experiences, and abuse.
- The Victim spirit – they deem themselves the victim and create situations where they become the victim.

An offender spirit also tends to operate through those who seek to take advantage of others. This often applies to rapists, pedophiles, traffickers, abusers, controllers, and narcissistic personalities. Individuals with an offender spirit carry the ability to transfer their seed into others. This is the reason that many who are victimized by them have some form of an offender spirit, whether it be becoming a rapist, molester, trafficker, abuser, etc., having some propensity for these attributes, or engaging in lesser perversions or adverse behaviors of these characteristics (e.g. a woman who has been raped becomes promiscuous, a child that has been molested grows up to be sneaky in their actions, someone that has been freed from sex trafficking struggles with sexually seductive behaviors). The offender spirit seeks to recycle and procreate itself. Psychological theories support this concept of unhealed victims using the same sort of abuse on others as an unconscious mechanism to reclaim the personal power that was stripped from them. Therefore, it is important that if you have experienced an offending spirit to cast this spirit out while also being healed from the root issues of your experience.

Spirit Of Division - This spirit comes for the unity of a relationship. It prevents people from agreeing and walking together as one or in unison with one another. It constantly causes conflicts that are often rooted in pride, self-focus, and a person being more focused on their agenda, needs, and desires rather than caring about the other person or the fullness of the relationship.

Spirit Of Divorce - This spirit attacks the covenant union of a relationship. This spirit can operate as a generational curse or as a personal curse on someone. People can also send curses that release this spirit into relationships or interject situations that cause doors of divorce to open. This spirit also operates by causing a person to be disloyal, untrustworthy, unfaithful to their vows, and a goal-breaker. The person is unable to keep their word - their agreement - their vow - therefore constantly breaching the covenant of the relationship. The more breaching that occurs, the more the foundation and walls of the relationship crumble, causing exposure to separation, destruction, and divorce.

Spirit Of Singleness - Whether in friendships or marriages, this spirit wants people to be alone. It does not want people to have partners, covenants, or reliable people they can walk with in a relationship. This spirit can be a generational curse brought upon the family line through sin, especially perversion, adultery, fornication, idolatry, and witchcraft. It can also be a curse released due to a vow a person has made due to hurtful experiences in relationships. A person can also be bewitched by someone speaking a spell/hex on them and, until it is broken, that blocks them from being able to have successful relationships or to be married. When people claim us as mates in the spirit, this can block our ordained mate from seeing us. This is the reason it is important to break vows with old lovers, boyfriends, girlfriends, and those that may be a potential mate but not "the one." In this day, it is even more important to cast down vows that people made as they fellowship with us on social media. People are quick to inbox someone and claim they are their husband/wife. These witchcraft claims can lock us down into a spirit of singleness and hinder marriage and healthy sustaining relationships to enter our lives. This spirit can also operate with a spirit of barrenness where a person is being blocked from their rightful position to bear children. It can also operate as sickness against the person's reproductive organs where they cannot procreate, have a challenging time procreating, or lose the child if they do procreate.

Spirit Of Trauma - Trauma is due to deeply disturbing, overwhelming, appalling, and distressful experiences. These situations can occur in relationships or in life in general. When these experiences occur, they can lodge shock and awe in our hearts, souls, and minds. Many people literally feel this shock as numbness, pain, panic, or blockages in their bodies. When these experiences are not dealt with, the enemy uses them as an open door to release a spirit of trauma into our lives. Usually, that spirit is lodged where we are experiencing the literal manifestation of shock and awe and, sometimes, can enter our lives immediately upon the impact of that experience. The spirit of trauma and any other spirits that accompany it must be cast out, along with being delivered and healed of the trauma that was experienced before complete wholeness can manifest. Otherwise, the person will continue to be triggered by the impact, thoughts, and feelings of the experience and have a trying time engaging, trusting, resting in, and feeling safe in a relationship. They will have their walls up, experience constant anxiety and fear, and a tendency to connect and disconnect from the person and the relationship.

Bewitchment - This spirit, or witchcraft act, is done through the casting of a spell by releasing words, hexes, vexes, and incantations upon a person so that they are bound to a person or that relationship. This can also cause one to be bound in their life and cannot operate in their free will to choose their path and to be successful. Bewitchment can be done by a person within the relationship, or they may solicit the help of an outside source that performs witchcraft. A very controlling or manipulative person can use verbal abuse and overbearing words to bewitch a person. The bewitched person may experience hallucinations, delusions, constant negative thoughts, confusion, mind-binding, mind-blinding, depression, mood swings, doom, gloom, fear, or an uncontrollable drawing to, or reliance on the person that bewitched them. They may feel they need to get out of the relationship but may not have any willpower to do so. Or if they do, they will be fearful, often like something is after them, or as if they are going to die if they do not return to the relationship. This is because some of the curses accompany death spells and so spirits of doom and gloom work with bewitchment to keep the person scared and bound to the relationship. These "doom and gloom" spirits have also been known to cause affliction, hardship, and tragedy when a person leaves the one who has bewitched them.

Sometimes sex is used to bewitch a person and to keep the person bewitched. When we have sex with someone, our souls become tied to one another. If that person is a witch, warlock, or operate in witchcraft, they can use the soul tie through sex to lock their partner into the relationship. Until the soul tie is broken, the bewitched person will be drawn to the other and to continue having intercourse with them. The bewitched person will feel addicted to the person and to having sex with them. They will also feel controlled and manipulated but will feel helpless getting out of the relationship.

Bewitching relationships are often tumultuous and draining. There will be constant drama, tension, psychological games and play on words, entrapment through words and situations, suspicion, and confusion. The bewitched person will constantly feel like life and blood are being sucked out of them as they are being controlled, seduced, and manipulated by the other person.

Sometimes spells are placed on jewelry, trinkets, and other items that are given to partners to keep them bound to the person and the relationship. These items should be thrown away to help break the spell.

SEXUAL PERVERSION IN MARRIAGE

> FROM THE BEGINNING, SATAN SOUGHT TO DISTORT, ATTACK, PERVERT, & DESTROY COVENANT MARRIAGE!

Spirits that attack marriage are covenant Breaking Spirits - they seek to destroy the divine origin and union to which God created marriage and family.

They seek to steal, kill, and destroy the seed, reproduction, and fruit of marriage so that children and the continual lineage of Godly lineage cannot praise God from generation to generation.

*The first demon to come against - husband and wife - to infiltrate marriage - was the serpent Satan (Study **Genesis 1-3**).*

Adam and Eve were already the purist form of God's supernatural knowledge, vision, and identity. Satan deceived Eve by making her believe she would have more knowledge, enlightenment, and God like identity than she already had. But truly eating of the tree of God and evil opened up a third eye and portal to sin and death.

***Genesis 3:4-5** And the serpent said unto the woman, Ye shall not surely die: For God doth know that in the day ye eat thereof, then your eyes shall be opened, and ye shall be as gods, knowing good and evil.*

This one incident opened their marriage to the following spirits and issues.

In the garden of Eden, we saw where an attack against one spouse had the ability to distort, curse, and change the identity and course of the entire marriage. Satan often utilizes a divide and conquer tactic where he aims to find small pockets to separate married couples. Offense, stress, frustration, dishonor, mistrust, disagreement, inadequacy, pride, usurping, seduction, lust, perversion, self-sabotage, etc. are used to divide and release an assignment to infiltrate one partner or the other. From these postures of sin, Satan entices with another vision that overrides the love, hearts, and vision for one's spouse and the marriage covenant. Let's review some of the spirits of the Garden.

Spirits From the Garden of Eden
- Spirit of Deception
- Seduction
- Sins of the Flesh & the World
- Spirits of Death, Hell, & the Grave
- Spirit of Knowledge

- Spirit of Usurping God's Order & Authority
- Spirit of This World
- Spirit of Shame, Guilt, Condemnation & Hiding (Adam & Eve tried to hide their nakedness & sin)
- Spirit of Impurity (Unrighteousness, Unholiness, Loss of Virtue, Innocence)
- Spirits that Cause Rejection & Erred Operations of True God Identity
- Spirits Of Demonic Counsel: The word translated as "*counsel*" in the original Hebrew is a noun that means "*something that provides direction or advice as to a decision or course of action.*" It also means the following:

    - An end result through consultation.
    - An action made from deliberation (consideration, reflection, pondering, brooding, discussion, debate, slow and careful movement of thought and a lack of haste).

    Demonic counsel enters the chat when you yield your ear to words, accusations, and information that does not align with God's truth and his word. It also is strengthened by communion. When you should be communing with your spouse, God, healthy supports, accountability partners, mentors, teachers, leaders, yet isolate or entertain carnal and ungodly things, you are housing and making a space for demons to find comfort in your life.

Eve communed with the serpent of demonic counsel and instead of taking his false claim back to God or her husband, she overestimated her own truth, worth, purity, strength, and wisdom. She thus allowed the demonic seed of Satan to take root and produce fruit in her heart. From that place, her sin was born.

Demonic Counsel Operates Through Spirits Of:		
Spirit of Deception	Spirit of the Vagabond & Wanderer (Displaced from God & in destiny)	Spirits of Justifications
Spirit of Disobedience	Spirits of Mistrust, Doubt, Unbelief	Spirits of Entitlement
Spirits of Oneness & Isolation	Spirits of Inadequacy & Insecurity	Spirits & Operations of Permissive Will (our will & desires) Versus God's Perfect will
Spirits Of Rejection	Spirits of Mistrust, Doubt, Unbelief	Spirits of Blindness
Spirits of Anti-submissiveness		Deaf & Dumb Spirits
Spirits Of Rebellion	Spirits of Blindness	Spirits of Control
Spirit of the Orphan	Spirit of The Thief, Killer & Destroyer	Spirits of Self-Idolatry
Spirit of Abandonment	Spirits of Control	Spirits of Fear
Spirit of Dissociation	Spirit of Delusion & Hallucination	Spirit of Elation & Grander, Fantasy & Higher Consciousness

***Jeremiah 7:24** But they hearkened not, nor inclined their ear, but walked in the counsels and in the imagination of their evil heart, and went backward, and not forward.*

***Psalm 1:1-6** Blessed is the man that walketh not in the counsel of the ungodly, nor standeth in the way of sinners, nor sitteth in the seat of the scornful.*

We dispute demonic counsel through exposing the enemy and always remaining in oneness with God, covenant, and the godly vision he gives for our lives and covenant relationships.

We must recognize the power of godly covenant, relationship with God and those he put in our lives, and intentionally draw to our supports rather than:

- Isolate from them
- Connect and disconnect from them
- Reject or fail to pursue the accountability, safety, protection, and truth godly covenant brings to our lives
- Sit in spaces and places that open the door to demonic counsel
- Commune and entertain demons and worldly voices and wisdom

***Mark 10:8-10** And the two shall become one flesh'; so then they are no longer two, but one flesh. Therefore what God has joined together, let not man separate." In the house His disciples also asked Him again about the same matter.*

To combat these spirits, you must know and have vision for who you are individually, who your partner is individually, and who you all are as a whole. When you lack security in these areas, demonic counsel can come in and distort, attack, pervert, and destroy you and what God has for your life. Your mind becomes twisted in thinking that it is not of God, which causes you to mishandle the blessings, people, covenants, opportunities, plans, and purposes, that he has given you. SHUT THE DOOR TO COVENANT BREAKING SPIRITS

MY LORD!

Genesis 2:18 And the Lord God said, It is not good that the man should be alone; I will make him an help meet for him.

When Satan fell from heaven, he took a third of the angels with him.

Revelations 12:4 And his tail drew the third part of the stars of heaven, and did cast them to the earth: and the dragon stood before the woman which was ready to be delivered, for to devour her child as soon as it was born.

Revelations 12:9 And the great dragon was thrown down, that ancient serpent, who is called the devil and Satan, the deceiver of the whole world—he was thrown down to the earth, and his angels were thrown down with him.

These angels known as the sons of God - perceived women as beautiful and took them as wives.

Genesis 6:2 *That the sons of God saw the daughters of men that they were fair; and they took them wives of all which they chose.*

<u>Fair</u> in the Hebrew is *tôb; tôbâ* and means:
1. good (as an adjective) (well)
2. beautiful, best, better, bountiful, cheerful, at ease, fair (word), (be in) favour, fine, glad, good (deed, -lier, -liest, -ly, -ness, -s), graciously, joyful, kindly, kindness, liketh (best), loving, merry, most, pleasant, pleaseth, pleasure, precious, prosperity, ready, sweet, wealth, welfare, (be) well ((-favoured))
3. welfare, benefit, good things, welfare, prosperity, happiness, good things (collective) bounty
4. good, pleasant, agreeable pleasant, agreeable (to the senses)
    a. pleasant (to the higher nature)
    b. good, excellent (of its kind)
    c. good, rich, valuable in estimation
    d. good, appropriate, becoming
    e. better (comparative)
    f. glad, happy, prosperous (of man's sensuous nature)
    g. good understanding (of man's intellectual nature)
    h. good, kind, benigngood, right (ethical) n m
    i. a good thing, benefit, welfare
    j. welfare, prosperity, happiness

k. good things (collective)good, benefit, moral good

The act of lusting upon woman is how perversion and the altered ideologies of marriage covenant entered the earth. It is also the reason these fallen angels took themselves wives and felt they should live like husbands with human women.

Lust - An intense or excessive sexual desire or appetite; uncontrolled or illicit sexual desire or appetite; lecherousness; a passionate or overmastering desire or craving; ardent enthusiasm; zest; relish.

Galatians 5:16-19 *This I say then, Walk in the Spirit, and ye shall not fulfil the lust of the flesh. For the flesh lusteth against the Spirit, and the Spirit against the flesh: and these are contrary the one to the other: so that ye cannot do the things that ye would. But if ye be led of the Spirit, ye are not under the law. Now the works of the flesh are manifest, which are these; Adultery, fornication, uncleanness, lasciviousness.*

<u>*Lusteth* in this passage is the Greek word *epithymeo*, and means:</u>
1. to set the heart upon, long for
2. covet (to desire wrongfully, inordinately, or without regard for the rights of others)
3. to turn upon a thing
4. to have a desire for, to lust after
5. to lust for forbidden things

***Matthew 5:28** But I say unto you, That whosoever looketh on a woman to lust after her hath committed adultery with her already in his heart.*

The Greek word for *looketh* is *blepo* and not only means *"to look with the natural eye, but to discern, see, perceive by the senses, to see with the mind's eye to gaze upon."*

Lust will have a person and even a demonic entity coveting for something that they are not supposed to have or that is not theirs to have. **It will have them operating contrary to their nature and original intent.** The person or demonic entity will have an ungodly, unhealthy, or demonic appetite for things that are forbidden, things that God deems wrong, things that are unnatural, things that are against God's laws, principles and boundaries, or errored in how they desire or engage a person, place, or thing.

Lust begins in the flesh – generally the eye gates, the spiritual and natural senses, the imagination of a person or the mind's eye. As lust is fed, it opens a third eye where the person begins to desire that which it is looking upon in a wrong way. Inside that third eye, they begin to meditate on that which they are looking at. They commune and entertain thoughts and demons that create an uncontrollable craving and appetite for what they are gazing upon.

Demons live and operate in these demonic realms, so their appetites and literal beings are already opened to the third eye. They are reprobate so even though they know Jesus Christ is Lord and recognize holy things, they are incapable of seeking redemption. They will always seek the lustful, perverted, twisted, anti-Christ nature of a person, place, or thing.

1John 2:16 *For all that is in the world, the lust of the flesh, and the lust of the eyes, and the pride of life, is not of their Father, but is of the world.*

<u>Pride</u> in Greek is *alazoneia* and means:
1. Braggadocio, i.e. (by implication) self-confidence: boasting, pride, empty, braggart talk
2. An insolent and empty assurance, which trusts in its own power and resources and shamefully despises and violates divine laws and human rights
3. An impious and empty presumption which trusts in the stability of earthy things

Lust is a worldly ambition. It is prideful – haughty. Once the flesh is fed, it increases in pride and fills the person and demonic entity with an empty assurance that they should, can, and need to have what they are lusting for. The person or demonic entity begins to trust in the truth of what lust is feeding them through their adulterous – mind's eye – the third eye. They become driven to want the lusts of the world – the cravings they are having and become prideful in their pursuit to obtain – covet it.

This is how believers result in believing that certain sexual acts are godly and lawful in and out of marriage when they are unholy and impure. Their lust has exalted itself above purity, righteousness, holiness, and the truth that we serve a holy God. He will never agree with perversion.

He will never agree with sex outside of marriage.
He will never agree with same-sex relationships.
He will never agree with sex toys and sex stores.
He will never agree with you masturbating and the exalting of your imagination.
He will never agree with making your spouse dress up and act like porn stars or your favorite secular idol – your entertainment eye candy - just so you can commit adultery with your demonic imagination.
He will never agree with swinging and partner swapping.
He will never agree with you touching and marrying little children.
He will never agree with you raping anyone, not even your spouse.
He will never agree with trafficking anyone.
He will never agree with your fetishes and sadistic sex acts.
He will never agree with your fetishes or weird proclivities.
He will never agree with your down low behavior.
He will never agree with sex with demons.
He will never agree with sex sacrifices or sex upon altars.
He will never agree with sex in dreams, visions, or spiritual realms.
Though he will bless the child, he prefers children born in marriage.

He will never agree with demons having children.
He will never agree with demons impregnating human women.

If you study the biblical definition of perversion, one of its meanings is *'twisted thinking.'* Let's process perversion.

Perversion – Any of various means of obtaining sexual gratification that is generally regarded as abnormal. Pathology of perversion is defined as a change to what is unnatural or abnormal. The condition of being corrupt. It is a deviation from the original and a twisting of the truth to cause distortion, misalignment, and deviation. It is an ideology and/or a spirit that leads people away from the truth regarding God, his word, his righteousness, his will, and plan for their mind, body, soul, lives, and destiny.

Pervert - To affect with perversion, corruption, twisted ideology; to lead astray morally, to turn away from the right course, to lead into mental error or false judgment, to turn to improper use; misapply, to misconstrue or misinterpret, especially deliberately; distort.

Lustful sexual acts that are improper or operate outside the boundaries of God fall under perversion. So basically, this entire chapter discusses behaviors and demonization that are rooted in perversion.

Philippians 2:15 *That ye may be blameless and harmless, the sons of God, without rebuke, in the midst of a crooked* *and perverse nation, among whom ye shine as lights in the world.*

Perverse in Greek is *diastrephō* and means:
1. to distort, i.e. (figuratively) misinterpret, or (morally) corrupt: — perverse(-rt)
2. turn away, to turn aside, to oppose
3. plot against the saving purposes and plans of God
4. to turn aside from the right path, to pervert, corrupt

These spirit entities in **Genesis 6** saw the goodness of who the woman was and decided to take them as wives. The wives did not recognize this as perversion and had children with these fallen angels.

***Genesis 6:1-6 The Amplified Bible** Now it happened, when men began to multiply on the face of the land, and daughters were born to them, that the sons of God saw that the daughters of men were beautiful and desirable; and they took wives for themselves, whomever they chose and desired. Then the LORD said, "My Spirit shall not strive and remain with man forever, because he is indeed flesh [sinful, corrupt—given over to sensual appetites]; nevertheless his days shall yet be a hundred and twenty years." There were Nephilim (men of stature, notorious men) on the earth in those days—and also afterward—when the sons of God lived with the daughters of men, and they gave birth to their children. These were the mighty men who were of old, men of renown (great reputation, fame). The LORD saw that the wickedness (depravity) of man was great on the earth, and that every imagination or* *intent of the thoughts of his heart were only evil continually. The LORD regretted that He had made mankind on the earth, and He was [deeply] grieved in His heart.*

One of the main reasons God does not want us to engage in sexual acts outside of his original plan of marriage covenant is because it opens our lives up to wicked imaginations. The more we feed our imagination, the more it breeds sin, evil, wickedness, perversion, and death. We wonder why people can be so heartless, evil, twisted, it is through appetites that have been fed upon through wicked imagination.

All the other twisted mindsets and ideologies regarding marriage, families, gender neutrality, ungodly sexual acts, have been birthed from this demonic covenant between the fallen angels and the women who married them. The more we have feasted upon these sensual appetites as mankind, the more wretched they have become throughout generations. Demons oppress people so that their imaginations become more wicked and stronghold to their workings.

Galatians 5:16-26 *This I say then, Walk in the Spirit, and ye shall not fulfil the lust of the flesh. For the flesh lusteth against the Spirit, and the Spirit against the flesh: and these are contrary the one to the other: so that ye cannot do the things that ye would. But if ye be led of the Spirit, ye are not under the law.*

Now the works of the flesh are manifest, which are these; Adultery, fornication, uncleanness, lasciviousness, Idolatry, witchcraft, hatred, variance, emulations, wrath, strife, seditions, heresies, Envyings, murders, drunkenness, revellings, and such like: of the which I tell you before, as I have also told you in time past, that they which do such things shall not inherit the kingdom of God.

But the fruit of the Spirit is love, joy, peace, longsuffering, gentleness, goodness, faith, Meekness, temperance: against such there is no law. And they that are Christ's have crucified the flesh with the affections and lusts. If we live in the Spirit, let us also walk in the Spirit. Let us not be desirous of vain glory, provoking one another, envying one another.

Spirits From Marriages Between The Fair Women & Fallen Angels
Spirit of Pride
Spirit of Lust (Lust of the eyes, flesh, prides of life)
Spirit of Covetousness, Jealousy, Envy, Greed, Possessions, (The fallen angels wanted to be God, then they wanted what God had with man)
Spirit of Mammon (The purpose of man, marriage, and family became about money, power and fame and less about the original intent to which God designed it)
Spirits of Gluttony & Greed (Excessively craving, indulging and becoming full of things that taste good but are not godly or healthy)

Spirit of Idolatry (Mankind began to worship themselves and their own desires and worship and serve demons, demonic systems and kingdoms)
Spirit of Division (Mankind was separated from God and his covenant with them)
Spirit of Divorce (mankind divorced God's covenant of marriage and married demons, thus entering covenant with them)
Spirits of Perversion (Twisted thinking; twisted sexual acts; evil wicked acts)
Spirits of Filth
Spirits of Uncleanliness
Spirits of Poverty
Spirits that Cause Sensual Appetites
Spirits that Cause Wicked Imaginations
Spirits of Corruption
Spirits of Lawlessness (Breaking the covenants & boundaries of God)
Spirits & Operations of Witchcraft (The more there was cross breeding between women and demons, the more mankind grew a lust to serve idols and idolatrous kingdom and systems from which these demons where a part of)
Spirits of Dishonor, Disrespect, Disregard

Godly Marriage is Honorable
God honors marriage and wants us to honor it.

Hebrews 13:4 *Marriage is honourable in all, and the bed undefiled: but whoremongers and adulterers God will judge.*

Honorable in the Greek is *timios* and means:
1. valuable, i.e. (objectively) costly, or (subjectively) honored, esteemed, or (figuratively) beloved
2. dear, honorable, (more, most) precious, had in reputation
3. as of great price, precious, held in honour, esteemed, especially dear

Undefiled is *amiantos* in Greek and means:
1. unsoiled, i.e. (figuratively) pure: — undefiled
2. not defiled, free from that by which the nature of a thing is deformed and debased, or its force and vigour impaired

Dictionary.com defines *undishonored* as:
1. lack or loss of honor, disgraceful or dishonest character or conduct
2. disgrace; ignominy; shame
3. an indignity; insult
4. a cause of shame or disgrace
5. to deprive of honor; disgrace; bring reproach or shame on
6. to rape or seduce

We like to think that an undefiled bed means we can do what we desire because we are married. But if there are acts that bring shame, dishonor, reproach, and disgrace upon our spouse and even upon God, then our bed is subject to defilement. If we are making our spouses engage in acts, they are uncomfortable with, even if there are areas of their soul and identity that need to be healed regarding intimacy, we could be defiling our marriage bed. As we examine the definitions, some acts could be considered rape when seduction is done in a form of manipulation and control rather than *Eros* love and a desire to romanticize your mate. We could be subjecting the marriage bed to defilement.

When defilement enters the marriage bed, we are operating in Aheb love rather than *Eros* love. We are succumbing to a love that is driven more by perversion than the innate desires of sex and intimacy that God instilled in us.

Eros Love Versus Burning Lust
We will talk about *Eros* love in greater detail in this book. You can refer to pages 305 to 306 and 325 to 327 if you prefer to know more now. However, *Eros* love is the romantic love, admiration, esteem, passion, and sexual intimate, physical attraction between a man and a woman. It is the love a man or a woman have for a partner of the opposite sex that they romantically admire and would desire to marry. *Eros* love is often misconstrued and even tainted with lust. Even though it is a healthy innate love, if *Eros* love is not properly governed or filtered through a pure mind, heart, and soul, it can cause people to fall into fornication, adultery, and inappropriate sexual or lustful behaviors. This type of love is intended for marriage and should not be intricately engaged, or ignited, outside of

matrimony. After marriage, *Eros* love can be fully awakened and is essential for the wellness of sexual intimacy and the strengthening of the relationship bond within the marriage covenant.

1Corinthians 7:9 The Amplified Bible *But I say to the unmarried and to the widows, [that as a practical matter] it is good if they remain [single and entirely devoted to the Lord] as I am. But if they do not have [sufficient] self-control, they should marry; for it is better to marry than to burn with passion.*

Galatians 5:22-23 *But the fruit of the Spirit is love, joy, peace, longsuffering, gentleness, goodness, faith, Meekness, temperance (self-control): against such there is no law. And they that are Christ's have crucified the flesh with the affections and lusts. If we live in the Spirit, let us also walk in the Spirit. Let us not be desirous of vain glory, provoking one another, envying one another.*

The Greek definition of self-control aka temperance (egkrateia) is the virtue of one who MASTERS his desires and passions, esp. his sensual appetites.

WHEWWWW! LET'S JUST PONDER THAT

DEFINITION FOR A MOMENT!

That is a powerful definition.

God is requiring us to be a master of self-control and is letting us know that it is part of what enables us to be virtuous. Since it is a fruit of the spirit, it is a part of his identity, his nature, his character. We, therefore, possess the ability through the Holy Spirit – his presence on the inside of us to master self-control. We just must engage by our spirit and not through our flesh and emotions. When our flesh and emotions guide us, we operate in a lack of self-control which can lead us to **BURNING!**

Dictionary.com defines *temperance* as:
1. moderation or self-restraint in action, statement, etc.
2. habitual moderation in the indulgence of a natural appetite or passion, especially in the use of alcoholic liquors
3. total abstinence (as in liquors and the like)
4. self control - control or restraint of oneself or one's actions, feelings, etc.

Apostle Paul is not saying that everyone is required to get married. He is offering a solution for those struggling with self-control in the area of sexuality, which is the inability to abstain from having sex. This solution does not assert that everything goes in the marriage bed. It simply places the blessing of having sex in its proper context which is in a marriage.

Apostle Paul is also addressing the issue of self-control centered around igniting a burning passion of *Eros* before its time. He is saying it is better to marry than to let the passion that has been awakened cause you to sin and even to succumb to eternal judgement that can result in persistent sin, unrepentant sexual sin, and the idolatry of sex being the raging drive – Lord - of your life.

<u>*Burn* is *pyroō* in Greek and means:</u>
1. to kindle, i.e. (passively) to be ignited, glow (literally), be refined (by implication), or (figuratively) to be inflamed (with anger, grief, lust): — burn, fiery, be on fire, try
2. to burn with fire, to set on fire, kindle to be on fire, to burn, to be incensed, indignant
3. make to glow full of fire, fiery, ignited, of darts filled with inflammable substances and set on fire
4. melted by fire and purged of dross (waste or worthless matter, coal of little value, the scum formed, usually by oxidation, on the surfaces of molten metals)

The concept of burning is not to be taken lightly. This definition reveals how a lack of self-control breeds an inflamed fire that can cause grief, anger, lust, and a constant passionate burning that is difficult to put out. Such a burning can result in purging out - burning out - God's fruit (nature) of purity, righteousness, holiness, virtue from within you, where you are SHIFTED to a form of lower value. The more out of control you are, the more you become fashioned and identified by the burning lust itself rather than who you are in God.

When we lack self-control as singles, we open our lives to sexual sin that God never meant for us to experience. This is because the passion that is guiding us, leads us to fulfilling the lust of the flesh, vain imaginations, and demonic appetites that God did not create us to experience. Often what we witness on TV where people argue, hit and emotionally attack one another then they are aroused and begin to have sex is rooted in burning lust. The fact that you are aroused in anger is an indication of a deeper unhealthy root. But many people, even married couples, will feed this arousal. This opens the door to a spirit of deception entering the relationship that starts fights to feed the couple's elation of burning lust. Some couples are not able to have sex without arguments and abusive behaviors. Many start to use inordinate and abusive sexual objects and acts to further feed this burning lust. When married, they justify it as an undefiled bed. But God will never approve of us arguing and abusing one another to engage in sexual intimacy.

So many ungodly and perverse acts that people assume are appropriate in marriage come from **sin out of wedlock.** And even those who remain virgins until marriage, take the scripture of an undefiled bed and think they can engage in anything. Yet *Galatians 5:22-23* lets us know that self-control is a fruit of the spirit for EVERY BELIEVER even as Apostle Paul addresses self-control in this text with singles. Here are some more scriptural insights on the fruit of self-control.

Titus. 2:11-12 *For the grace of God has appeared that offers salvation to all people. It teaches us to say "No" to ungodliness and worldly passions, and to live self-controlled, upright and godly lives in this present age.*

1Corinthians 9:27 *But I keep under my body, and bring it into subjection: lest that by any means, when I have preached to others, I myself should be a castaway.*

New Living Bible *No, I strike a blow to my body and make it my slave so that after I have preached to others, I myself will not be disqualified for the prize.*

1Thessalonians 4:3-5 *For this is the will of God, even your sanctification, that ye should abstain from fornication: That every one of you should know how to possess his vessel in sanctification and honour; Not in the lust of concupiscence, even as the Gentiles which know not God.*

> **STRIKE YOUR BODY WITH A BLOW SUCH THAT YOU DO NOT PREACH TO OTHERS YET BECOME A CASTAWAY! WHEWWW!**

The Power of Purity & Sanctification
We think purity means abstaining and self-control, but purity means sanctification.

1Thessalonians 4:3-4 *For this is the will of God, even your sanctification, that ye should abstain from fornication: That every one of you should know how to possess his vessel in sanctification and honour.*

<u>Sanctification</u> in Greek is *hagiasmos* and means:
1. purification, i.e. (the state) purity
2. concretely (by Hebraism) a purifier
3. holiness, sanctification, consecration
4. the effect of consecration
5. sanctification of heart and life

Sanctification is about being restored in innocence, holiness, and purity according to the standard and will of God. Sanctification is a state of separation unto God.

All believers enter this state when they are born of God: "You are in Christ Jesus, who became to us wisdom from God, righteousness and sanctification and redemption"

1Corinthians 1:29-31 *That no flesh should glory in his presence. But of him are ye in Christ Jesus, who of God is made unto us wisdom, and righteousness, and sanctification, and redemption: That, according as it is written, He that glorieth, let him glory in the Lord.*

Burning Lust Activation:
1. Spend time journaling personally and together to process the revelation you learned in this chapter. Be detailed and mindful with embodying the revelation and

seeking to absorb all the insights, deliverance, healing, and freedom God has for you.
2. Whether single, dating, or married, ask God to reveal areas where you need deliverance from burning lust and perversion. Journal what he says.
3. Whether single, dating, or married, ask God to show you areas where you have crossed boundaries as it relates to intimate sexual encounters. Ask God to reveal to you how these burning lusts and perversions entered your life. Journal what he says and spend time asking him to guide you in repenting, uprooting and healing from root issues, closing doors, and breaking free from demonic oppression. Journal your deliverance and healing process and experiences with God. Seek deliverance and inner healing if necessary.
4. Ask God to give you some keys to stay free. Journal what he says. Implement these keys in your daily lifestyle. Seek deliverance and inner healing if necessary.
5. Make fasting and consecration a common part of your walk so that you can kill your flesh from burning lust, as well as break mind, heart, and soul strongholds, soul ties, and cycles, patterns, and propensities related to burning lust.
6. If you are married, the more you are honest with one another in sharing and completing this activation together, the greater the purging of your marriage bed and ability to restore your sexual intimacy in healthy fulfillment.

HEALTHY COMMUNICATION SKILLS

Communication is the lifeline of a God-centered marriage.

Proverbs 18:21 says, *"Death and life are in the power of the tongue."*

Words can build up or tear down, so couples must speak with love, honesty, and grace.

James 1:19 *reminds us to be "quick to listen, slow to speak, and slow to anger."*

True communication isn't just talking, it's listening, understanding, and seeking unity.

When couples communicate God's way, they strengthen their bond and reflect His love in their marriage.

<u>***Communication Wellness***</u> - Expressing thoughts and feelings in a healthy manner. Learning communication skills, conflict resolution skills, anger management, social skills, interpersonal skills, and emotional wellness. Setting

goals and practicing the applicable tools until they become a lifestyle in your relationships and household. Pursuing counseling, mediation, and/or accountability partners if necessary to heal and grow in these skills.

Sexual intimacy begins outside the marriage bed. You want great love making, great laughter, great memories, unashamed vulnerability, learn how to communicate. Learn healthy communication wellness so you can effectively manage and communicate your thoughts and feelings properly. You have **NO EXCUSE** in this area as you can google these skills, practice and implement them in your marriage and daily interactions. You can also purchase my, *"Divine Art To Healthy Communication Skills,"* and *"Maintaining Emotional Wellness"* Ebooks.

It is your responsibility to think, feel, perceive, communicate, behave, and respond in a godly manner. Grow up and take responsibility for maturing in the areas you need to be transformed so your spouse will trust you and so you can be a healthy partner that BUILDS the marital covenant rather than tears it down.

HUSBANDS – Just because you are a man, this does not mean you should not know how to express your thoughts and feelings. God himself knows how to express himself. You were made in his image. You are, therefore, capable of expressing yourself. It is a matter of learning healthy skills in this area, while allowing yourself to live naked, unashamed, and vulnerable with your partner.

WIVES – You are capable of expressing your thoughts and feelings, without being overbearing, demanding, nagging (to annoy by persistent faultfinding, complaints, or demands), or tearing down your partner. The best way to a man's heart is to feed his manhood – make him feel like a man you trust, love, honor, and adore. The best way to get a man to communicate and be vulnerable with you, is to accolade him, build him up, and treat him like a man. Build him up in who God says he is and who God wants him to be. Stroke his ego regarding the things you desire from him and build him up in the capability to fulfill them.

When a man is constantly fed negativity, it becomes a chore and just another thing on his list to complete. This feeds any inadequacies or stress challenges they have rather than quickening them to want to fulfill your request. Create opportunities to do things with them so they feel supported. Also, recognize when you are asking them to do things that they do not have the capacity to do. You discern this when you are constantly asking them to do something, and they do not do it or hit and miss with completing it. Either do it yourself or have someone from the outside complete it. Remember you are an adaptable help meet, so help and cover your husband rather than continuously uncovering him with your words and complaints of what they are not or cannot do. Remember the key is to implement the vision that works for your marriage not the perception you and the world have for covenant relationship.

It is important to note that as a covenant couple, you are NEVER the enemy to one another. The minute you all view one another as an enemy, a door to offense, separation, blindness, doubt, mistrust, strife, revenge, retaliation, and punishment has manifested in and/or around you. Such a posture lends to covenant breaking, especially through thoughts and behaviors of division and divorce.

Learning Your Partner
Learning one another's personality types that are generally defined by our identity, calling, upbringing, experiences, ethnicity, belief systems, habits, quirks, pet peeves, interests, love languages, behaviors and responses, emotional operations, and uniqueness, etc. is so essential in relationships.

Learning people, or in this instance your partner, helps you to embody grace and love for who they are and not who you want them to be. It helps you to understand how they may think, feel, respond, and you are regarding how they SHIFT and flow while lending grace for any transformation needed or just simply honoring one another's similarities and differences. This also aides in not taking things personal that could be misinterpreted as rejection, resistance, dishonor, refusal but is more of just who the person is. People have freewill and no matter how much you see their potential to change and be a better person, they have to want that for themselves, God has to want it for them, and they have to be willing to surrender their freewill to make that potential a reality. There will be some instances where people will be resistant to change due to disobedience, they do not have the revelation and vision for self-improvement in that area, they do not have the capacity to change, or what you are experiencing is simply who they are. Regarding a person's personality helps you in not taking someone's actions personally or their process with God personally. You are able to regard where they are in life, who they are, and not deflect their issues on to yourself.

When you are dating, even though you may not like everything about your spouse, you should marry because you like that person's personality. If you do not really like the person, DO NOT MARRY THEM. If you are tolerating that person's personality, DO NOT MARRY THEM. If you think you can change them into what you want, DO NOT MARRY them.

- ✓ As the person you are dating shows you who they are **BELIEVE** them.
- ✓ As Holy Spirit reveals to you who the person really is **BELIEVE HOLY SPIRIT.**
- ✓ Ask Holy Spirit to reveal the person's true personality to you so you will not make excuses for who they really are.
- ✓ Process with God if this is what HE is signing you up for in marriage. If he does not say this is your portion, **DO NOT MARRY THIS PERSON.**

If you are already married yet personality differences and challenges are impacting your marriage, I am decreeing that you and your spouse will **DO THE WORK**, to learn one another's personalities and implement the revelation in this section. Commit to falling in love all over again and work on learning one another, honoring the reality of one another, even as you set goals to work on becoming a better YOU for yourself, God and your spouse. Forgive one another for past personality challenges you have taken personally, and endeavor to implement a clean slate of learning to like one another and to fall in love all over again. You never know what you might discover about yourself, your spouse, and God during this venture of love. Believe me, it is better to posture here than to remain dreading the person you married and not like who they are and who they continue to become.

Transitions Times & Seasons
Every transition reveals something new about you and your partner. It is important to discern and understand times and seasons in relationships and when you all have evolved and matured in life, God, destiny, and purpose because your needs, desires, expectations, drive, stamina, physical abilities and presentation, and health wellness may change. Such changes may require learning one another in this new dimension in life and having grace for one another as you evolve in your communication style, love language, and honor one to another.

It will be important to respect where one another is in your personal walks, resist comparison, jealousy and envy, and create a culture of continuously honoring and empowering one another. The enemy will come for your unity through this avenue. He will seek to cause division, strife, unworthiness, rejection, insecurity, sabotage, destiny murder, etc., by making you all feel unequally yoked because God uses each of you differently or because you are in different times and seasons of maturity regarding salvation, discipleship, training and equipping, and walking in evolving in your personal destinies.

Please know that if you are truly journeying with God, you are right where you need to be. What is on the inside of you and how God operates through you is what he needs, your spouse needs, your marriage needs, those that are tied to your destiny needs. Your unique personality will also play a factor in how God uses you. Authority is not in volume and extreme expression, it is in the power of the name, redemptive blood, identity, glory, confidence, grace, and covenant relationship with Jesus Christ. Do not require one another to perform or be something God is not saying. Empower one another to be your unique selves where you cultivate true authentic God identity personally and in your covenant marriage.

Escapism & Dissociation

Dictionary.com defines *escapism* as:
1. the avoidance of reality by absorption of the mind in entertainment or in an imaginative situation, activity, etc.
2. an inclination to or habit of retreating from unpleasant or unacceptable reality, as through diversion or fantasy

Please understand the following truths:

- ✓ Your spouse cannot have a relationship with you when you live in the fantasy world of your subconscious or unconscious mind.

- ✓ Your spouse cannot be the fantasy person you have and communicate with in your mind.

- ✓ Your spouse cannot hear the thoughts and dialog you are having with them inside your head. Therefore, you cannot respond passively aggressively about what you have not verbally communicated yet have communed with through the fantasy spouse you are married to in your head.

- ✓ Your spouse cannot have a relationship with you when you have dissociated, disconnected, and isolated from them and the relationship and retreated inside yourself, inside the thoughts and fantasies of your mind, or physically isolated from them in some form or fashion.

- ✓ Please know that when you have to go into an isolated space or you storm into a back room every time conflict or challenges ensue, that too is a form of escapism and dissociation. You are leaving the present reality to live and commune in your fantasy world amongst yourself. This can be like having a third person in the marriage. Your spouse is having to contend with the extra personality or spouse you have created in your head. And in some instances, it is a demonic spirit because such behaviors open the door to demonic activity as you are communing in second heaven spheres of influence. Please note that this is different from needing space to calm down, reflect, and pray, so you can return and engage in conflict resolution. Conflict resolution is healthy, escapism and dissociation are unhealthy, draining, time consuming, and are covenant breaking behaviors.

Dictionary.com defines *dissociation* as: "*the splitting off of a group of mental processes from the main body of consciousness, as in amnesia or certain forms of hysteria.*" Many people dissociate where they enter the unconscious realm of their mind or even astral project (their soul leaves their body) from their body to avoid uncomfortable situations or conversations. They often do not hear, feel, or experience what is being spoken or done and if they do, they may not take any responsibility for it or feel led to do anything since they have disconnected from the reality of the experience.

Many people who have experienced traumatic life situations engage in this type of behavior. They can be exceedingly difficult to communicate with, and it can be difficult to get them to be accountable for change. Sometimes dissociation can cause a literal split in their personality so the spouse may be dealing with two distinct people depending on the conversation. When this part of the personality is present, the person may:

- Regress into trauma behaviors and responses.

- SHIFT into a deaf and dumb or stupor response where they are incapable of hearing or retaining what is being said.
- Regress to a little girl or little boy spirit.
- Deflect by changing the conversation or playing the victim even though they may be the offender or the one that needs to accept responsibility and change.
- Connect and disconnect in their thoughts, feelings, love languages, and covenant partnership position.

If you use escapism or dissociation as a form of communication, you need deliverance and inner healing and then you need to learn healthy communication skills, healthy coping and stress management skills, and balanced emotional wellness to completely close the doors to these behaviors. Such behaviors make you and your spouse miserable. Take responsibility to heal so your relationship does not suffer.

Power Of Agreement
Amos 3:3 Can two walk together, except they be agreed?

The Message Bible *Do two people walk hand in hand if they aren't going to the same place?*

Couples must want harmony, peace, oneness, and the soundness of covenant that agreement SHIFTS into their lives.

Keys To Possessing Amos 3:3 In Marriage:

Having a heart for harmony and a spirit of agreement for the will, purpose and plans of God.
Possessing a spirit of quick repentance and forgiveness.
Living through godly transparency and vulnerability with your spouse and God.
Desiring and seeking to continuously evolve in godly character.
Possessing a love for righteousness - righteousness (the condition of being in right stand-ing with God where even if you feel you are in right standing with your partner your standard is not how they respond, but what God is saying and unctioning you to do).
Having and honoring marriage accountability partners.
Recognizing and pursuing a lifestyle of continual deliverance and healing.
Honoring your spouse's voice and who God is them.
Know true unconditional love and sacrificing yourself to give and receive love as God requires.

Honoring One Another's Voice

- Do not marry anyone you are not willing to listen to.
- Do not marry anyone you cannot honor the God in them.
- Do not marry anyone you do not have a heart or pursuit to get to know and love the God in them.
- If you are already married, realize that your partner is a unique representation of God and has his voice on the inside of them. It is ridiculous for you to honor the preacher's voice, the prophet's voice, your supervisor's voice, your friends voice, but not the person you sleep with, have sex with, and have vowed to love and cherish unto death. The fact that this is an issue reveals that true godly love, submission, and communication,

has not been cultivated in the foundation of the marriage. There could also be some unresolved issues that need to be addressed and forgiven. Familiarity and taking one another for granted may also have entered the relationship and overridden grace, love, honor, and the heart of God for one another.

Honoring one another's voices is a part of submission. According to ***Ephesians 5:22-33***, wives are to submit to husbands as unto the Lord and husbands are to love their wives like Christ loves the church. Both are to demonstrate honor, respect, and regard for one another like you would God. Neither party should be rejecting the voice of God, therefore, you should not be refusing to honor what one another says. Abuse, neglect, demonic oppression/possession, witchcraft, idolatry, leading one another astray, should be the only reasons you would resist listening to one another.

Heal in the areas that cause you and your partner to disregard one another's voice.
Ask God to give you a love for one another's voice so you honor the God in one another.
Ask God to give you his eyes for your spouse so you love them and honor them like he does.
Practice respecting one another's voice and searching out with God how to confirm with him what you all are speaking to one another.
When you become familiar with one another, reground yourselves, and be intentional about honoring and

> regarding one another. Focus on consciously not taking one another for granted. **SHIFT RIGHT NOW!**

Healthy Communication & Conflict Resolution Skills

Some of this chapter is from Dr. Taquetta Baker's book, "Healing the Wounded Leader".

Learn healthy communication and conflict resolution skills, role model, and teach others how to communicate and resolve conflict. Interrogation is when forceful, threatening, battering questions and statements are used to obtain information.

Interrogation is not communication. It puts people on the defense and guard where they do not feel comfortable or safe to share information. It also causes people to feel pressured to share information or agree with statements that may not necessarily be the truth or their truth. Such communication should be avoided in your marriage as it comes across as controlling and manipulative.

Conflict does not mean disconnect or divorce. You hear me couples! CONFLICE DOES NOT MEAN DISCONNECT OR DIVORCE!

It just means all parties involved have a challenge to work through and that is okay. Challenges teach us a lot about one another and enable us to take the relationship to a deeper dimension of unconditional love, forgiveness, patience, godly character, and grace as they process and mature personally and in relationship regarding who each person is individually and to one another. Do not be afraid of conflict. Learn to embrace it as a part of life and relationships, especially your marriage. The key is learning how to communicate and resolve conflict in a biblical healthy manner. The biblical applicable keys below will bless you, however, my "***Annihilating The Powers Of Church Hurt***" has a detailed chapter on biblically examining and resolving conflict.

In dating, engagement, and marriage you will warn, rebuke, and correct one another. But your posture needs to remain in trusting God with your partner and with the outcome of what is shared. This is the reason honoring one another's voice, honoring the power of agreement, knowing one another's personality types, and having grace for one another is so important.

Active Listening & Proper Questions For Resolution

Active listening is being able to work to understand one another, consider the thoughts and feelings of others, explore, and examine one's thoughts, feelings, and perceptions efficiently, agree to disagree, set goals to improve relationship whether you agree or disagree, and dispel matters respectfully.

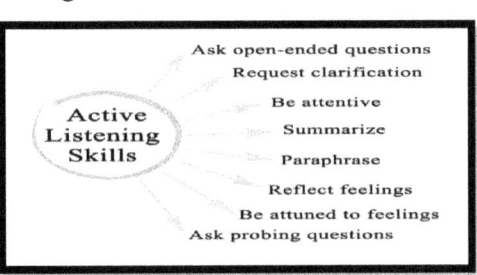

Be open to embrace conflict and challenges when they occur and know that you can mature and evolve within yourself, that person, and that situation.

Before seeking to resolve conflict that is challenging or where you are not mature in conflict resolution, first spend time processing your thoughts and feelings with God. Exchange his character, fruit, thoughts and feelings for yours.

Break the powers of demonic bondages that would oppress your thoughts and feelings.

Process your situation with God and ask him for his truth regarding what has occurred as this will enable you to consider both sides.

Ask God for revelations and strategy for resolving the conflict and implement what he says. This is important because God will tell you:

> How to present the need to have a discussion to resolve conflict.

When to address the situation and ask for a time of conflict resolution.
Where to have the meeting to discuss the conflict.
Who should be there as sometimes a witness or mediator may be needed.
What to do to partner with him.
What he is going to do as you are obedient to him.
What to say and what not to say.
How to express your thoughts and feelings so you can be heard and regarded.

Open Ended Questions Versus Closed Ended Questions:

Open-end questions cannot be answered with a simple 'yes' or 'no,' and require the client to elaborate on their points.

Open-ended questions allow you to listen to the person's perspective, identify information that they are not speaking or that is hidden within what they are sharing, observe body language for unconscious thoughts, feelings, behaviors, and triggers, while listening to the Holy Spirit for revelation and insight about how to process what they are sharing and how to resolve the conflict.

Closed-ended questions provoke limited responses that may cause people to become defensive, negative, and pessimistic, while sharing minimal information from a posture of protecting and justifying their perspective, versus exploring and processing comfortably and progressively. I recommend using closed-ended questions as little as possible.

Open-ended questions begin with:

What (reveals facts, information, and considerations)
When (reveals timing, seasons, proceedings, follow up information, patterns, and cycles)
Where (reveals location, environment, and situations)
How (provokes thoughts, feelings, consideration, exploration and processing)
Could (allows processing of alternative perceptions, thoughts, feelings, and behaviors)
Who (reveals people, targets, and options)
Provides opportunities for expounding information that is shared:
Explain that a bit more
Share more about that
Elaborate on that

Closed-ended questions begin with:

Is
Are
Do
Can
Should
Why (can cause defensiveness and feeling the need to justify actions so limit the use of why questions)

Journal some of your open-ended questions and use them when you and your partner come together to discuss challenging matters. Endeavor to be polite and regarding.

Focus on operating through the character, heart, and nature of God no matter what the person has done to you or how you feel about the person.

Be mindful of what really is the person's issue, them being an open door to being used against you by the enemy, and how demonic spirits cause conflict, division, and breeches that would steal, kill, and destroy relationships, opportunities, success, process, progress, honor, mutual respect. Be mindful to resolve conflict in a healthy manner.

John 10:10 *The thief cometh not, but for to steal, and to kill, and to destroy: I am come that they might have life, and that they might have it more abundantly.*

Colossians 3:12-17 *Put on therefore, as the elect of God, holy and beloved, bowels of mercies, kindness, humbleness of mind, meekness, longsuffering; Forbearing one another, and forgiving one another, if any man have a quarrel against any: even as Christ forgave you, so also do ye. And above all these things put on charity, which is the bond of perfectness. And let the peace of God rule in your hearts, to the which also ye are called in one body; and be ye thankful. Let the word of Christ dwell in you richly in all wisdom; teaching and admonishing one another in psalms and hymns and spiritual songs, singing with grace in your hearts to the Lord. And whatsoever ye do in word or deed, do all in the name of the Lord Jesus, giving thanks to God and the Father by him.*

1Thessalonians 5:11 *Therefore encourage one another and build each other up, just as in fact you are doing.*

WHEN RESOLVING CONFLICT, IMPLEMENT THE FOLLOWING STEPS:
Stay focused and listen attentively. As the person is sharing, posture yourself in a place of resolution while putting yourself in the other person's shoes. You are striving to hear through their heart posture and who they are and how what has occurred impacted them.
Ask open ended questions rather than closed ended questions that put people on the defense. This helps you come across as more resolution focused than accusatory or like a prosecutor.
Do not attack. Express that these are your thoughts and feelings and allow the person a chance to explain themselves. Encourage them to give you the same opportunity. "I" statements are good because you are expressing how you perceived the situation without outright attacking or blaming. This is beneficial in instances where misperceptions have occurred.
Repeat what you need clarity on so the person can correct or elaborate on what they said. Remember, clarity brings knowledge and knowledge is power.
Be okay with conflict and disagreement; it is what makes us unique. When you embrace conflict as a part of healthy communication, you will resolve conflict quicker and easier.
Stay focused on resolving the matter and not allowing challenging thoughts and emotions to shut down the

conversation.
Emotions and challenging thoughts are going to arise. But they should not rule your ability to be tempered, meek and articulate. Focus on communicating through your spirit and the character of God rather than your emotions.
Be conscious to commune with God in your mind. Ask him to speak through you and to guide you in your responses.
Be honest and express your thoughts, feelings, concerns and disagreements in a calm and respectful manner.
Pay attention to nonverbal communication and undertones. Be open to addressing these forms of communication.
Be discerning when the conversation stops being about you and the person and SHIFTS to exposing unresolved issues. This happens a lot in leader/member relationships. Leaders are often a catalyst for healing mother, father, teacher and authority figure wounds.
After resolving challenging situations, engage in small talk to restore joy, peace and ease within the relationship interactions.
Start and end times of conflict with prayer. Forgive where necessary, cleanse out hurtful feelings and thoughts; restore trust, honor, love and validation from one to another.
Do not take phone calls or texts unless it is an emergency.
The inability to communicate your needs, thoughts, desires and motives, is the result of a deeper issue. Even if you were not taught healthy and effective

> communication, you are mature enough to stop using your upbringing and past as an excuse. Deal with your underlying root issues while receiving deliverance and healing. You are also mature enough to learn the tools needed to communicate your thoughts, feelings and motives in a healthy manner.
>
> Stop engaging in the generational and relational cycles that cause you to be broken and unhealthy. Do not let people draw you into generational and relational cycles that God has delivered you from.
>
> The only person that can bring value to your words, thoughts and feelings is you. If you cannot express them, do not expect anyone else to give them a voice or value them.

Pray & Study The Bible Together
Prayer and studying the Bible is the highest form of communication. They connect a couple to God and to one another. They continuously transform each person into being what God wants and breeds a spirit to want to be like God and be obedient to God. They allow God to be the head of the marriage covenant, and places God as the head and center of the marriage. God is able to reveal continual marital vision, and that couple is filled with the supernatural capability to bring it to pass.

Because the husband is the head of the marriage and family, you have the capacity to intercede, override demons and strongholds, SHIFT forth breakthrough with a kingly authority of sonship that is greater than your wife. God put you first and made you the head, so demons must obey you – the earth must obey you. When you grasp this revelation and start to walk in it, your  marriage and family will experience blessings, harvest, freedom, and overflow beyond your imagination. Possess a spirit to want to pray and want to gather your family consistently to pray. Be the head through your disposition as a man and son and allow God to reign kingly dominion into your life, marriage, and family.

PURSUING GOD'S UNCONTAINABLE LOVE

Some of this revelation is from my, "Power Of Purity" Manual.

You may have heard of the terms *love tank* and *love languages*. Dr. Gary Chapman coined the term *"love tank"* in his book, *"The Five Love Languages,"* where he contends every person has a love tank. He believes that our love tank is filled up and depleted based on interactions with our partners, family members, and those we are in a relationship with.

I first want to state that if you are requiring others to always fill your love tank, you will always be depleted. You must fill your own love tank up through your relationship with God and then build yourself up in his love.

Please know that love languages are generally based on our personalities, our desires, what we think we need, our mindsets and perceptions, and our experiences. Love languages therefore only allow us to experience a measure of God's love rather than the vastness of his love. The vastness of God's love is found in the following scriptures.

1Corinthians 13:4-8 Charity suffereth long, and is kind; charity envieth not; charity vaunteth not itself, is not puffed up, Doth not behave itself unseemly, seeketh not her own, is not easily provoked, thinketh no evil; Rejoiceth not in iniquity, but rejoiceth in the truth; Beareth all things, believeth all things, hopeth all things, endureth all things. Charity never faileth: but whether there be prophecies, they shall fail; whether there be tongues, they shall cease; whether there be knowledge, it shall vanish away).

*1Corinthians 13:4-8 **New Kingdom James Bible** Love suffers long and is kind; love does not envy; love does not parade itself, is not puffed up; does not behave rudely, does not seek its own, is not provoked, thinks no evil; does not rejoice in iniquity, but rejoices in the truth; bears all things, believes all things, hopes all things, endures all things. Love never fails.*

Love is God! God is love. Love is the identity of God. We are the prototype of him. We therefore possess the capacity to love like he loves.

Love is obedience in action. This is the reason it is a commandment. God commands us to experience love and to pursue the fulfillment love brings into our lives with him and with one another.

God requires us to love with all that is within us. When we love to this capacity, we are seeking to express the fullness of his love on the inside of us. This allows love to be immeasurable, limitless, and everlasting. This allows love to move, SHIFT, and advance the way it is supposed to in our lives. As love should never be boxed in. Love should always evolve, grow, and mature.

Let me say it again! God's love is eternal, vast, and inexhaustible. We put God's love in a box of what we want to experience. Therefore, we put limits on how it can be expressed to us.

> **GOD'S LOVE CANNOT BE CONTAINED!**

GOD'S LOVE IS UNCONTAINABLE!

Its capacity is infinite. When you grasp this revelation, you will pursue all the love God has for you. You will not let personalities, gender, people, experiences, fear, dictate and determine how much of God's love you experience. You will seek to give it and expect God to bestow it upon you. You expect him to find ways to demonstrate his love to you.

When we love like God, we allow ourselves to experience who he is as love. We allow him to bless us as he demonstrates and fulfills his expressions of love and prosperity of love in and around us.

In *1Corinthians 13*, we discern that the more you give love the more love continues to give to you and that person you are loving. Such love goes beyond who you think you should be loved, or how a person should be loved. God's love for us is constantly growing, constantly maturing, constantly demonstrating a new dimension of who he is and who we are to him. When we love like him, we keep falling more in love with the heart to love, and the grace to love like he loves.

You will expect him to place people – the God designed mate - in your life that can love you the way he wants you to be loved. For every experience of withholding of love, you know God will create a situation for you to experience what was trying to be stolen from you. And the more you and your spouse learn to freely give love, the more it will reveal love in your marriage covenant.

You will not worry about who cannot love you correctly because you recognize that your pursuit to want to give and receive as God requires, has activated HIS love around you.

There is a continuous dying to self and surrendering to God in marriage that resurrects new and fresh capacities of love. This continuous igniting of resurrection power restores that marriage couple back into right standing with God and with his creation of marriage before the fall of man to sin in the garden of Eden.

***Genesis 2:25** And the man and his wife were both naked and were not ashamed or embarrassed.*

God wants married couples to be open, vulnerable, unconcerned, unashamed, guiltless, pure, and virtuous before one another.

His pursuit and expression of love allows for this. When love is boxed in, it opens the door for shame, embarrassment, sin, and wanting to hide from God and one another. Couples must want and pursue this depth of love and keep on feeding it until it becomes a natural part of their relationship communication. They have to pursue this beyond touch and sexual intimacy. This requires learning to love like God loves and seeking his vision for how to love their partner.

Seek to love one another like God loves as this is the ultimate, and most valuable love you can give one another. Ask God for grace for your partner, his eyes and heart for that person, and patience to grow in love with them. Endeavor to continuously love and fall in love with your partner more and more each day and ask God to give you the ways and the heart to do that. Continuously pray for your spouse and your covenant relationship. Prayer brings forth love, vision, compassion, and manifested purpose where you constantly have God's mind, will, and purpose for your spouse and what God desires the relationship to be and advance into for his glory.

Understand that relationships are a journey and growing in love is a journey. You are not arriving at a destination. You are evolving in covenant manifestation. Recognize that love languages can change with age, maturity, healing and deliverance, times and seasons. Communicate consistently, be attentive, and regard these changes and transitions so that you can honor and navigate to new dimensions of love properly with God and your spouse. There also must be a posture that your reward to give love comes from God first and he will fill you to overflow, directly or indirectly, or through others, even as he teaches you and your partner to freely love. This is important because true agape love – the unconditional love of God – is given and received without conditions. When you start to focus on what is being reciprocated from what you give, your love tank experiences depletion.

Jesus never cared about the love posture of people's hearts; he only cared about being an example and intercessor of God's unconditional love.

Matthew 22:36-40 Master, which is the great commandment in the law? -- Jesus said unto him, Thou shalt love the Lord thy God with all thy heart, and with all thy soul, and with all thy mind. This is the first and great commandment. And the second is like unto it, Thou shalt love thy neighbour as thyself. On these two commandments hang all the law and the prophets.

ALL MEANS EVERY WHIT – WHOLE – COMPLETELY!

Taquetta's Kingdom Wellness Love Languages are not to box you in but to activate you in expressing God's unconditional love. Use them as a guide to grow with God in being a catalyst of his identity of love.

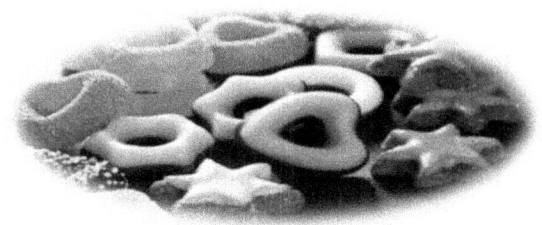

1. **Words Of Affirmation** – Building up with words and acts of agape love, support, attentiveness, affection, praise, encouragement, compliments, excitement for who the person is and who they are evolving into. Display grace and mercy as they work on goals, strategies, and endeavor to be better and to be successful.

2. **Gifts** – Heartfelt and strategic gifts that bestow honor, gratitude, consideration of that person, special occasions, etc., while demonstrating that the person is special and valued. Gifts can be simplistic acts of kindness and sensitivity to what the person enjoys, loves, or is favorable to that person. Hearing God for how to bless and honor that person. Blessings and giving to them in a way that demonstrates the heart of God for that person.

3. **Acts Of Service** – Being self-sacrificing, willingly blessing, and sowing into the person, bearing the person up in life endeavors, assisting in efforts to ease burdens, workloads, and life challenges.

4. **Quality Time** – Providing one-on-one time, personal attention, undivided attention, being a listening ear, and

displaying to that person who they are, what they are saying, and what they are doing is important.

5. **Loyal, Committed, & Faithfulness** – Ability and capacity to remain loyal, committed, and faithful to the relationship, life matters, one's goals and strategies to God, to what God is speaking and requiring for oneself personally, to others, and the relationship.

6. **Physical Touch** – Kissing (i.e. on the cheek, forehead, lips, hand), hugging, holding hands, massages, cuddling, sitting close together, dancing, head rubs, playing in hair, sexual intercourse, etc. Most people claim physical touch is their love language. Many have not developed their love language beyond physical touch and always gravitate to this love language, especially intimate kissing, sexual stimulation, and intercourse. Physical touch, however, is innate and is generally everyone's love language. We all have an innate desire to belong, to be touched, and to be close. This is an automatic love language that should be displayed within the biblical boundaries of the relationship as when *Eros* (intimate love) is aroused before the appropriate time is difficult to contain. Recognizing what each person can handle regarding physical touch and honoring proper boundaries and biblical standards is vital to help ensure not succumbing to sexual sin. I implore each person not to test flesh or to tempt one another. You want to build other areas of your love language and physical touch outside of sexual stimulation and intercourse. This will build your intimacy, romance, connectivity, and honor to please

and explore one another in ways that build a full capacity of love and touch.

7. **Receiving Of Love Languages** - Avoid rejecting, resisting, non-embracing, or connecting and disconnecting from love that is available and being displayed.

8. **Communication Wellness** - Expressing thoughts and feelings in a healthy manner. Learning communication skills, conflict resolution skills, anger management, social skills, interpersonal skills, and emotional wellness. Setting goals and practicing the applicable tools until they become a lifestyle in your relationships and household. Pursuing counseling, mediation, and/or accountability partners if necessary to heal and grow in these skills.

9. **Expressing Appreciation & Honor** – Display thankfulness, grace, and appreciation for the self-sacrificing, submission, servanthood, blessings, and honor that is being given.

10. **Honor, Respect, & Dignity** - Honor and respect can be vital for some people, especially men, leaders, people called to platforms, and high positions. Culture can also be a factor in the affirmation of honor and respect. Sometimes people's positions, purposes, and callings cause them to experience lots of dishonor so they will require this to be filled by loved ones. Build them up in accolades, scriptures, God identity, and vision so they can be empowered in healthy divine honor and respect.

When this is not fulfilled the person will succumb to pride, control, pessimism, and demonic counsel. They will seek ways to assert their right to be honored and respected. This will breed conflict and division rather than unity and Godly confidence and dignity.

11. **Intellectual Stimulation** – Possessing the ability to intellectually understand and communicate, empower one another with knowledge and truth, provide intellectual and/or educational invigoration. This tends to be especially important to people who pursue constant knowledge, pursue high educational attainment and success, like to read books, and study or explore unique topics and experiences.

12. **Spiritual & Biblical Stimulation** – Possessing the capability to impart and empower one another spiritually and biblically, honor who each other are in God, honor the way he uses each of you, regard godly revelation and insight, and evolve in God realities together.

13. **Financial Generosity/Benevolence** – Ability to financially bless and provide rewards, provision, and opportunities for destiny advancement. Land, buildings, investments, grants, scholarships, positions, and favors, are also included in this love language. Some people enjoy having money to bless others.

14. **Self-Care** - I would contend that self-care is the greatest love language of all. Loving oneself well so you can give love well - love from a healthy love tank -

freely give what you receive from yourself and God. (***Philippians 2:3-4, Matthew 10:8***)

Uncontainable Love Activation:
1. Journal what you learned from this revelation and how to apply it to your life and relationships, in this case your marriage.

2. Spend five minutes thanking God for the ability to express his love in unique ways.

3. Spend five minutes thanking God for growing your revelation and understanding of his love and asking God to fill you with new dimensions of his love.

4. While communing with your spouse, journal what your love languages are.

5. While communing with your spouse, journal what their love languages are.

6. While communing with your spouse, share with one another as you journal how each of your love languages empower you personally.

7. While communing with your spouse, share with one another as you journal the impacts of not having your love languages validated and fulfilled and how this would affect each of you personally.

8. While communing with your spouse, pray for five minutes then ask God what demonstrations of love he wants you all to express to one another in this season of your relationship. Set three goals you all can implement to improve immediately.

9. While communing with your spouse, ask God the ways you need to submit and surrender to him and your spouse where your love for him, your spouse, and the marriage constantly resurrects, grows and matures infinitely.

10. Pray together and ask God what areas he wants you all to fulfill and mature with one another as it relates to love languages. Set three goals to build these love languages that God highlights.

11. Study **Genesis 2:25, I Corinthians 13:4-8, Matthew 22:36-40, and Ephesians 5:22-33.** Ask God to teach you how this is his identity and greatest dimensions of love and the foundation of marriage covenant. Ask him to teach you how to be immeasurable in love with your spouse. Set three personal and marital goals to evolve in God's uncontainable love.

12. Overtime, seek to grow in all the love languages listed where they become the fullness of your relationship and continue to ask God how to love one another so he can constantly fill you all up with the immeasurable power and expression of his love.

MARITAL INTIMACY BY AKEYSHA

Akeysha Headley has been married for 15 years and counting. She helps to mentor dating, engaged, married, and struggling couples. She has a remarkable success rate of bringing deliverance, healing, and sustaining success to these covenant relationships.

Akeysha's Keys To Fulfilling Marital Intimacy:

Intimacy takes time! Do not expect your spouse to just hit the ground running with knowing you. Time also means you must be intentional about intimate time spent.

Your needs and desires will change over time. The only way to know this is to communicate them. Do not be afraid to try new things that are within the realm of respect and honor...but fun and enjoyable.

Change your view of intimacy as being just pleasure to one of serving. You are serving your spouse, and your spouse is serving you. This will ensure you both achieve pleasure.

PRAY TOGETHER!!! Prayer draws you to a vulnerable place with God and each other. As you draw closer to Him together, your sexual intimacy will reap the benefits.

Intimacy does not start in the bed! It starts with how you are guarding, building, and governing each other's soul (mind, will, emotions).

Keep distractions out of your bedroom. For some couples that may mean no TV or turning off screens at a certain time, setting boundaries with your children, or even limiting what topics are allowed for discussion in the bedroom. Your bedroom is a place of meeting! Be present!

BONUS: Design and decorate the bedroom together. This will allow both parties to feel like this is a place for you both, even down to picking the new comforter. It matters!

Intimacy Activation: Journal how to utilize these tips in building intimacy with your spouse. Spend time together setting three goals you can work on as you consider these intimacy strategies.

MARITAL INTIMACY BY PRAISE

Coach Praise's famous moto to couples is, "There is no sex in heaven so you might as well enjoy it now!" She has sixteen years and counting of experience in being a relationship expert on various ministerial, community, and global platforms, while also mentoring dating, engaged, and married couples.

When it comes to strengthening intimacy:

Couples must understand that intimacy started with God.

Genesis 2:25 New King James Bible *And they were both naked, the man and his wife, and were not ashamed.*

The marriage bed is a place of honor. Both parties must honor each other's preferences, likes, and dislikes.

Hebrews 13:4 King James Bible *Marriage is honourable among all, and the bed undefiled; but fornicators and adulterers God will judge.*

Sex was made by God, and it is pure. Both hearts must be pure towards it.

Proverbs 5:15, 17-18 New International Bible *Drink water from your own cistern, running water from your own well. Let them be yours alone, never to be shared with strangers. May your fountain be blessed, and may you rejoice in the wife of your youth.*

Sex is for the purpose of procreation. Sex is also a symbol of the two becoming one in the place of intimacy. It is a symbolism of coming into the presence of God for communion, worship and then being blessed as you surrender in expression of worship, praise, and thanksgiving unto the Lord.

Intimacy benefits both spouses. It empowers healthy relationships. If there is no foundation of intimacy then consistent sex will be challenging, especially for the wife. Build intimacy through daily romance, affirmations, honor, blessings, help, and building in love together.

Both men and women have a lot to enjoy from intimacy. It strengthens the bond of both agape (unconditional) and *Eros* (romantic) love. The Songs of Solomon cover the satisfaction that intimacy provides to married couples.

Desire to be satisfied during intimacy and not just tolerate the experience. Make it your responsibility to please your mate and to be pleased by your mate. This is your godly right as a married couple.

Song of Songs 7:11-12 New International Bible *Come, my beloved, let us go to the countryside, let us spend the night in the villages. Let us go early to the vineyards to see if the vines have budded, if their blossoms have opened, and if the pomegranates are in bloom— there I will give you my love.*

Intimacy Activation: Journal on how to use these tips in building intimacy with your spouse. Spend time together setting three goals you can work on as you consider these intimacy strategies:

10 Reasons Why Sex Is Important To Your Marriage:

Trey & Lea's StrongerMarriageWorkshops.com

1. Sex cultivates oneness.
2. Sex is great for your heath.
3. Sex is a great de-stressor.
4. Sex strengthens your marriage.
5. Sex is intimate conversation.
6. Sex creates a bonding agent.
7. Sex reconnects you as a couple.
8. Sex conveys love, desire and selflessness.
9. Sex can help you get through tough times.
10. Sex is God ordained.

MARITAL INTIMACY BY TAQUETTA

Biblical Sexual Intimacy is a combination of physical and emotional connectivity between a husband and wife that involves trust, vulnerability, loyalty, love, submission, self-sacrifice, communication, intentionality, and care. It can include emotional bonding, romance, foreplay, and other forms of physical intimacy, in addition to intercourse.

Biblical Intimacy is a close, familiar, sacred, safe, private, protected, fortified, verbally, emotionally, and physically affectionate, interpersonally knitted relationship that builds and evolves through a godly covenant.

Sexual intimacy and intimacy in general are foundationally needful attributes to a marriage covenant.

Both are vital to being able to conceive and have children. Many married couples claim to want children but have not made intimacy and sexual intimacy a priority in their marriage. They have not cultivated natural intimacy where spiritual intimacy can become supernaturally sound in and around their covenant marriage, their reproductive organs, their marriage bed, their wombs, and ability to conceive.

The first revelation key I want to speak to frustrated married couples who want to conceive is, "YOU HAVE TO HAVE SEX TO GET PREGNANT!" Often, I am quite taken aback when married couples act like the need to have intimacy and sex is not a requirement for pregnancy. I am also shocked by the lack of priority or intentionality that is given to marital intimacy. Most couples want all the benefits of marriage without the work. Truth is that marriage is work. Intimacy in any relationship, friendship, or otherwise, requires work.

Relationships are what you make of them.

What you invest, is what it produces.

What you do not invest, results in a lack of production.

This is for any relationship, especially marriage.

Intimacy Healing Activation: Take five minutes to process this revelation with God and your spouse. Repent for any disregarding of intimacy and sexual intimacy. Journal where you need to improve. Journal two goals to work on improving immediately in this area.

Cultivating Supernatural Intimacy

I would contend that there are those married couples that God is not allowing to conceive without building intimacy. Some people get to birth any kind of way, as God is just striving to get his offspring in the earth. But there are some, that God is saying, "*this child, this vision, this offspring, must be birthed through a supernatural womb that has been cultivated in intimacy*." You and your spouse may be those God has chosen.

This could be because of:

- ✓ Your personal callings.

- ✓ The vision God has for your marriage and what it is representing in the earth.

- ✓ Personal and generational strongholds you are breaking or personal and generational blessings within your offsprings and bloodlines.

- ✓ **JUST BEING CHOSEN BY GOD TO BIRTH HIS WAY!**

You will not know if this is you until you ask God!

Birthing Activation: Take five minutes to thank God that he is head of your life and all it entails.

Ask God if you are chosen to birth forth by his divine formula of healthy intimacy. Ask him what is so important about your marriage, your womb, your seed, your offspring, that intimacy is vital to how you birth. Journal what he reveals to you all.

Spend ten minutes thanking him for the revelation and declaring that you surrender your marriage, your womb, your seed, your offspring to his plan and purpose.

Spend five minutes embracing your spouse in two new levels of intimacy verbally and physically. Journal any differences you all experience.

ARE YOU A COMMUNICATOR?

Sexual intimacy begins outside the marriage bed. Learn healthy communication skills, conflict resolution skills, coping skills, interpersonal skills, social skills, anger management, and emotional wellness so you can effectively manage and communicate your thoughts and feelings properly. You have **NO EXCUSE** in this area as you can google these skills, practice and implement them in your marriage and daily interactions. You can also purchase my, *"Divine Art to Healthy Communication Skills,"* and *"Maintaining Emotional Wellness"* eBooks.

Emotional connection is vital to intimacy. Learning to be expressive and vulnerable with one another is one of the best gifts you can give your covenant relationship. It is key to comforting one another, empowering one another, being considerate of one another, having grace for one another, and to bringing one another pleasure and joy as you evolve in relationship together.

Emotional connection is essential to intertwining - knitting your souls together in *Eros* love. *Eros* love is romance love that God created for marriage.

> ***Eros love*** is the romantic love, admiration, esteem, passion, and attraction between a man and a woman. It is the love a man or a woman has for a partner of the opposite sex that they romantically admire and would desire to marry. *Eros* love is often misconstrued and even tainted with lust. Even though it is a healthy innate love, if *Eros* love is not properly governed or filtered through a pure mind, heart, and soul, it can cause people to fall into fornication, adultery, and inappropriate sexual or lustful behaviors. This type of love is intended for marriage and should not be intricately engaged, or ignited, outside of matrimony. After marriage, *Eros* love can be fully awakened and is essential for the wellness of sexual intimacy and the strengthening of the relationship bond within the marriage covenant.

When couples are disconnected from one another emotionally and fear expressing their thoughts and feelings to one another, insecurity regarding intimacy and rejection of expressing emotions to one another, creeps in the marriage and marriage bed and makes intimacy difficult. It causes intimacy to be detached, and void of the excitement and emotional zeal needed to make *Eros* love.

YOU MUST build emotional connectivity daily.

Make it a necessary part of your communication and love language with one to another.

Be healed of past childhood issues so they do not hinder your ability to communicate and grow in healthy relationship with your spouse and those who are in your life. Go to counseling, inner healing or have a deliverance session. Do what is necessary to heal so you can live and evolve in a healthy marriage covenant.

Share sexual intimacy issues and trauma experiences with your spouse so they can display honor and patience with you as you grow together in intimacy. This is vital because your spouse is looking forward to the gift of sex and intimacy with you as a married couple. Do not deprive them by making them pay for what others did to you or any shame you have regarding past sexual encounters and present sexual bondages. Seek healing with God, a counselor, and/or a deliverance minister, while taking responsibility to live in this new life of intimacy and wellness with your mate.

YOU ARE WORTH THIS SHIFT AND SO IS YOUR MATE AND YOUR MARRIAGE!

Do not make excuses for poor communication skills, degenerative character, and immature behavior. Marriage and sexual intimacy are for adults. Grow up and take responsibility in maturing in the areas you need to be transformed so your spouse will trust themselves with you and so you can effectively communicate your needs and desires in and outside the marriage bed.

Intimacy Healing Activation: Take five minutes to thank God for his God identity on the inside of you.

Spend five minutes thanking God for being an intimate communicator and that he has placed this innate ability – identity - to effectively communicate your emotions, thoughts, and feelings on the inside of you.

Repent for any immature or detached emotions. Repent to God and your spouse for anyway this has affected the marriage covenant.

Explore where you and your partner need to heal and grow in this area. Set three goals you can work on immediately to improve emotional connectivity.

HONOR IS ESSENTIAL!

Spend five minutes embracing your spouse in two new levels of emotional connectivity. Journal any differences you all experience.

Honor is EVERYTHING in a marriage. God honors marriage and wants us to honor it.

Hebrews 13:4 *Marriage is honourable in all, and the bed undefiled: but whoremongers and adulterers God will judge.*

<u>Honorable</u> in the Greek is *timios* and means:
4. valuable, i.e. (objectively) costly, or (subjectively) honored, esteemed, or (figuratively) beloved
5. dear, honorable, (more, most) precious, had in reputation
6. as of great price, precious, held in honour, esteemed, especially dear

Be quick to repent anytime honor has been violated. If your spouse believes they have been dishonored, be open to quickly humbling yourself and doing what is necessary to restore the power and trust of honor. This strengthens intimacy. When your spouse feels safe and valued, it draws them into a greater love language and zeal for intimacy.

Please understand that intimacy is innate and needful in marriage. For you are called to fulfill your spouse sexually.

It is part of the covenant you entered when you agreed to marry. Regarding this truth is essential to a healthy marriage and healthy intimacy. The moment you think it is okay to have a sexless or intimate-less marriage, you have put your marriage, your spouse and yourself in danger.

1Corinthians 7:3-5 The husband should fulfill his marital duty to his wife, and likewise the wife to her husband. The wife does not have authority over her own body but yields it to her husband. In the same way, the husband does not have authority over his own body but yields it to his wife. Do not deprive each other except perhaps by mutual consent and for a time, so that you may devote yourselves to prayer. Then come together again so that Satan will not tempt you because of your lack of self-control.

1Corinthians 7:5 The Message Bible Abstaining from sex is permissible for a period of time if you both agree to it, and if it's for the purposes of prayer and fasting - but only for such times. Then come back together again. Satan has an ingenious way of tempting us when we least expect it.

Ingenious means extremely intelligent, cleverly inventive, constructive, or resourceful.

The enemy will INVENT scenarios and opportunities to fulfill for your spouse what you neglect.

Do not become an open door for dishonor and sin by neglecting your spouse and yourself in this area of your marriage.

Both parties should make it their responsibility to maintain healthy intimacy even if health challenges are a factor. It is also important not to allow life stressors, business, children, etc., hinder intimacy.

Ask God to heal you of anything that would hinder you from desiring, loving, and enjoying intimacy. Learn yourself, your body and your mate. Build intimacy and evolve in it as you progress in your marriage covenant.

Intimacy Activation: Spend five minutes thanking God for the innate gift of sexual intimacy.

Repent to God and your spouse for anyway you have been neglectful and dishonoring in your marriage and regarding sexual intimacy.

Pray together while rededicating your marriage, your bodies, and your covenant back into godly alignment of honor with God and one another. Journal your experiences after you have done this.

Set three goals to implement immediately to restore honor in your marriage covenant. Journal your goals and hold one another accountable to them.

HONORABLE MARRIAGE BED!

Do not do anything in the marriage bed that your spouse is not comfortable with as this is HONORING. When your spouse shares discomfort in any manner, take time to listen, and make changes together. Do not pressure one another to cross boundaries where there may be perceptions of dishonor, discomfort, or disregard. Instead do what is naturally pleasing and allow your trust and safety with one another to build intimacy in areas where your spouse will then feel open to other areas of intimacy.

Undefiled is *amiantos* in Greek and means:
3. unsoiled, i.e. (figuratively) pure: — undefiled
4. not defiled, free from that by which the nature of a thing is deformed and debased, or its force and vigour impaired

Dictionary.com defines *undishonored* as:
7. lack or loss of honor, disgraceful or dishonest character or conduct
8. disgrace; ignominy; shame
9. an indignity; insult
10. a cause of shame or disgrace
11. to deprive of honor; disgrace; bring reproach or shame on
12. to rape or seduce

We like to think that an undefiled bed means we can do whatever we desire because we are married. But if there are acts that bring shame, dishonor, reproach, and disgrace upon our spouse and even upon God, then our bed is subject to defilement. If we are making our spouses engage in acts, they are uncomfortable with, even if there are areas of their soul and identity that need to be healed regarding intimacy, we could be defiling our marriage bed. As we examine the definitions, some acts could be considered rape when seduction is done in a form of manipulation and control rather than *Eros* love and a desire to romanticize your mate. We could be subjecting the marriage bed to defilement.

When defilement enters the marriage bed, we are operating in Aheb love rather than *Eros* love. We are succumbing to a love that is driven more by perversion than the innate desires of sex and intimacy that God instilled in us.

We think purity means abstaining and self-control, but purity means sanctification.

1Thessalonians 4:3-4 For this is the will of God, even your sanctification, that ye should abstain from fornication: That every one of you should know how to possess his vessel in sanctification and honour.

Sanctification in Greek is *hagiasmos* and means:
1. purification, i.e. (the state) purity
2. concretely (by Hebraism) a purifier
3. holiness, sanctification, consecration
4. the effect of consecration
5. sanctification of heart and life

Sanctification is about being restored in innocence, holiness, and purity according to the standard and will of God.

Sanctification is a state of separation unto God.

All believers enter this state when they are born of God: *"You are in Christ Jesus, who became to us wisdom from God, righteousness and sanctification and redemption."*

***1Corinthians 1:29-31** That no flesh should glory in his presence. But of him are ye in Christ Jesus, who of God is made unto us wisdom, and righteousness, and sanctification, and redemption: That, according as it is written, He that glorieth, let him glory in the Lord.*

Marriage in and of itself produces sanctification even to the point where it can make an unbelieving spouse holy unto the Lord. The believing sanctified spouse, causes the entire household to be considered holy. **WOW!**

1Corinthians 7:14 For the unbelieving husband is sanctified by the wife, and the unbelieving wife is sanctified by the husband: else were your children unclean; but now are they holy.

Husbands are to love their wives such that the love itself sanctifies and cleanses the marriage with the word of God.

1Corithians 5:25-27 Husbands, love your wives, even as Christ also loved the church, and gave himself for it; That he might sanctify and cleanse it with the washing of water by the word, That he might present it to himself a glorious church, not having spot, or wrinkle, or any such thing; but that it should be holy and without blemish.

Though the marriage bed is undefiled, there are some sexual operations that will never be godly. It is important to regard this truth and allow God into your sexual intimacy communication so he can share with you his boundary lines. Also hold one another to what is honorable between you and as you live through the biblical principles of God's word. I highly recommend by manual, *"The Power Of Purity,"* to further bring clarity, truth, deliverance, and healing in this area.

Romance one another. Learn one another's love languages, likes and dislikes inside and outside the marriage bed. Seek ways to romance one another, bless one another and bring joy and love to one another. This builds emotional connectivity and empowers the desire and drive for intimacy. Romance is not rocket science. You can google romance and receive all kinds of examples of how to be romantic. I recommend Jackie Green's manual, "*The Marriage Vault.*" Among other great wisdom keys, she shares eighty-eight ways to be romantic with your spouse.

Seek wise counsel ONLY from those who will encourage you to honor your spouse, and that will help to keep your marriage bed undefiled. Be mindful of what you speak about your spouse and the way you present them to that person. Even if they are someone you can be very relaxed and open with, be mindful of words that tear down as opposed to build you, your spouse, and your marriage covenant. This helps you to engage your spouse with a pure heart of grace and dignity no matter what challenges you all are going through. Your eyes continue to be set on who you all are together and the love you are building with one another. You are also able to keep pure eyes for who God is in your spouse and the reason God put you all in covenant together.

Seek medical help if sexual intimacy becomes difficult whether that be physically or emotionally. Sometimes, this can be an indication of a health issue, hormonal or chemical imbalance, or stress factors that are hindering the bodies response to intimacy. Do not let these issues go on for prolonged periods of time. Most of them can be rectified with changes in diet, exercise, medications, supplements, essential oils, self-care regimens, counseling, inner healing, and/or deliverance. Understand that your neglect in this area not only affects you but your spouse and the harmony of your home. Be open to doing what is necessary to maintain intimacy.

Do not withhold emotional connection opportunities, communication, or intimacy. Always be willing to draw close and to create opportunities for closeness.
Do not punish your spouse by withholding intimacy. Always agree when you are going to abstain from intimacy. Endeavor to keep your promises and agreements surrounding intimacy, and do not go to long without having intimate fellowship.

1Corinthians 7:1-6 *Now concerning the things of which you wrote to me: It is good for a man not to touch a woman. Nevertheless, because of sexual immorality, let each man have his own wife, and let each woman have her own husband. Let the husband render to his wife the affection due her, and likewise also the wife to her husband. The wife does not have authority over her own body, but the husband does. And likewise the husband does not have authority over his own body, but the wife does. Do not deprive one another except with consent for a time, that you may give yourselves to fasting and prayer; and come together again so that Satan does not tempt you because of your lack of self-control.*

INTIMACY ACTIVATION

1. Spend five minutes thanking God for his gift of honor in marriage and the marriage bed.

2. Spend five minutes declaring to God how honor is essential and how you will honor your marriage, your spouse, and your marriage bed.

3. Spend five minutes praying with your spouse in this area.

4. Spend five minutes with your spouse just resting before God.

5. Journal with your spouse areas where your marriage is honorable. Praise and honor one another for these acts of honor in your marriage.

6. Journal with your spouse areas where you all need to improve your honor towards one another in your marriage.

7. Journal with your spouse areas where you all need to sanctify your marriage bed.

8. Set three goals you all can implement immediately to improve in honoring one another in marriage and your marriage bed. Set honorable goals to hold one another accountable in these areas.

WAYS TO INCREASE AROUSAL

COUPLES, I am going to share SOME keys to help with healthy PURE sexual intimacy. I trust God will lead you further in this area or you can reach out to myself, Coach Praise, or Coach Akeysha for more insights in this area.

Sex and romance, even the experience of intercourse itself, starts outside of the marriage bed. It starts with building honor, fondness, regard, love, joy, pleasure, excitement, closeness, passion, romance and a desire, willingness, and openness to draw and build a desire for intimacy with one another.

Spend time doing fun and romantic adventures throughout the day and week and allow your communication and interactions to build intimacy and desire for making love.

Spend time being intentional with doing life together, making decisions together, and conquering trials together. This builds intimacy and desire for making love.

The more couples trust and lean on one another, the deeper the bond of intimacy matures, thus maturing the desire to please one another and to experience intimacy together.

Take moments together throughout the day to build care, attentiveness, romance and intimacy. Examples, hugging and/or kissing for 20 seconds before leaving and when entering one another's presence, sending text messages of appreciation, care, concern, romance, writing and speaking poetry or singing songs to one another, light caresses and touches as you engage one another throughout the day; playful romantic engagement that entail saying and doing things to make one another laugh, smile, feel affirmed, valued, impassioned, or naturally or romantically loved; intentionally touching  and bonding (cuddling) while sitting with one another, watching movies, before you go to bed at night, throughout the night, and when you awaken in the morning. Create and take opportunities to rest together, be together and enjoy one another's company daily, throughout the day, and make or schedule longer intentional time for this a few times a week.

Continual compliments and affirmation build appreciation, affection, and increase love. Be mindful not to gloss over, disregard, disconnect, or take these moments for granted. Be intentional to embrace them every time they are given so this becomes the lifestyle of your relationship.

Massages with lotions and oils help with relaxation, de-stressing, and attentiveness to caring and learning one another's bodies and responses to pleasure, while building arousal. This also helps the body, especially the pleasure points and sexual organs to relax and yield to pleasure and receiving intercourse.

Light touches of the body with the fingertips and palms of the hand builds arousal and *Eros* love. Especially as the person receiving focuses on relaxing, being loved, being pleasured, and becoming one with their mate.

Learn one another's physical pleasure points and being intentional to love and arouse one another in these areas can aide in relaxing for intercourse and can teach the body to relax, yield and embrace longer times of intercourse. The more the body is taught to relax and recieve pleasure, the more it will relent to receiving love in a healthy *Eros love* way, rather than pint up pressure and rushing lust or passion.

Map of Erogenous Zones

SCALP
From a gentle head massage to a more BDSM hair pull, the scalp is an underrated erogenous zone.

EARS
Some light earlobe play is all the rage.

ARMPITS
A spot that rarely gets touched and often gets tickled is an infamous sensitive zone!

HANDS/FINGERS
Most of the human hand's 17,000 touch receptors are literally at your fingertips.

LOWER STOMACH & INNER THIGHS
Great zones for anticipation. "Where are they headed next?" your brain wonders. Your body will respond accordingly.

VULVA
"Because the internal and external structure of the clitoris is larger than most expect, much of the surface area of the vulva is considered to be an erogenous zone," says Carpenter.

Stars of this area: clitoris, g-spot

LIPS
A multi-purpose zone. Try mouth-to-mouth...or maybe a finger to the lips of your partner.

NECK
Licking or sucking here is often a great place to show your partner some love.

NIPPLES
The chest region (including breasts) is sensitive for any gender—and generally reserved for people you're more intimate with.

BUTT
Whether it's a light touch or a firm hand, this area is one hyper-sexualized zone that often lives up to the hype.

FEET
This famously fetishized body part isn't a pleasure center for everyone—but those who love feet find myriad ways to enjoy them.

PENIS
"The frenulum, or the ridge below the head of the penis, is usually the most sensitive part for folks with penises."

Other notable mentions: prostate, testicles, perineum

Men – **HUSBANDS** - are givers so they can automatically receive pleasure without much arousal. Women – **WIVES** - you are receivers. A husband does not know how your body is receiving unless you tell them. Your body may need time to adjust and receive pleasure and physical oneness. The wife initiating and leading intimacy can increase receptivity, romance, passion, and sexual pleasure. This also teaches the husband your rhythm, the art, quality, expression, grace, beauty, creativity, and skills of love making; how your body and his body responds to pleasure; patience with sexual intimacy, your comfortability and willingness to explore, and how to love through emotional and spiritual interaction and not just physical body responses.

> **ATTENTION WIFEY!** WIVES YOU ARE A RECEIVER! **DO NOT** PUT THE RESPONSIBILITY ON THE YOUR HUSBAND TO KNOW HOW YOU ARE RECEVING AND TO KNOW HOW TO PLEASE YOU!
>
> GIVE YOURSELF A VOICE AND A GODLY RIGHT TO BE PLEASED BY EXPRESSING AND COMMUNICATING YOUR THOUGHTS AND FEELINGS REGARDING INTIMACY.

Let's just ponder the truth of this insight for a moment.

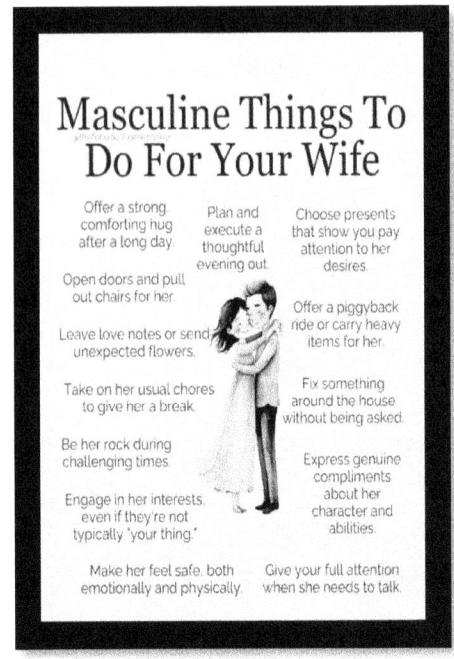

Sometimes, the wife being on top while giving and receiving expressions of physical love can be pleasurable for her and her husband and prepare the genitals, especially hers for oneness. Lightly thrusting the genitals together, while being on top of your husband increases arousal and the desire for oneness. Using a small amount of lubricant (suggestion Astroglide lubricant) on both of your genitals will also help with arousal and preparing the woman's body for entry.

The husband making sure his wife has had an orgasm before intercourse can increase receptivity to her vagina receiving the penis and her enjoying sexual intercourse.

HUSBANDS be mindful to love your wife and make sure she enjoys love making just as much as you do. Also, asking your wife if she is ready for intercourse can help gauge where her body is rather than just assuming she is where you are. WIVES do not abuse your bodies or bruise your emotions by enduring pain and challenges during love making. Be honest if you need more time to be aroused or to posture in receive mode. Allow God's gift of sex to do what it is intended to do for you, which is to give you honor, passion, pleasure, and love, even as you receive it. Be okay if more time is needed to communicate and engage in love making to help the body to fully posture for intercourse.

HUSBAND if you and/or your wife is a virgin, or if you and your wife have been abstaining from sex for a while, be patient with yourselves. Be patient with her and be patient with the process of love making, especially your initial experiences of sexual intercourse. Do not rush her in doing something her body is not ready for. Doing so can cause trauma around sex and make her resistant to wanting to engage in sexual intimacy. Be patient, learn her body, let her learn, and allow yourselves to work together to attain consummation of your marriage. Do not shame or condemn her and do not let it be a stab to your manhood if time is needed in this area. The more you all work together to build *Eros* love, the stronger your foundation will be, and the greater your love language will be in the future.

Virgins, I want to share that the hymen is a small piece of skin that generally surrounds (but does not cover) the vaginal opening. The hymen can wear down naturally over time from doing activities, or tear during penetration of the vagina. If it has not worn down with daily activities, it will be there on your wedding night. It can sometimes feel like something is tearing during the initial experience of sex. This may be painful, but it is a natural process of your body coming into marital sexual intimacy. WIVES, your body type and your ability to receive pleasure will determine the duration of pain in that initial experience and whether you will experience this a few more times. But eventually your body will adjust to your husband and to sexual intercourse. And if you use the keys in this chapter, you will SHIFT in being able to give and receive love with pleasure and ease.

Reading Songs of Solomon together and to one another and laughing about how wild it is can help to relax and embrace sex as an intimate God designed blessing that he has given to your marriage covenant. This can help build communication and open your *Eros* love to the spiritual vision of intimacy within your marriage union.

TYPES OF LOVE IN THE BIBLE
Storge – Empathy bond
Philia – Friend bond
Eros – Romantic love
Agape – Unconditional "God" love
Aheb - Inordinate love. This type of love can be rooted in lust, perversion, unseemingly acts or conversations, wicked, evil, domineering, sadistic, or abusive acts; doing things that are not natural to the body, gender roles, and godly creation; engaging in what God has decided is NOT orderly, proper, or appropriate.

Eros Love is the romantic love, admiration, esteem, passion, and sexual intimate, physical attraction between a HUSBAND and a WIFE. It is the love a man or a woman has for a partner of the opposite sex that they romantically admire and would desire to marry.

Eros is an English word that means "erotic." *Eros* was the word often used to express sexual love or the feelings of arousal that are shared between people who are physically attracted to one another. The word was also used as the name of the Greek god of love, *Eros* (the Romans called him "Cupid"). In New Testament times, this word had become so debased by the culture and the church that it is not used even once in the entire New Testament. Yet God has designed sex for husband and wife. His desire is for you to experience *Eros* love in your marriage covenant.

Bible References of Eros Love
Genesis 2:18,24
Proverbs 5:18-19
Song of Songs 4:9-10 (the entire book)
1Corinthians 7:5
Hebrews 13:4

Eros Bible Truths
Eros love is a gift from God to husbands and wives. It is God's creation and idea. He wants you to enjoy marriage and intimacy.
Healthy *Eros* love takes work, but marriage is work. It is a daily work of building the vision of covenant marriage together as a lifestyle. The more you yield to what God desires and requires for marriage, the

less the work feels like a chore. The identity of who you are as one God chose to be married, evolves as you rest in the blessing, fulfillment, call and purpose to marriage as a lifestyle.
Eros can intensify with communication, patience, grace, growing in love together, selflessness (agape love). It can diminish through pride, dishonor, disregard, abuse, impatience, and selfishness. The more you give of yourself by making an effort to please your mate and not just yourself, the more fulfillment and building of passionate Eros love manifests in your marriage covenant.
Eros is celebrated in the bond and holiness of heterosexual marriage. Outside of biblical marriage, biblical boundaries, and principles, *Eros* can become confusing, distorted, perverted, sinful, selfish, idolatrous, and abusive. It can also open doors to demons entering a person's life, the marriage bed, the dream realm, and covenant.

Eros Love Activation:

1. Spend time journaling what you learned from this chapter. Share your journal entry with your spouse.
2. Spend time cleansing yourselves with the blood of Jesus of any past or present traumas and misconceptions you have had regarding sex. Spend time exploring these areas with God and together as a couple and asking him to heal you all personally, generationally, and together as a married couple.
3. Set three to five goals to work on to improve your *Eros* love in your marriage covenant. Do regular check ins to make sure you are achieving your goals, growing in *Eros*, and to implement new goals as you mature in life personally and together.

I AM DIVORCED NOW WHAT?

One of the greatest revelations I have learned from counseling people through divorce is that divorce is just an event in life! It is not the end, nor the full identity of your life.

> DIVORCE IS JUST AN EVENT IN LIFE! IT IS NOT THE END, NOR THE FULL IDENTITY OF A PERSON'S LIFE!

People come to counseling feeling helpless, destitute, shameful, guilt ridden, condemned, regretful, and doomed. But there is indeed life after divorce.

- ✓ There is deliverance and healing after divorce.
- ✓ There are lessons to be learned and implemented from divorce to make better decisions after divorce.
- ✓ There is life to pursue after divorce.
- ✓ There is joy and fulfillment after divorce.
- ✓ There is sustaining success after divorce.
- ✓ There are relationships and dating after divorce.

- ✓ There is remarriage after divorce.
- ✓ There is fulfilled marriage and the ability to live through ordained godly covenant after divorce.
- ✓ There are children to raise God's way, even though you, and they have experienced divorce.
- ✓ There are children to conceive with your new covenant mate after divorce.
- ✓ There is evolving destiny to live daily with God whether single, waiting, or re-married after divorce.

Divorce can be messy, traumatic, and enraging, but it is not an experience that you cannot overcome with God.

Divorce only defines you in a negative way if you allow it to define you that way.

Divorce only defines you by how you decide to let your experience impact your life.

Divorce is not an experience that you cannot take charge over and choose with God how it impacts your life.

I share these truths so that you will not be stuck in the divorce experience. These truths can help you SHIFT into pursuing a deliverance and healing process with God.

God does hate divorce, but divorce was allotted in the laws of Moses because of transgressions and challenges people were having in their marriages. God hates divorce because he is a covenant-keeping God. He originated his plan for mankind, and who he is as their God, inside the constitution of marriage and family. When the foundation of marriage is broken, it impacts the generational alignment, blessings, and heritage of family, while opening doors for foreign gods to govern the bloodline.

Divorce is death. It kills abundant life within people, marriage, and family. God is eternally focused on and desires longevity and overflowing life with those he is in covenant with. God's hatred is not towards you, per say, as a divorcee, as you would have to do something very horrid for God to hate you. God will always hate divorce, even though he understands the reasons divorce occurs. He understands that divorce entered in through the Fall of mankind in the garden – through the division that came from Satan pitting Adam and Eve against God. God does hate divorce itself because of the separation this causes that he never desired to have with mankind and with marriage and family. This will never change. We should all hate divorce and want to be married for life. We should all want to be covenant keepers who regard the eternal loyalty and fruitfulness it releases into our lives and generational lines. So, even if we experience or witness divorce, we should never become used to it or cultivate it as the norm. It should always be an experience we despise and never want to see in operation.

Please know that God would never want you to remain in a marriage where you, your children, or loved ones are being ABUSED, in any way. Though there are biblical grounds listed in the Bible for divorce such as adultery and death, God wants us to use wisdom and seek spiritual guidance where we hear him clearly regarding divorce. Study the scriptures listed in the table regarding divorce.

by gbaskerville | Jul 28, 2020 | Divorce Bible Verses, Do I have biblical grounds for divorce?

From the website lifesavingdivorce.com
THREE CHRISTIAN VIEWS OF DIVORCE

Christian view	Number of acceptable reasons to divorce	Verses used to support this view
Biblical View	4 reasons 1. Adultery/sexual immorality 2. Physical neglect/abuse 3. Emotional neglect/abuse 4. Abandonment by unbeliever	Ex. 21:10-11, Deut. 21:11-14, Genesis 2:24, Mal. 2:13-16, Mark 10, Matt. 5:31-32, Matt. 19:8, 1 Cor. 7:15. Plus verses telling us not to associate with people with serious sins, including all types of abuse and sexual immorality: 1 Cor. 5:11-12, Eph. 5:3-7, 2 Tim. 3:1-5. Those who don't care for their family are worse than unbelievers: 1 Tim. 5:8
New Testament Only View	1 or 2 reasons 1. Adultery/sexual immorality 2. Abandonment by unbeliever	Gen. 2:24, Mal. 2:13-16, Mark 10, Matt. 5:31-32, 1 Cor. 7:15
Permanence View	0 (no acceptable reasons for divorce)	Gen. 2:24; Mal. 2:13-16, Mark 10

Examine the grounds for divorce for where wisdom is required. Wisdom is the principal thing. It is where repentance and guidance from God is essential to not lead to unnecessary suffering in a marriage that simply has died, and resurrection is not possible. I make this statement because freewill is always a factor in every circumstance.

Proverbs 4:7 *Wisdom is the principal thing; therefore get wisdom: and with all thy getting get understanding.*

I have helped people process through seeking God for whether they are to divorce. Some of them have been told to stay and God has given a reason and plan for that. Others have been told to leave, and God has given a reason and a plan for that decision. I share this to say, allow God into the process and trust him with what he will reveal. This way you will not only have biblical truth but his will and purpose for your life.

Separation & Reconciliation
Before considering divorce, explore with God whether he is requiring separation and reconciliation. It would be beneficial to enter professional, Bible-based counseling immediately when divorce is being considered and process with God how to contend for, or how to leave a marriage. I have found that those who do this have a clear, divine vision, are able to heal quickly, and can SHIFT to what God is speaking to them with faith to trust their future regardless of whether God is requiring them to stay or leave the marriage. I have also witnessed marriages completely dissolve in divorce, then, in a later season, God restores the marriage. God is always about redemption, reconciliation, and restoration. He is a repairer of that which is breached, so do not think it is strange if he desires and requires you to repair your broken marriage.

Isaiah 58:12 *And they that shall be of thee shall build the old waste places: thou shalt raise up the foundations of* *many generations; and thou shalt be called, The repairer of the breach, The restorer of paths to dwell in.*

ICorinthians 13:7 *Love never gives up, never loses faith, is always hopeful, and endures through every circumstance.*

Restoration takes work, but if God is requiring it, you, that mate, and your marriage covenant is worth the work. God has divine purposes for the reason he will perfect it and work it for the good of all. The restoration will boast of an exceeding weight of glory regarding his grace, mercy, unconditional love, supernatural forgiveness, applicable tools for transformation, and how salvation redeems marriage and family.

Please understand that restoration is NOT recapturing what you have lost. The breach of that relationship changed both parties and the dynamics of the relationship. Something died or has entered a place of resuscitation even if it can be resurrected. Therefore, it is important to examine who both of you all are now, what the marriage has SHIFTED into, and work from this position so that God can make each of you and the marriage better than it was. Through this place, God will restore what needs to be in this new SHIFT in your marriage, while leaving behind all that is unbeneficial to the marriage covenant.

The greatest skills and characteristics needed for restoration are:

- ❖ Conflict Resolution Skills.
- ❖ Communication Skills.

- ❖ Emotional Wellness.
- ❖ Patience for one another and the process toward wholeness.
- ❖ Grace, mercy, and the ability and willingness to forgive quickly.
- ❖ Relinquishing and not living in the past, while consciously living in the present and focused on the future.
- ❖ Learning God's true purpose for marriage and family and grounding those foundational truths into your restoration process.
- ❖ Seeking and living through godly vision of what the restoration should look like and evolve into, while being obedient to the part of the vision he gives and allowing your obedience to reveal further vision.
- ❖ Recognizing that you all are not perfecting yourselves; God is perfecting each of you and the marriage.
- ❖ Make consistent prayer, Bible study, fasting, consecrating, vision casting, and destiny alignment a part of your marriage covenant.
- ❖ Honor one another's voice and who each of you are in God. Dishonor is a major marriage covenant breach. Do not marry, or remarry, anyone you do not honor or listen to. Study honor and submission with each other and practice it until it becomes innate in your interactions with one another.
- ❖ Divorce should never be an option. Never enter a marriage with the mindset that you can always divorce no matter what would be considered legal or justifiable grounds for it. Posture yourself and

your mindset regarding marriage in a place that there will be nothing you and your mate cannot get through, there will be things that you and your partner will never experience, and whatever you do experience, God is able to assist you with whatever is in that season of marriage. Cleanse any ideologies, perceptions, and bloodline propensities out of your lives and generations that would have either of you considering divorce as an option. As you re-commit, endeavor to marry for the fullness of your life.

Psalm 138:8 *The LORD will perfect that which concerneth me: thy mercy, O LORD, endureth for ever: forsake not the works of thine own hands.*

This is the reason I recommend a counselor to assist with the restoration process. The counselor will identify, direct you all, and teach you each of the skills you need to be successful.

I recommend the manual, "*Kingdom Marriages and Vault Marriages*" by Apostle Jackie Green when God is requiring restoration of a marriage. She also suggests the book, "*First Aid for A Wounded Marriage*," by Marilyn Phillips. These manuals will equip you through your restoration journey.

Heal & Avoid Litigation
Take time to heal. You deserve this season of healing. You deserve the time it takes to

- Learn yourself in this new place you have SHIFTED into.
- Learn God and build relationship with him in this new place.
- Become one in wholeness within your own identity.
- Learn what type of mate you desire and deserve.
- Learn to believe again for marriage.

Make sure you are in a consistent tangible place of healing before pursuing dating for marriage. Tangibility means you have consistent fruit that healing from the divorce has taken place in your life.

Make sure you are truly legally divorced - not separated, not in a divorce proceeding, not contemplating divorce - but completely, legally, divorced before pursuing dating for marriage. If you do meet someone during this time, place them into a friendship relationship until you are *LEGALLY DIVORCED*. **DO NOT** pursue them as a potential mate until you are actually divorced. No matter how you package this, it is **ADULTERY** if you or the other person is still legally married. This person is someone else's husband or wife. No matter how much you justify the reasons they can be with you, you cannot claim someone else's spouse. No matter how much you try to make it be God, God will not approve of you pursuing or posturing yourself as someone's mate in this situation, as he will not violate his word.

***Proverbs 6:32** But whoso committeth adultery with a woman lacketh understanding: he that doeth it destroyeth his own soul.*

Adultery is one of the major things God despises. Anytime we serve other gods, put other people and things above him, he deems it adultery. It provokes him to jealousy and wrath. If he is this challenged in his own character regarding adultery, what reasons do we think he would justify or approve our actions for divorce. Please know that adultery is not just sexual sin, for the word says the following:

***Matthew 5:28** But I say unto you, That whosoever looketh on a woman to lust after her hath committed adultery with her already in his heart.*

The Greek word for *looketh* is *blepo* and not only means *"to look with the natural eye, but to discern, see, perceive by the senses, to see with the mind's eye to gaze upon."*

<u>*Blepo* in Greek means:</u>
1. to see, discern, of the bodily eye
    A. with the bodily eye: to be possessed of sight, have the power of seeing
    B. perceive by the use of the eyes: to see, look descry
    C. to turn the eyes to anything: to look at, look upon, gaze at
    D. to perceive by the senses, to feel
    E. to discover by use, to know by experience
2. metaph. to see with the mind's eye

- A. to have (the power of) understanding to discern mentally, observe, perceive, discover, understand
- B. to turn the thoughts or direct the mind to a thing, to consider, contemplate, to look at, to weigh carefully, examine
3. in a geographical sense of places, mountains, buildings, etc. turning towards any quarter, as it were, facing it

This passage of scripture reveals that looking entails thoughts, perceptions, concepts, ideologies, feelings, emotions, expressions, flesh, needs, desires, will, plans, and purposes.

MY LORD!

Let's just ponder the truth of that for a moment.

When we entertain (look) upon a thing long enough, we can open portals that feed false narratives and ideologies in our mind, heart, and soul that are more about what our flesh and desires want than what is the true will and purpose for our lives. We can become so zealous to have our desires fulfilled, that we begin to make what we desire to be God.

We can use scriptures and reasonings in ways that feed the lies that what we want is legal and aligned with God. Such entertaining can also open the portals to communing with demons that speak as if they are God. These demons will build strongholds of false ideologies into our lives where we justify the adulterous acts we are engaging in.

Another way this operates is people will find themselves in a stronghold of their desires so that they will not seek God for truth. They will contend that this specific person is their mate, and they will align as the person's mate, all while hoping and praying things work out in their favor. The waster spirit enters to steal time and focus, while further strengthening the person to commit adultery where the enemy will gain a foothold in that person's life. Because they lack direction, they waste time waiting on a mate that may not be God's ordained covenant partner for their lives. I have had people come to counseling bound in this area. Many of them have spent months and years lusting after a mate that legally is not available to them that places them in a stronghold to promises they cannot fulfill. Because the relationship is based on emotional adultery and false promises, it takes a while to untangle them from the soul ties that have entangled them into adultery, even if there are no physical, sexual interactions. This leaves them striving to understand how there is a legal ground for adultery if they have not had sex, but looking and entertaining is adultery to God according to laws in spiritual realm.

Adultery has spiritual and natural ramifications that will be tangible in your life, that person's life, and whatever relationship you all are building. Adultery will be a scar and a tare that grows up with the wheat of your relationship and will have to be weeded out to purify the foundation of the relationship and to stop the way the enemy uses this open door to attack you, that person, and whatever relationship you all are building. Study the Parable of the Sower in *Matthew 13:1–23, Mark 4:1–20, Luke 8:4–15*. One major way the enemy uses this door of adultery is through the legislation of litigation.

The Spirit Of Litigation – Litigation entails a dispute over legal rights and obligations that can often be disputed in a court proceeding. Often, when it comes to a situation, positioning, systematic proceeding, judicial matter, property or land dispute, legal matters of marriage, separation, or divorce, or other judicial proceedings, if the enemy cannot hinder a person from being victorious, he will look for legal ways in policies, procedures, or spiritual and natural principles, standards, and laws in effort to attack, delay, deny, frustrate, overthrow, thwart, or wreak havoc in a person's life. These litigations may be legal and have merit, but the enemy's main reason for using this tactic is to prosecute, charge, indict, sue, shame, scandal, disbar, terminate, dissolve, or annul an agreement so that the person can no longer be successful or obtain occupancy for what God is releasing to them.

These efforts are also for the purposes of nullifying the jurisdiction to which God wants that person to govern with dominion in their lives, bloodline, regions, and/or spheres of influence as the enemy is always seeking to have legal ground and claim to the lineages, territories, and spheres that God wants a person and their heritage to possess. Territorial governance is the greatest blessing a person can have because he who owns the land and sphere has the greatest authority - kingly authority.

Sometimes litigation can be spiritually illegal, but the enemy will use natural laws and procedures that are legal to challenge and attack a person. Spiritually, the person has not done anything wrong for the enemy to attack, so he will find a clause in a natural policy or procedure to attack a person. We will see this in employment, business, and marketplace endeavors; school and educational matters, business and entrepreneurial dealings; economic and financial situations, political proceedings. The enemy may also litigate natural policies, procedures, and/or laws of a company, worldly systems, contracts, binding agreements, or a moral position of integrity to attack a person's finances, character, progress, process, and success.

There are also instances where open doors of compromise - subtle, unrecognized, or unrepentant sins - disobedience and sin against the laws and standards of God can be used to assert litigation in areas of a person's life. Until the sin is repented of and the doors of sin are closed, the enemy can assert litigation to attack a person. Especially if the person is an intercessor standing in the gap for others or a bloodline curse breaker.

***Zechariah 3** Then the guiding angel showed me Joshua the high priest [representing disobedient, sinful Israel] standing before the Angel of the LORD, and Satan standing at Joshua's right hand to be his adversary and to accuse him. And the LORD said to Satan, "The LORD rebuke you, Satan! Even the LORD, who [now and ever] has chosen Jerusalem, rebuke you! Is this not a log snatched and rescued from the fire?" Now Joshua was clothed with filthy (nauseatingly vile) garments and was standing before the Angel [of the LORD]. He spoke to those who stood before Him, saying, "Remove the filthy garments from him." And He said to Joshua, "See, I have caused your wickedness to be taken away from you, and I will clothe and beautify you with rich robes [of forgiveness]." And I (Zechariah) said, "Let them put a clean turban on his head." So they put a clean turban on his head and clothed him with [rich] garments. And the Angel of the LORD stood by. And the Angel of the LORD [solemnly and earnestly] admonished Joshua, saying, "Thus says the LORD of hosts, 'If you will walk in My ways [that is, remain faithful] and perform My service, then you will also govern My house and have charge of My courts, and I will give you free access [to My presence] among these who are standing here.*

Satan is generally in the court of heaven using these litigations to contend against a person's life, prayers, promises, and prophecies. He wants to take back what God has said rightfully belongs to that person or to make the person look disqualified and/or illegal, such that what God is saying is theirs is taken. Handling these matters in the court of heaven, repenting when necessary to break any legal ground, while standing in the truth of God's promises, prophecies, and who he has purposed the person to be and do, are the greatest weapons against the spirit of litigation. Also know that God will overthrow Satan for the person and all those attached to them, as we discern this in Zechariah three. God will not allow Satan to use these litigation proceedings to hinder a person's victory. It is important for the person to trust this truth as they walk out these types of experiences. God will prevail with restoration, restitution, and victory!

Isaiah 43:1-4 The Message Bible *But now, GOD's Message, the God who made you in the first place, Jacob, the One who got you started, Israel: "Don't be afraid, I've redeemed you. I've called your name. You're mine. When you're in over your head, I'll be there with you. When you're in rough waters, you will not go down. When you're between a rock and a hard place, it won't be a dead end— Because I am GOD, your personal God, The Holy of Israel, your Savior. I paid a huge price for you: all of Egypt, with rich Cush and Seba thrown in! That's how much you mean to me! That's how much I love you! I'd sell off the whole world to get you back, trade the creation just for you.*

You can learn how to legislate in the courts of heaven in my manual, *Gatekeeping Regions for God's Glory.*

When this principle of litigation is not regarded, it opens doors to covenant breaking spirits to begin operating in your life and marriage.

- ❖ The enemy also uses the legalities of this principle to wreak havoc in other areas of your life as you will experience a lot of contention in areas where you should witness the safety, protection, blessings, favor, goodness, promises, and prophecies of God in your life.

- ❖ If you are a bloodline breaker and have stood interceding and contending for the bloodline, the enemy uses this principle to snatch back territory that you have worked hard to overtake. Especially in areas where you have contended for purity, godly marriages, success, and destiny attainment.

- ❖ The enemy will use this door to attack your children and future generations. Especially those who are destined for greatness in the family line or those who are dependent upon your curse breaking stance to align with godly destiny.

Save yourself, and a potentially good marriage covenant, some hassle by going through the proper procedures to be in alignment with God and to close up any doors the enemy will use against what can be legally and divinely joined together for kingdom fulfillment. If you have engaged in litigation do the following to break yourself free:

- ❖ Spend time with God repenting for adultery personally and generationally and acts of litigation.
- ❖ Break soul ties with the person you are in adultery with.

- ❖ Break soul ties with any demons in your bloodline, or that person's bloodline, that have laid claim to you, your soul, and your lineage.
- ❖ Renounce ways you have postured as that person's spouse and command the webbing to be destroyed to free your mind, heart, soul, emotions, flesh, will, plans, purposes, destiny, and calling.
- ❖ Close up demonic portals that would give demonic spirits further access to commune and feed you lying thoughts and fleshly energies that would draw you to lust and adultery.
- ❖ Search out with God and journal what caused you to posture in this manner. Be honest with yourself and deal with these areas in your soul.
- ❖ Spend time seeking truth from God regarding who you are, who he is, the standards he has for your life and a mate, and the reasons this was adultery so you can embody and stand in truth regarding the reality of your experience, what you deserve in a mate, and the truth of God regarding the mate he has for you.
- ❖ Pursue a couple of accountability partners that can speak truth to you, question you when necessary, and hold you to the standards, truths, and realities that are needed to keep this door closed in your life, and to walk in covenant with you for what God truly has and is requiring for your life. ***Proverbs 11:14*** *Where there is no counsel, the people fall; But in the multitude of counselors there is safety.*

Divorce Healing Activation:

- Explore ways you need to forgive yourself, your ex, and others that may be factors in the divorce. Spend a season with God in a process towards complete forgiveness.

- Explore, journal with God, and spend time with him healing from all anger, resentment, shame, guilt, condemnation, pity, helplessness, hopelessness, regret, failures, betrayal, infidelities, financial hardships and challenges, grief over the loss of family, friends, relationships, the marriage itself, the experience of death through divorce, broken promises, unfulfilled goals, visions, and aspirations, any issues around ALL children and how they are impacted by the marriage and divorce, separation and divorce proceedings, fear of dating and being married again. Consider a season of counseling and deliverance to process this area completely.

- Spend time breaking soul ties. From my manual, *Kingdom Keys to Governing Relationships*:

When you get divorced, it is best to break the soul ties with your former spouse. Many people have a difficult time moving forward because their souls are still tied to their ex-spouse. The covenant of marriage must be repented for and broken in the spirit realm, and soul ties must be cleansed and broken so you can be free from all that was deposited and shared while married. It is important to break and cleanse these soul ties. This can be done by:

- ❖ Spending time before the Lord identifying every ungodly soul tie.
- ❖ Confessing and repenting for your role in the soul tie.
- ❖ Forgiving your soul tie partner and forgiving yourself for engaging in the soul tie.
- ❖ Breaking and removing the soul tie. Be sure to call out every person's name you have a soul tie with; go through these steps, and break and remove each tie.
- ❖ Using the blood of Jesus and the fire of God, cleanse yourself of all ungodly deposits, and command any parts of your soul, heart, mind, and identity to be restored back to you.
- ❖ Though there are godly soul ties, sometimes we can become too familiar with one another and take one another for granted. This causes us to behave towards one another in ways that can be inordinate, unbecoming, possessive, or dishonoring. To avoid such behaviors, I suggest occasionally breaking any ungodly soul ties that have formed through familiarity, misunderstanding, miscommunication, lack of regard, being more to one another than God has said, becoming lax in the relationship, fleshly, or imbalanced in your interaction then declaring that only the godly soul tie you are to have with

that person remains or is re-established.

- Explore ways you could have included God in your dating, your engagement, and marital process to ensure you were entering into a godly covenant.

- Explore and journal areas you compromised, settled, and operated more through the potential rather than reality of who that person was, who and where you were in life, and what marriage is really about.

- Explore and journal what you learned about yourself and marriage as it relates to your experience.

- Explore and journal what you learned about your ex, yourself in relation to your ex and marriage, and what you learned about God.

- Explore and journal what you need to be more mindful of and do better going forward in embracing dating, engagement, and marriage.

<u>Court & Divorce Prayer Focus:</u>
Use this strategy when engaging in a divorce and divorce proceedings. Pray this consistently you experience until complete breakthrough:

- Call for favor and for God's will and direction to be made manifest in divorce agreements between the lawyers and of filing the paperwork.

- Pray for the courtroom of God to be in the room on the day(s) of your divorce proceedings. Call the day out and invite God, his heavenly kingdom, and the angels to be in your midst and in operation.

- Pray that divine justice be done on your behalf and that the court decisions be fair and of God's will.

- Cancel all attacks related to your character and your name. Decree that you have favor and a good name among those who are a part of the court proceedings.

- Cancel any attacks to steal from you, where the finances and assets are not divided properly or equally, or as it relates to what you agreed to with your lawyer.

- Pray for supernatural debt cancelation if necessary. That even as you would work to pay off debt, God would supernaturally grace you with some of your bills from marriage being divinely paid.

- Pray for the heart and love of who you are to be seen by the judge and the courts so that any future changes regarding assets, finances, land, or child custody battles can be considered and implemented.

- Pray to continually break the covenant spiritually and naturally with your ex.

- Break soul ties with your ex and family line and speak blessings over them regarding who they are, and at any time to your children.

- Pray for everything that was good in the marriage to be a blessing upon you and/or your children and ex, and for everything that was ungodly and negative to die with the divorce.

- Pray that your ex-SHIFTS further into the heart of who they need to be as a person and parent so that the children and any future interactions will be cordial and not tumultuous.

- Continue to cast out and cleanse any spirits that came upon you during the marriage or that would try to operate in and around you and your children.

- Pray that the generational curses of divorce to be broken off your life and lineage, and for you and your children to be restored in the divine truth of God's requirements and will for your family and marriage.

- Pray for your life to SHIFT into divine destiny with God and for that to be the only pathway open in your life and the life of your children.

- Thank God for showing up and showing out for you regarding paper filing and systematic procedures, court legislation, legal matters, agreements, and the nullifying of demonic spiritual workings and operations.

MANUAL REFERENCES

Books by Dr. Taquetta Baker

- *Keys To Sustaining The Vision Workbook*
- *Kingdom Keys To Governing Relationship*
- *Kingdom Wellness Counseling & Mentoring Manual, Volume I*
- *The Power Of Purity*

Books By Apostle Jackie Green

- *Kingdom Marriages*
- *Vault Marriages*

Websites

- *Blueletterbible.com*
- *Biblestudytools.com*
- *Dictionary.com*
- *Olivetree.com*
- *Strong's Exhaustive Bible Concordance Online Bible Study Tools*
- *The Map Of Erogenous Zones Photo is from https://dame.com/blogs/sexual-wellness/erogenous-zones-infographic*

MARRIAGE GATEKEEPING INDEX

Abuse – page 140, Spirit of Abuse -page 229
Active Listening Skills – page 275 to 277
Agreement In Marriage – page 271 to 273
Arrested Development – page 216 to 217
Bewitchment – page 233 to 235
Boundaries In Relationships – page 178
Build A Mate Syndrome – page 195 to 201
Building Marriage - page 7 to 44, Team Building - page 36 to 44
Burning Lust – page 255 to 261
Carnality & Wordliness – page 188 to 195
Choosing A Godly Mate – page 55 to 76, No Regarding Standards – page 178 to 180
Control & Manipulation – page 209, Control Through Jezebel & Narcissm & Ahab – page 223 to 228
Communication Skills - page 263 to 283, Conflict Resolution Skills - page 274 to 275, Conflicting Communication – page 180 to 181, Deaf & Dumb Spirit Hinders Communication – page 220 to 221
Dating & Engagement Strategies – page 52 to 54
Demons that destroy marriages/relationships – page 215 to 235, Perversion in marriage – page 236 to 261, Spirits From The Garden Of Eden – page 237 to 238, Demonic Counsel – page 239 to 242
Destiny & Marriage – page 151 to 154
Discipleship Impacting Relationships – page 186 to 187
Division – page 231
Divorce – page 231 to 232, I Am Divorce Now What? - page 328 to to 350
Enabling - page 208 to 209

Engagement – page 45 to 54, Engagement Dating – page 52 to 54
Entanglements Hinder Marriages – page 160 to 244
Eros Love – page 253 to 255, page 305 to 306, page 312, page 320, page 324 to 327
Escapism In Communication - page 268 to 270
False Obligations & Loyalties – page 206 to 208
Financial Marriage Help & Maturity – page 155 to 159
Fight, Flight, Freeze – page 165 to 166
Foundation In Marriage - page 7 to 44
Ghosting – page 211
Grooming – page 181 to 186
Help Meet – page 93 to 110
Honor – page 252 to 254, Honoring One Another's Voice – page 272 to 273, page 308 to 317
In-laws – page 139 to 144
Inordinate Affections – page 212
Insecurity & Low Self-esteem – page 210
Intentionality In Marriage – page 31 to 38
Intimacy – page 296 to 317, Increase Arousal – page 318 to 327
Iron Sharpening Iron – page 20 to 21
Love (Godly Love & Love Languages) – page 284 to 295, Unhealthy Love - page 209, Fear In Giving/Receiving Lord – page 221
Leaving & Cleaving – page 129 to 138
Learning Your Partner – page 265 to 266,
Lust – page 244 to 247
Marital Mentoring - page 1 to 6
Married Couples Please God – page 25 to 36, page 323

Narcissism – page 223 to 228
Offense – page 229 to 231
Open & Closed Ended. Questions – page 277 to 282
Passive Aggressiveness – page 218 to 219
People Pleasing – page 210
Perversion – page 247 to 251
Praying Couples – page 282 to 283
Pride (Leviathian) – page 219 to 220
Relationship Dependent – page 209 to 210
Rejection – page 221 to 222
Sanctification & Purity– page 259 to 260
Sabotage – page 218
Seasons & Transitions – page 267 to 268
Sexual Trauma – page 177
Singles Pleasing God – page 12 to 19, Spirit of Singleness – page 232 to 233
Situationships – page 204 to 205
Soulties – pages 22 to 24, page 201 to 204
Submission – pages 77 to 92
Trauma (Unhealed) – page 163 to 166, Trauma Bonding – page 167 to 177, Spirit Of Trauma 233
Undefiled - page 252 to 254, page 311 to 312
Victimization – page 217
Vision (Godly Vision For A Mate) – page 111 to 128, Godly Vision Activation – page 145 to 148
Warlock & Witch Hooking – page 213 to 214
Wisdom For Couples – page 149 to 150

Kingdom Shifters Product Line

Products available at kingdomshiftingbooks.com and amazon.com	
Books (Paperback, Kindle, and e-books available)	
Healing the Wounded Leader	There is an App for That
Apostolic Governing	Sustaining The Vision Workbook
Apostolic Mantle	Annihilating Church Hurt
Healing the Wounded Leader	Discerning the Voice of God
Release the Vision	Feasting in His Presence
Birthing Books That Shift Generations	Prayers that Shift Atmospheres
Atmosphere Changes (Weaponry)	Dismantling Homosexuality
Strategies for Eradicating Racism	Let There Be Sight
Kingdom Shifters Decree That Thang	Kingdom Watchman Builder on the Wall
Kingdom Heirs Decree That Thang	Kingdom Keys to Governing Relationships
Fivefold Operations – Manuals I, II, and III	Unmasking the Power of the Scouts – Volumes I and II
Processing Grief & Loss	Cultivating Destiny From The Womb
Kingdom Wellness Counseling & Mentoring Manual I	Deliverance From The Stronghold of Suicide

Truth About Willful Sin	Ascending Into Heavenly Realms
Gatekeeping Regions For God's Glory	KW Life Coaching Manual
Gatekeeping Your Covenant Marriage	Healing Families God's Way
Supernatural Birthing Journal	Kingdom Deliverance Journal
Deliverance Is The Children's Bread Volume I & II	Governing Divine Intel
Divine Art Of Communication	What Is Your Calling
Books for Liturgical / Interpretive Dance Ministries	
Dance & Fivefold Ministry	Dance from Heaven to Earth
Spirits that Attack Dance Ministers	Dancers! Dancers! Dancers! Decree That Thang
CD's	
Decree That Thang	Kingdom Heirs Decree That Thang
Teaching and Worship	

Quote—Apostle Jackie Green!

Marriage is God's invention and inspiration that is full of change, challenges and choices whether you are married five years or fifty years. Just when you think you know him or her, you discover something new about one another. Learn to love the discovery of God, yourself, and your mate. Want to grow and gatekeep all God has for you in the covenant vision of godly marriage!

SHIFT RIGHT NOW!

www.ingramcontent.com/pod-product-compliance
Lightning Source LLC
Chambersburg PA
CBHW070716160426
43192CB00009B/1213